Friends Forever

Peanuts: Friends Forever

Charles M. Schulz

Ballantine Books

New York

A Ballantine Books Trade Paperback Original

Copyright © 2015 by Peanuts Worldwide LLC

Published in the United States by Ballantine Books, an imprint of Random House,
a division of Penguin Random House LLC, New York.

BALLANTINE and the HOUSE colophon are registered trademarks of
Penguin Random House LLC.

The comic strips in this book were originally published in newspapers worldwide.

ISBN 978-0-8041-7951-5
eBook ISBN 978-0-8041-7952-2

Printed in the United States of America on acid-free paper

randomhousebooks.com

2 4 6 8 9 7 5 3 1

Book design by Donna Sinisgalli

Friends Forever

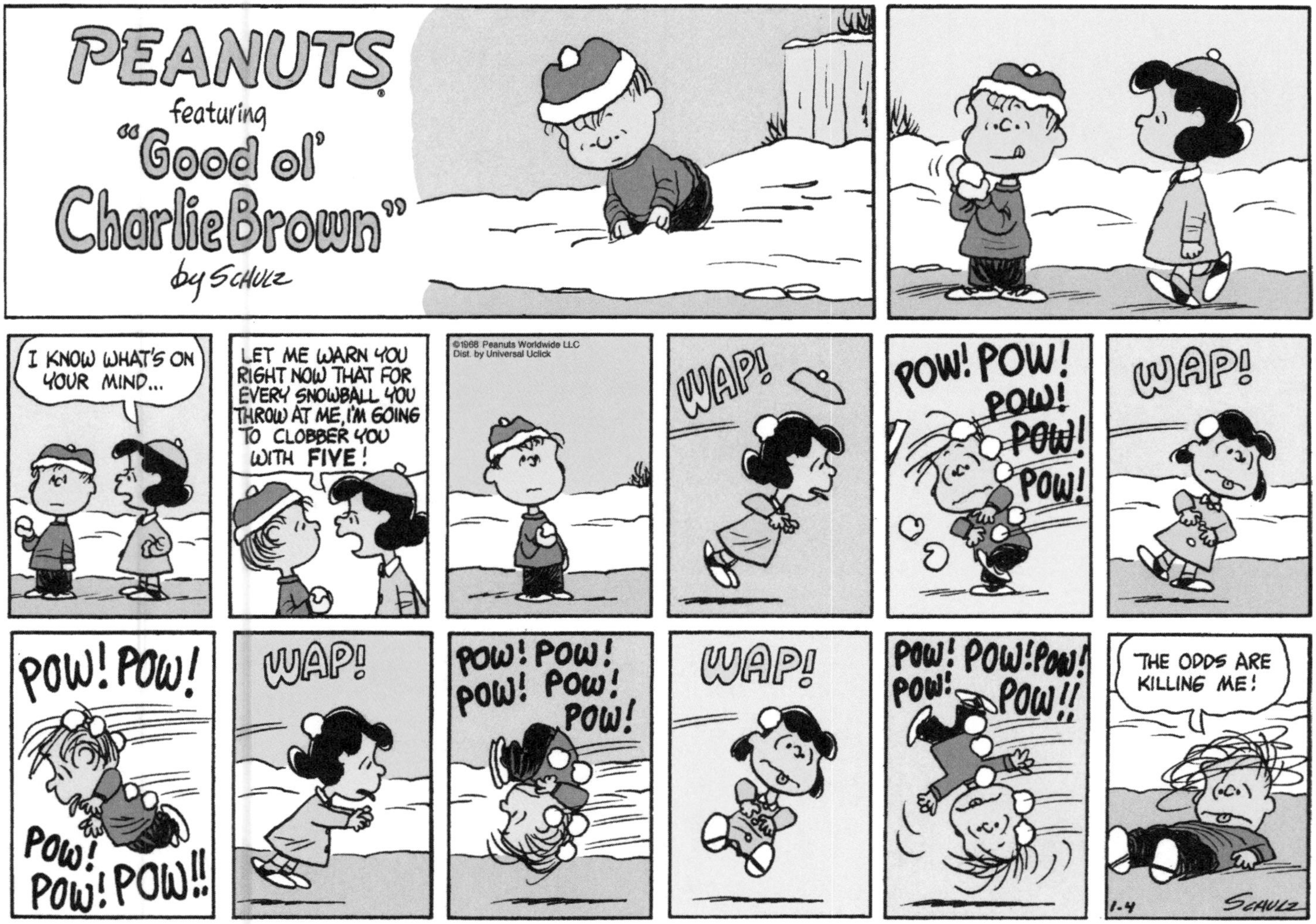
PEANUTS
featuring
"Good ol' Charlie Brown"
by SCHULZ
I KNOW WHAT'S ON YOUR MIND...
LET ME WARN YOU RIGHT NOW THAT FOR EVERY SNOWBALL YOU THROW AT ME, I'M GOING TO CLOBBER YOU WITH FIVE!
©1968 Peanuts Worldwide LLC Dist. by Universal Uclick
WAP!
POW! POW! POW! POW! POW!
WAP!
POW! POW! POW! POW! POW!!
WAP!
POW! POW! POW! POW! POW!
WAP!
POW! POW! POW! POW! POW!!
THE ODDS ARE KILLING ME!
1-4
SCHULZ

© 1966 Peanuts Worldwide LLC. Dist. by Universal Uclick
www.snoopy.com
AUGH!
1-4
NEVER SET YOUR STOMACH FOR A JELLY-BREAD SANDWICH UNTIL YOU'RE SURE THERE'S SOME JELLY!
SCHULZ

STUPID WEATHER!
www.snoopy.com
ARE YOU COMPLAINING AGAIN? DO YOU REALIZE THAT YOU SPEND ALL YOUR TIME COMPLAINING?
1-5
© 1965 Peanuts Worldwide LLC. Dist. by Universal Uclick
WHY SHOULDN'T I COMPLAIN?
IT'S THE ONLY THING I'M REALLY GOOD AT!
SCHULZ

YOU HAVE VERY NICE HANDS, VIOLET
www.snoopy.com
THANK YOU
I THINK NICE HANDS ARE IMPORTANT FOR A GIRL
1-6
© 1965 Peanuts Worldwide LLC. Dist. by Universal Uclick
I DON'T LIKE MY HANDS... THEY'RE TOO SKINNY
WHAT CAN YOU DO TO GAIN WEIGHT IN YOUR HANDS?
SCHULZ

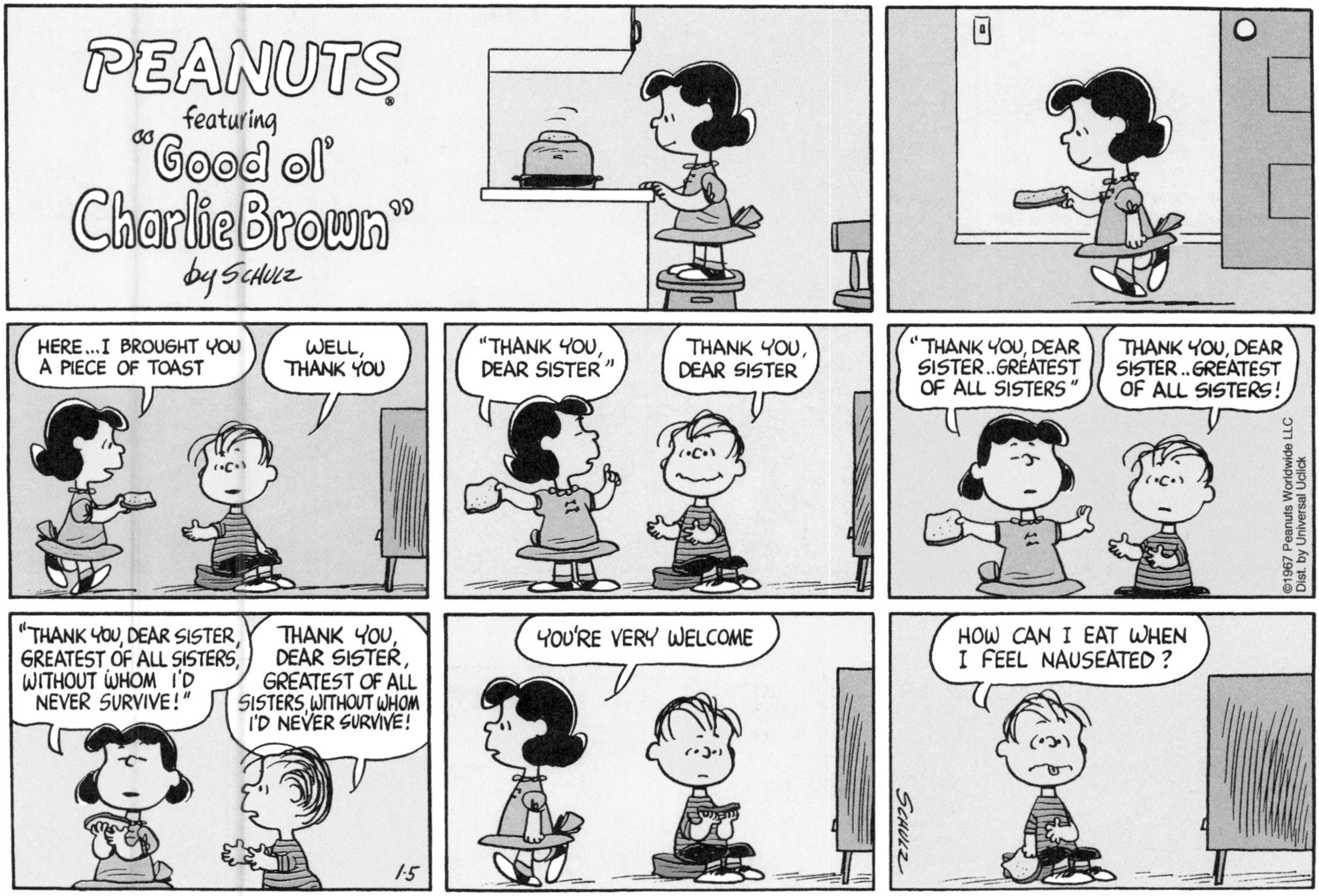
PEANUTS®
featuring
"Good ol' Charlie Brown"
by SCHULZ
HERE...I BROUGHT YOU A PIECE OF TOAST
WELL, THANK YOU
"THANK YOU, DEAR SISTER"
THANK YOU, DEAR SISTER
"THANK YOU, DEAR SISTER..GREATEST OF ALL SISTERS"
THANK YOU, DEAR SISTER..GREATEST OF ALL SISTERS!
©1967 Peanuts Worldwide LLC
Dist. by Universal Uclick
"THANK YOU, DEAR SISTER, GREATEST OF ALL SISTERS, WITHOUT WHOM I'D NEVER SURVIVE!"
THANK YOU, DEAR SISTER, GREATEST OF ALL SISTERS, WITHOUT WHOM I'D NEVER SURVIVE!
1-5
YOU'RE VERY WELCOME
SCHULZ
HOW CAN I EAT WHEN I FEEL NAUSEATED?

MOM SAYS TO GET YOUR COAT ON.. WE'RE GOING TO GO GET A MEASLES SHOT...
A MEASLES SHOT?
GOOD GRIEF, EVERY TIME I TURN AROUND, I GET SHOT FOR SOMETHING
WHAT DOES THAT PEDIATRICIAN THINK I AM, A DART BOARD?!
© 1967 Peanuts Worldwide LLC, Dist. by Universal Uclick
www.snoopy.com
SCHULZ
12-30

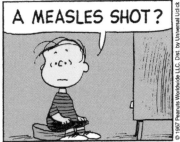

WHY DO I HAVE TO GET A MEASLES SHOT?
12-31
WHO EVER WORRIES ABOUT MEASLES? WHAT'S A LITTLE "RUBEOLA" AMONG FRIENDS?
© 1967 Peanuts Worldwide LLC, Dist. by Universal Uclick
YOUR STUPIDITY IS APPALLING!!!
www.snoopy.com
MOST STUPIDITY IS!
SCHULZ

A MEASLES SHOT... GOOD GRIEF!
WHY GET VACCINATED? WHY NOT JUST WEAR SOMETHING RED OR DRINK SOME ELDERBERRY BLOSSOM TEA?
© 1967 Peanuts Worldwide LLC, Dist. by Universal Uclick
THOSE ARE OLD WIVES' CURES
1-1
www.snoopy.com
SOME OF THOSE OLD WIVES WERE PRETTY SHARP!
SCHULZ

MY ARM HATES TO GET SHOTS
TELL YOUR ARM NOT TO WORRY... HERE, READ THIS...
1-2
"MEASLES IS THE MOST COMMON AND SERIOUS 'CHILDHOOD DISEASE'."......HMM...
© 1967 Peanuts Worldwide LLC, Dist. by Universal Udick
"COMPLICATIONS ARE MIDDLE-EAR INFECTIONS, PNEUMONIA AND EVEN BRAIN DAMAGE"....WOW!
www.snoopy.com
DID YOU HEAR THAT, ARM? IT'S GOING TO BE WORTH IT!
SCHULZ

WHAT ARE YOU PUTTING ON MY ARM? WHAT ARE YOU DOING?
1-3
IS THAT THE NEEDLE? IS THAT IT? ARE YOU DOING IT NOW? WHAT HAPPENED TO SUGAR CUBES?
© 1967 Peanuts Worldwide LLC, Dist. by Universal Udick
WHERE'S THE NEEDLE? WHERE'S MY ARM? WHAT ARE YOU.. AAUGH!
www.snoopy.com
WE JUST SHOT THE MEASLES!
SCHULZ

SO WE WENT OVER TO OUR PEDIATRICIAN'S, SEE...
1-4
AND LUCY AND I BOTH GOT MEASLES SHOTS... NOW, WE'LL NEVER GET MEASLES, ISN'T THAT GREAT?
© 1967 Peanuts Worldwide LLC, Dist. by Universal Udick
ISN'T IT WONDERFUL THAT SUCH A VACCINE HAS BEEN DEVELOPED SO THAT CHILDREN DON'T HAVE TO GET MEASLES, AND...
www.snoopy.com
I KNOW WHAT YOU'RE HINTING!!
SCHULZ

HURRY UP, CHARLIE BROWN! WE'LL BE LATE FOR SCHOOL!
www.snoopy.com
1-2
I WONDER IF HE READ "GULLIVER'S TRAVELS," AND WROTE HIS BOOK REPORT...
© 1965 Peanuts Worldwide LLC, Dist. by Universal Uclick
DID YOU FINISH IT, CHARLIE BROWN? WHEN DID YOU DO IT?
AT THREE O'CLOCK THIS MORNING!!!
SCHULZ

I KNEW I WAS RIGHT! I KNEW IT!
www.snoopy.com
THERE WAS A DAY JUST LIKE TODAY BACK IN 1935! THIS ISN'T A NEW YEAR AT ALL... THIS IS A **USED** YEAR!
1-8
I'M GOING TO WRITE A STRONG LETTER OF PROTEST...
© 1966 Peanuts Worldwide LLC, Dist. by Universal Uclick
WHO'S IN CHARGE OF YEARS?
SCHULZ

11-29
BLEAH!
© 1966 Peanuts Worldwide LLC, Dist. by Universal Uclick
WHAT IN THE WORLD **ARE** THOSE?
www.snoopy.com
SOUR MARSHMALLOWS!
SCHULZ

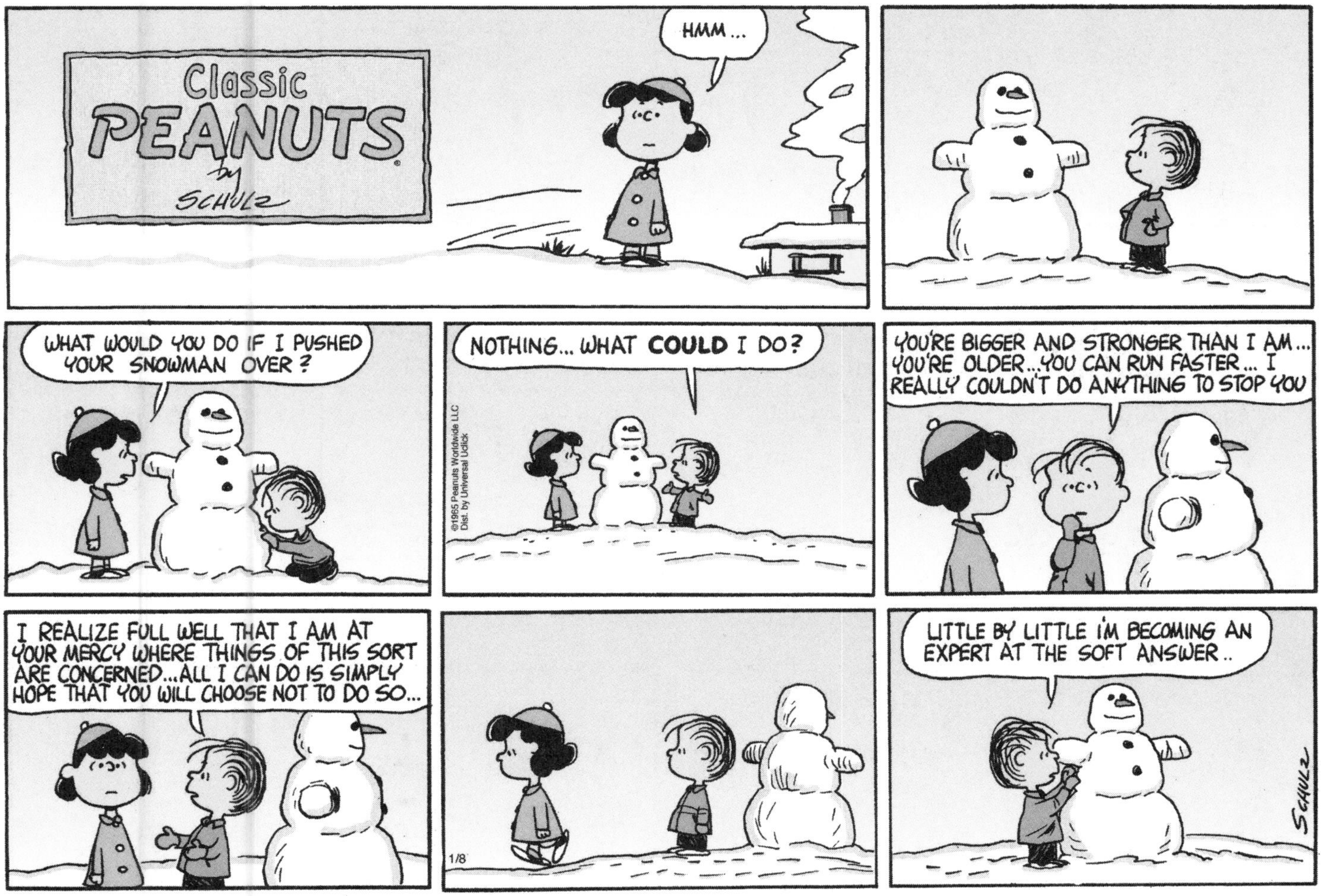
Classic PEANUTS by SCHULZ
HMM...
WHAT WOULD YOU DO IF I PUSHED YOUR SNOWMAN OVER?
NOTHING... WHAT **COULD** I DO?
©1965 Peanuts Worldwide LLC
Dist. by Universal Udick
YOU'RE BIGGER AND STRONGER THAN I AM... YOU'RE OLDER...YOU CAN RUN FASTER... I REALLY COULDN'T DO ANYTHING TO STOP YOU
I REALIZE FULL WELL THAT I AM AT YOUR MERCY WHERE THINGS OF THIS SORT ARE CONCERNED...ALL I CAN DO IS SIMPLY HOPE THAT YOU WILL CHOOSE NOT TO DO SO...
1/8
LITTLE BY LITTLE I'M BECOMING AN EXPERT AT THE SOFT ANSWER..
SCHULZ

WOULDN'T IT BE FUN TO GO TO AN OLD-FASHIONED BALL?
www.snoopy.com
YOU KNOW, ONE OF THOSE GRAND AFFAIRS WHERE ALL THE LADIES WEAR FLOWING GOWNS...
© 1965 Peanuts Worldwide LLC, Dist. by Universal Uclick
THE ORCHESTRA PLAYS STRAUSS WALTZES AND THE CEILING IS COVERED WITH BEAUTIFUL CHANDELIERS! WOULDN'T THAT BE FUN?
1-11
ESPECIALLY IF YOU KNEW HOW TO DANCE!
SCHULZ

MY DAD HAS A DENTAL APPOINTMENT TODAY
1-13
www.snoopy.com
YESTERDAY HE WENT TO SEE AN OPHTHALMOLOGIST
© 1965 Peanuts Worldwide LLC, Dist. by Universal Uclick
THE DAY BEFORE HE WENT TO SEE AN ORTHOPEDIST...
HE CONSIDERS IT ALL PART OF HIS COMPLETE PHYSICAL BREAKDOWN SINCE TURNING FORTY
SCHULZ

THERE'S MY "X"
NOW, DON'T MESS IT ALL UP... TRY TO BE NEAT!
© 1967 Peanuts Worldwide LLC, Dist. by Universal Uclick
1-16
www.snoopy.com
SCHULZ

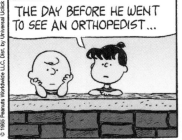

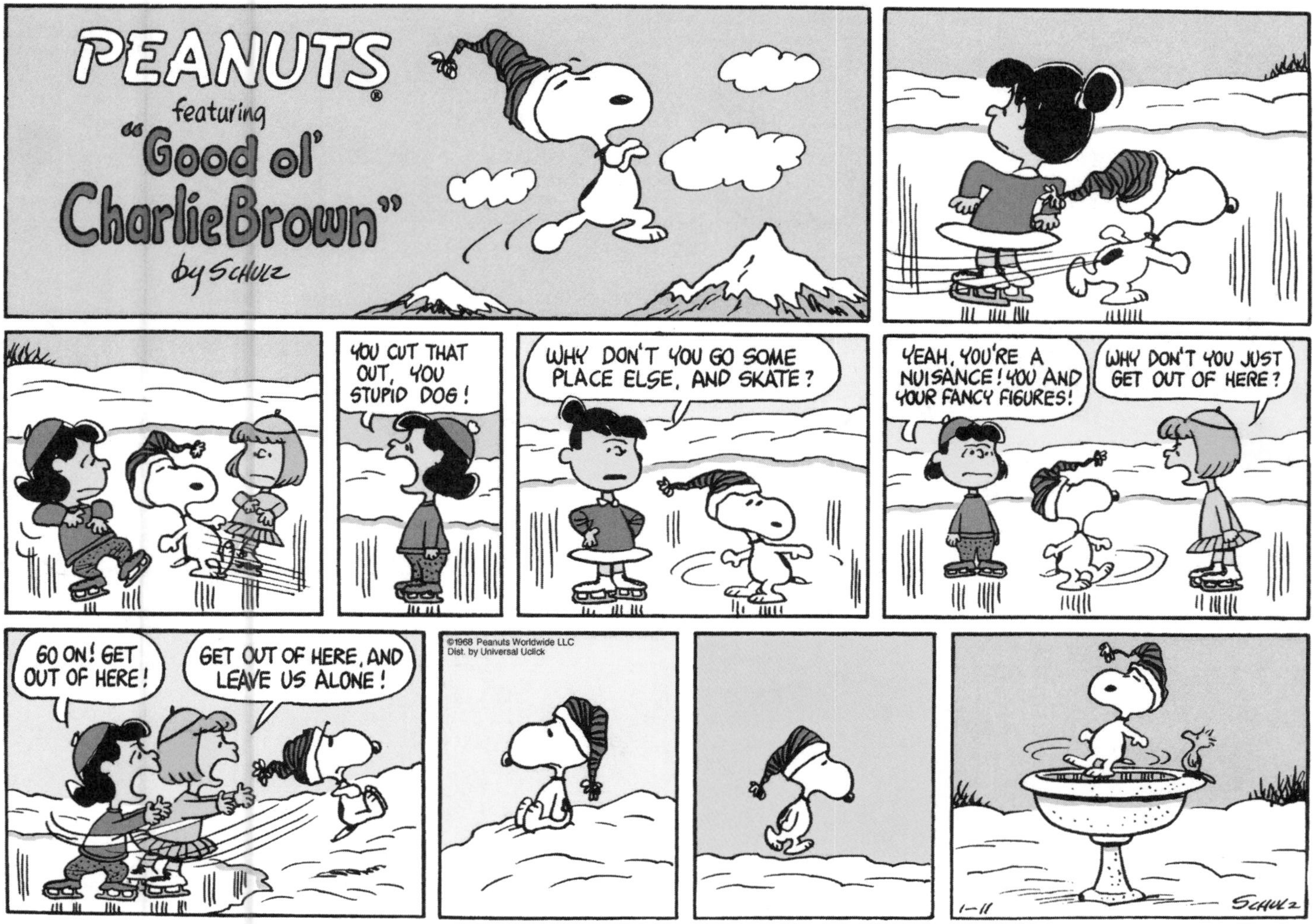
PEANUTS®
featuring
"Good ol' Charlie Brown"
by SCHULZ
YOU CUT THAT OUT, YOU STUPID DOG!
WHY DON'T YOU GO SOME PLACE ELSE, AND SKATE?
YEAH, YOU'RE A NUISANCE! YOU AND YOUR FANCY FIGURES!
WHY DON'T YOU JUST GET OUT OF HERE?
GO ON! GET OUT OF HERE!
GET OUT OF HERE, AND LEAVE US ALONE!
©1968 Peanuts Worldwide LLC
Dist. by Universal Uclick
1-11
SCHULZ

WHAT ARE YOU GRINNING ABOUT?
I'M NOT GRINNING...THIS IS MY DISARMING SMILE...
1-18
© 1967 Peanuts Worldwide LLC. Dist. by Universal Uclick
www.snoopy.com
A DISARMING SMILE DOESN'T STAND A CHANCE AGAINST MY **TOTAL-WARFARE FROWN**!
SCHULZ

DEAR MISS OTHMAR, I HOPE YOU ARE FEELING BETTER.
www.snoopy.com
I DON'T BLAME YOU FOR GETTING UPSET THE OTHER DAY.
1-18
© 1965 Peanuts Worldwide LLC. Dist. by Universal Uclick
YOU WERE A SIGHT RUNNING DOWN THE HALL SCREAMING AND THROWING THOSE ENVELOPES ALL OVER.
REST QUIETLY. DON'T WORRY ABOUT US.
YOUR PUPIL, LINUS
SCHULZ

WE'RE HAVING A TEST TODAY ON CHAPTER FOUR..
CHAPTER **FOUR**?! GOOD GRIEF, I STUDIED CHAPTER TWO!
© 1968 Peanuts Worldwide LLC. Dist. by Universal Uclick
I'M DOOMED...
1/20
www.snoopy.com
STUDYING THE WRONG CHAPTER IS LIKE CUTTING YOUR FINGERNAILS TOO SHORT!
SCHULZ

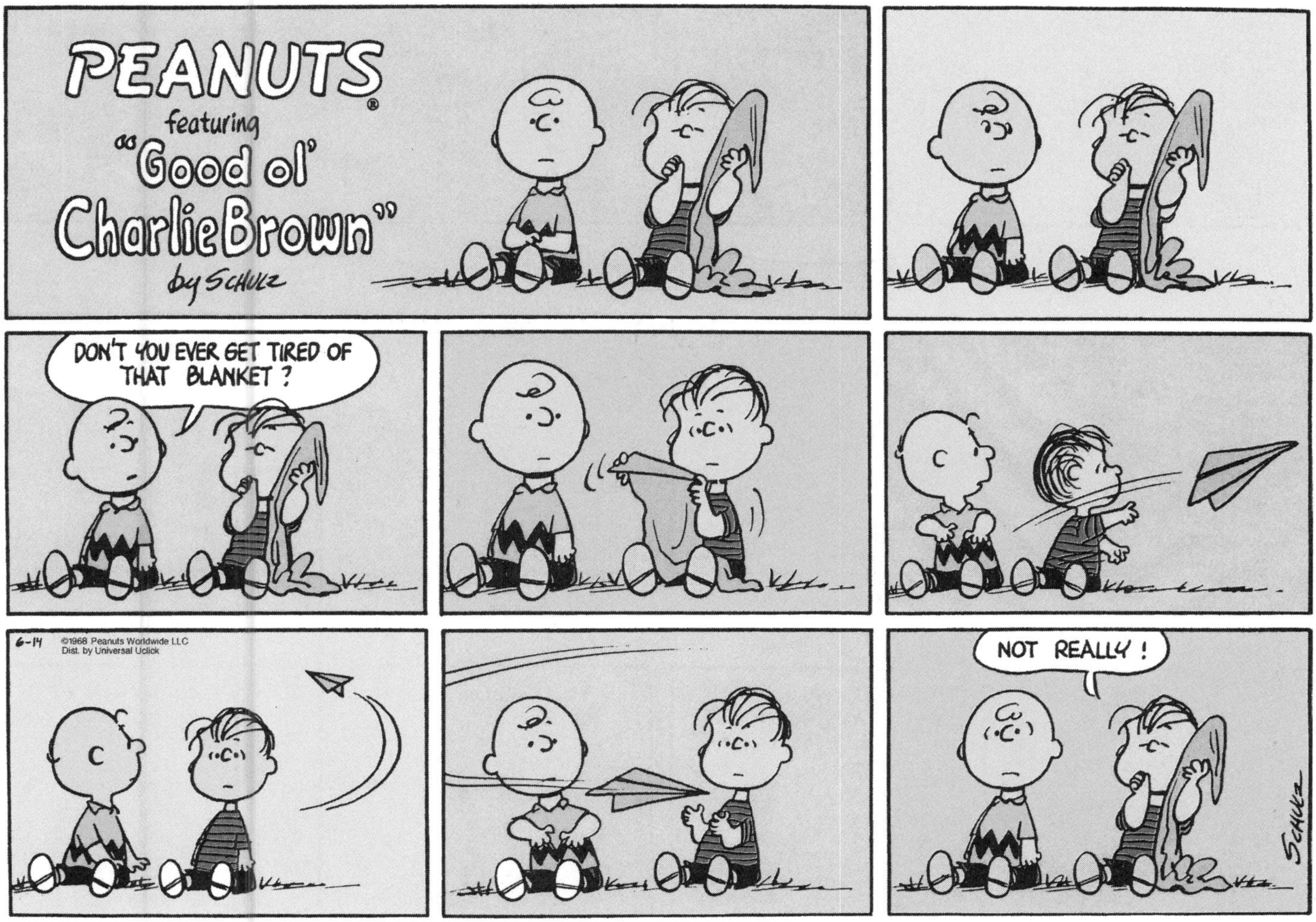
PEANUTS®
featuring
"Good ol' CharlieBrown"
by SCHULZ
DON'T YOU EVER GET TIRED OF THAT BLANKET ?
6-14
©1968 Peanuts Worldwide LLC
Dist. by Universal Uclick
NOT REALLY !
SCHULZ

THIS KID AT SCHOOL SAID I HAVE A FUNNY FACE...
IS IT ALL RIGHT IF I TELL HIM YOU'RE GOING TO SLUG HIM? YOU CAN BE MY KNIGHT IN SHINING ARMOR...
I'D RATHER YOU DIDN'T
WHAT KIND OF A KNIGHT ARE YOU?
I'M A DOVE KNIGHT
1-21
© 1968 Peanuts Worldwide LLC. Dist. by Universal Uclick
www.snoopy.com
SCHULZ

YOU STUPID KID, YOU THINK YOU'RE SO SMART!
I HAVE A BOY FRIEND WHO'S GOING TO CLOBBER YOU!
I'M NOT YOUR BOY FRIEND, AND I'M NOT GOING TO CLOBBER ANYBODY!
DON'T GO 'WAY! I HAVE TO TALK HIM INTO IT!!
1-22
© 1968 Peanuts Worldwide LLC. Dist. by Universal Uclick
www.snoopy.com
SCHULZ

THIS KID AT SCHOOL INSULTED ME, SEE?
NOW, WHAT I WANT YOU TO DO IS BITE HIM ON THE LEG TO HELP ME GET EVEN WITH HIM..
BITE SOMEONE...JUST TO GET EVEN?
HOW GAUCHE!
1-23
© 1968 Peanuts Worldwide LLC. Dist. by Universal Uclick
www.snoopy.com
SCHULZ

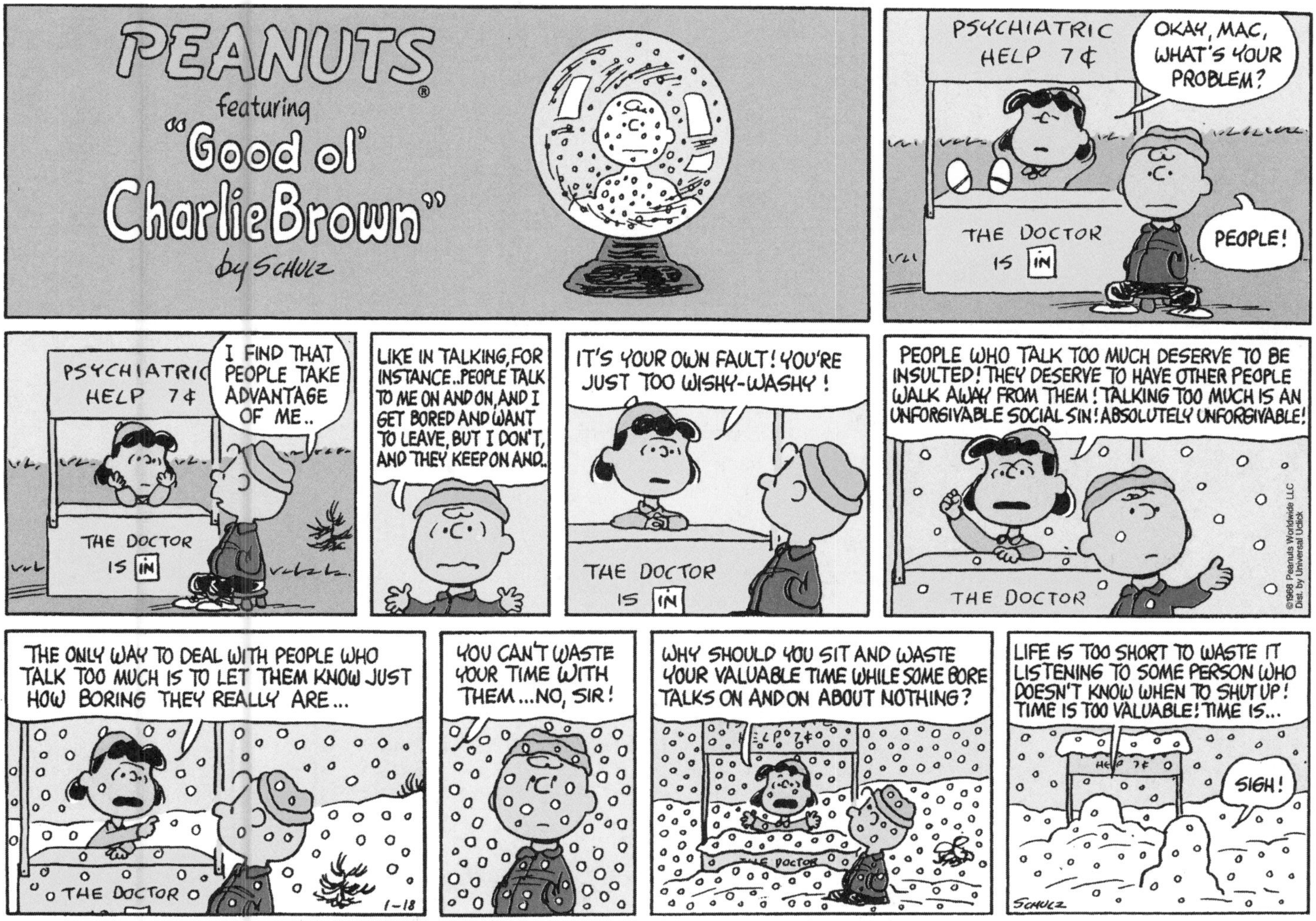
PEANUTS®
featuring
"Good ol' Charlie Brown"
by SCHULZ
PSYCHIATRIC HELP 7¢
OKAY, MAC, WHAT'S YOUR PROBLEM?
THE DOCTOR IS IN
PEOPLE!
PSYCHIATRIC HELP 7¢
I FIND THAT PEOPLE TAKE ADVANTAGE OF ME..
THE DOCTOR IS IN
LIKE IN TALKING, FOR INSTANCE..PEOPLE TALK TO ME ON AND ON, AND I GET BORED AND WANT TO LEAVE, BUT I DON'T, AND THEY KEEP ON AND..
IT'S YOUR OWN FAULT! YOU'RE JUST TOO WISHY-WASHY!
THE DOCTOR IS IN
PEOPLE WHO TALK TOO MUCH DESERVE TO BE INSULTED! THEY DESERVE TO HAVE OTHER PEOPLE WALK AWAY FROM THEM! TALKING TOO MUCH IS AN UNFORGIVABLE SOCIAL SIN! ABSOLUTELY UNFORGIVABLE!
THE DOCTOR
©1988 Peanuts Worldwide LLC
Dist. by Universal Uclick
THE ONLY WAY TO DEAL WITH PEOPLE WHO TALK TOO MUCH IS TO LET THEM KNOW JUST HOW BORING THEY REALLY ARE...
THE DOCTOR
1-18
YOU CAN'T WASTE YOUR TIME WITH THEM...NO, SIR!
WHY SHOULD YOU SIT AND WASTE YOUR VALUABLE TIME WHILE SOME BORE TALKS ON AND ON ABOUT NOTHING?
LIFE IS TOO SHORT TO WASTE IT LISTENING TO SOME PERSON WHO DOESN'T KNOW WHEN TO SHUT UP! TIME IS TOO VALUABLE! TIME IS...
SIGH!
SCHULZ

THIS SOUNDS LIKE A GOOD IDEA...
"TO KEEP FROM SLIPPING ON ICY SIDEWALKS, NAIL BOTTLE CAPS TO THE SOLES OF YOUR SHOES"
1-20
© 1967 Peanuts Worldwide LLC, Dist. by Universal Uclick
www.snoopy.com
I THINK YOU'RE SUPPOSED TO TAKE THE BOTTLES OFF!
SCHULZ

MY DAD LIKES TO HAVE ME COME DOWN TO THE BARBER SHOP, AND WAIT FOR HIM
NO MATTER HOW BUSY HE IS, EVEN IF THE SHOP IS FULL OF CUSTOMERS, HE ALWAYS STOPS TO SAY, "HI" TO ME...
© 1968 Peanuts Worldwide LLC, Dist. by Universal Uclick
I SIT HERE ON THE BENCH UNTIL SIX O'CLOCK, WHEN HE'S THROUGH, AND THEN WE RIDE HOME TOGETHER..
1-24
www.snoopy.com
IT REALLY DOESN'T TAKE MUCH TO MAKE A DAD HAPPY...
SCHULZ

© 1968 Peanuts Worldwide LLC, Dist. by Universal Uclick
NICE GOING...IT TOOK THAT STONE FOUR THOUSAND YEARS TO GET TO SHORE, AND NOW YOU'VE THROWN IT BACK!
1-19
www.snoopy.com
EVERYTHING I DO MAKES ME FEEL GUILTY..
SCHULZ

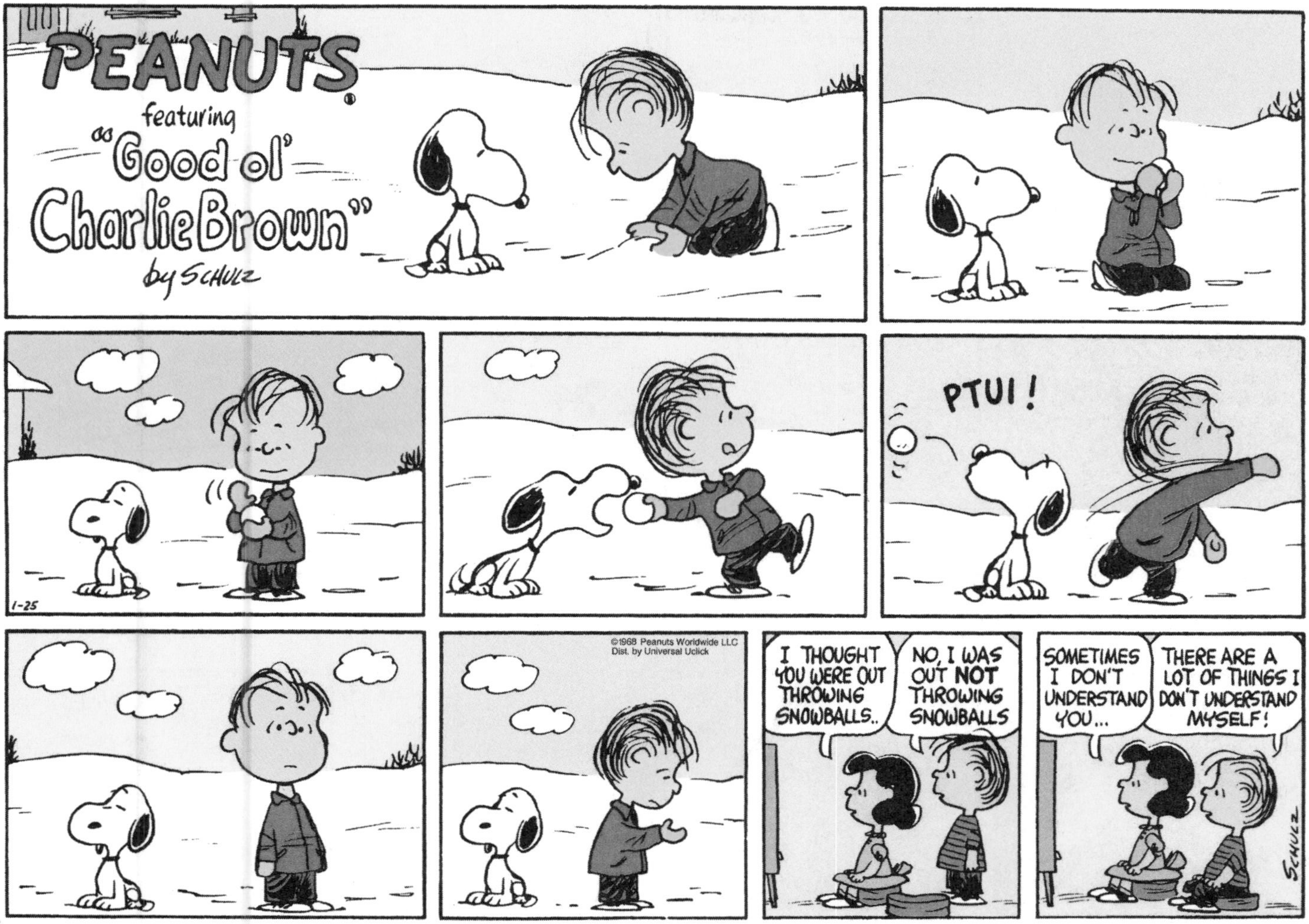
PEANUTS
featuring
"Good ol' Charlie Brown"
by SCHULZ
1-25
PTUI!
©1968 Peanuts Worldwide LLC
Dist. by Universal Uclick
I THOUGHT YOU WERE OUT THROWING SNOWBALLS..
NO, I WAS OUT **NOT** THROWING SNOWBALLS
SOMETIMES I DON'T UNDERSTAND YOU...
THERE ARE A LOT OF THINGS I DON'T UNDERSTAND MYSELF!
SCHULZ

ONE OF BEETHOVEN'S FAVORITE DISHES WAS MACARONI AND CHEESE
THE GIRL I MARRY MUST BE ABLE TO MAKE GOOD MACARONI AND CHEESE..
1-28
© 1967 Peanuts Worldwide LLC, Dist. by Universal Uclick
www.snoopy.com
HOW DID BEETHOVEN FEEL ABOUT COLD CEREAL?
SCHULZ

WHO'S CRABBY?
YOU'RE CRABBY!
www.snoopy.com
YOU'RE ALWAYS CRABBY! YOU'RE CRABBY IN THE MORNING, YOU'RE CRABBY AT NOON AND YOU'RE CRABBY AT NIGHT!
1-29
© 1966 Peanuts Worldwide LLC, Dist. by Universal Uclick
CAN I HELP IT IF I WAS BORN WITH CRABBY GENES?!
SCHULZ

HURRY UP... YOU'LL BE LATE FOR SCHOOL..
HERE...DON'T FORGET YOUR LUNCH..
© 1967 Peanuts Worldwide LLC, Dist. by Universal Uclick
SO LONG...HAVE A GOOD DAY..
1-30
www.snoopy.com
SURVIVE!
SCHULZ

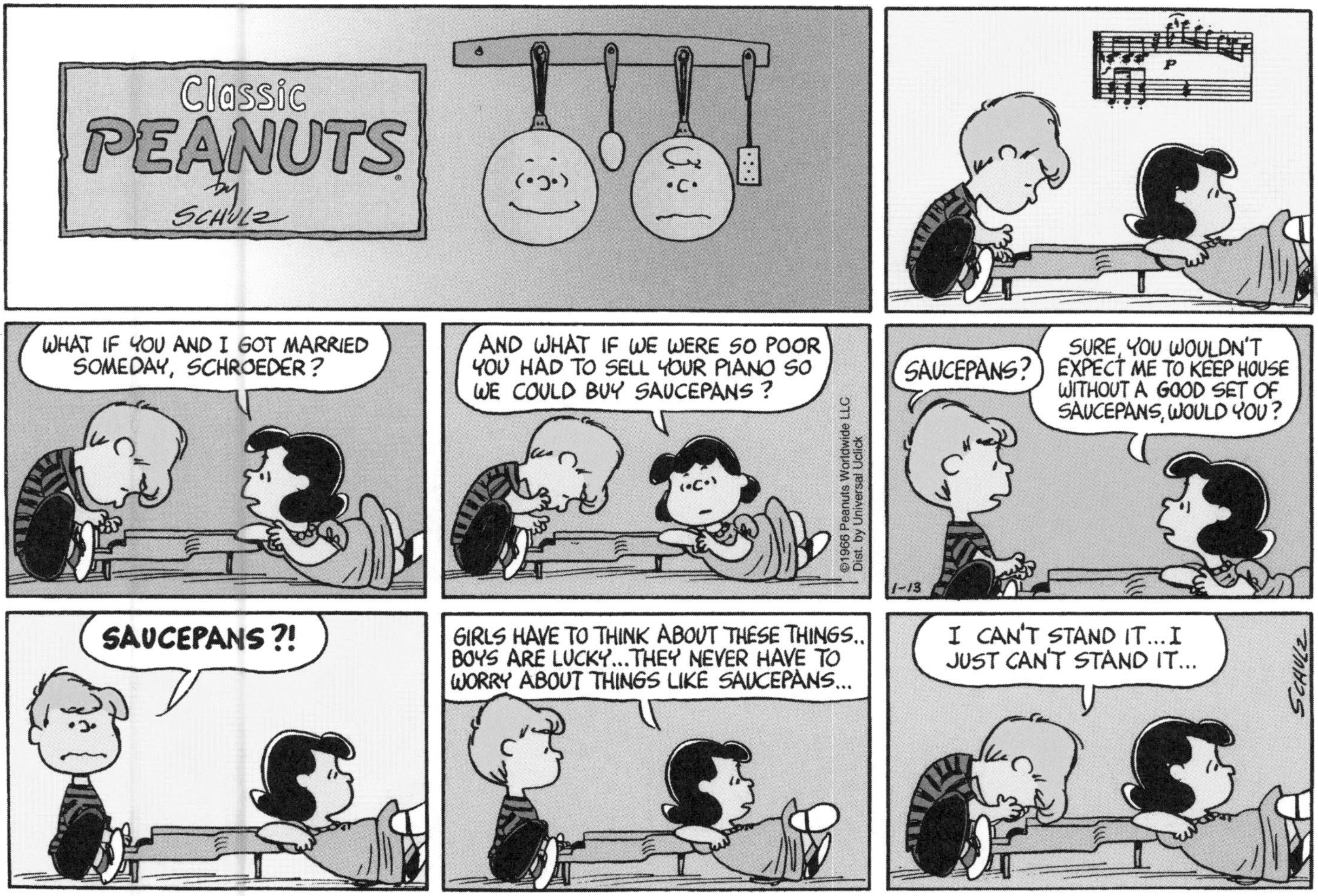
Classic PEANUTS by SCHULZ
WHAT IF YOU AND I GOT MARRIED SOMEDAY, SCHROEDER?
AND WHAT IF WE WERE SO POOR YOU HAD TO SELL YOUR PIANO SO WE COULD BUY SAUCEPANS?
©1966 Peanuts Worldwide LLC
Dist. by Universal Uclick
SAUCEPANS?
SURE, YOU WOULDN'T EXPECT ME TO KEEP HOUSE WITHOUT A GOOD SET OF SAUCEPANS, WOULD YOU?
1-13
SAUCEPANS?!
GIRLS HAVE TO THINK ABOUT THESE THINGS.. BOYS ARE LUCKY...THEY NEVER HAVE TO WORRY ABOUT THINGS LIKE SAUCEPANS...
I CAN'T STAND IT...I JUST CAN'T STAND IT...
SCHULZ

WELL! WHAT A SURPRISE..
THANK YOU VERY MUCH
2-1
© 1967 Peanuts Worldwide LLC, Dist. by Universal Uclick
THIS IS GOOD HOT CHOCOLATE
IT WOULD TASTE EVEN BETTER WITH A SKI LODGE AROUND IT!
www.snoopy.com
SCHULZ

YOU SPEND ALL YOUR TIME LYING ON TOP OF THAT DOG HOUSE..
2-2
THAT'S ALL YOU SEEM TO DO... YOU JUST LIE THERE AND LIE THERE
© 1968 Peanuts Worldwide LLC, Dist. by Universal Uclick
I JUST DON'T SEE HOW YOU DO IT!
LET'S NOT OVERLOOK THE POSSIBILITY OF GENIUS!
www.snoopy.com
SCHULZ

2-3
© 1968 Peanuts Worldwide LLC, Dist. by Universal Uclick
POOF!
www.snoopy.com
PICK A CARD... ANY CARD..
SCHULZ

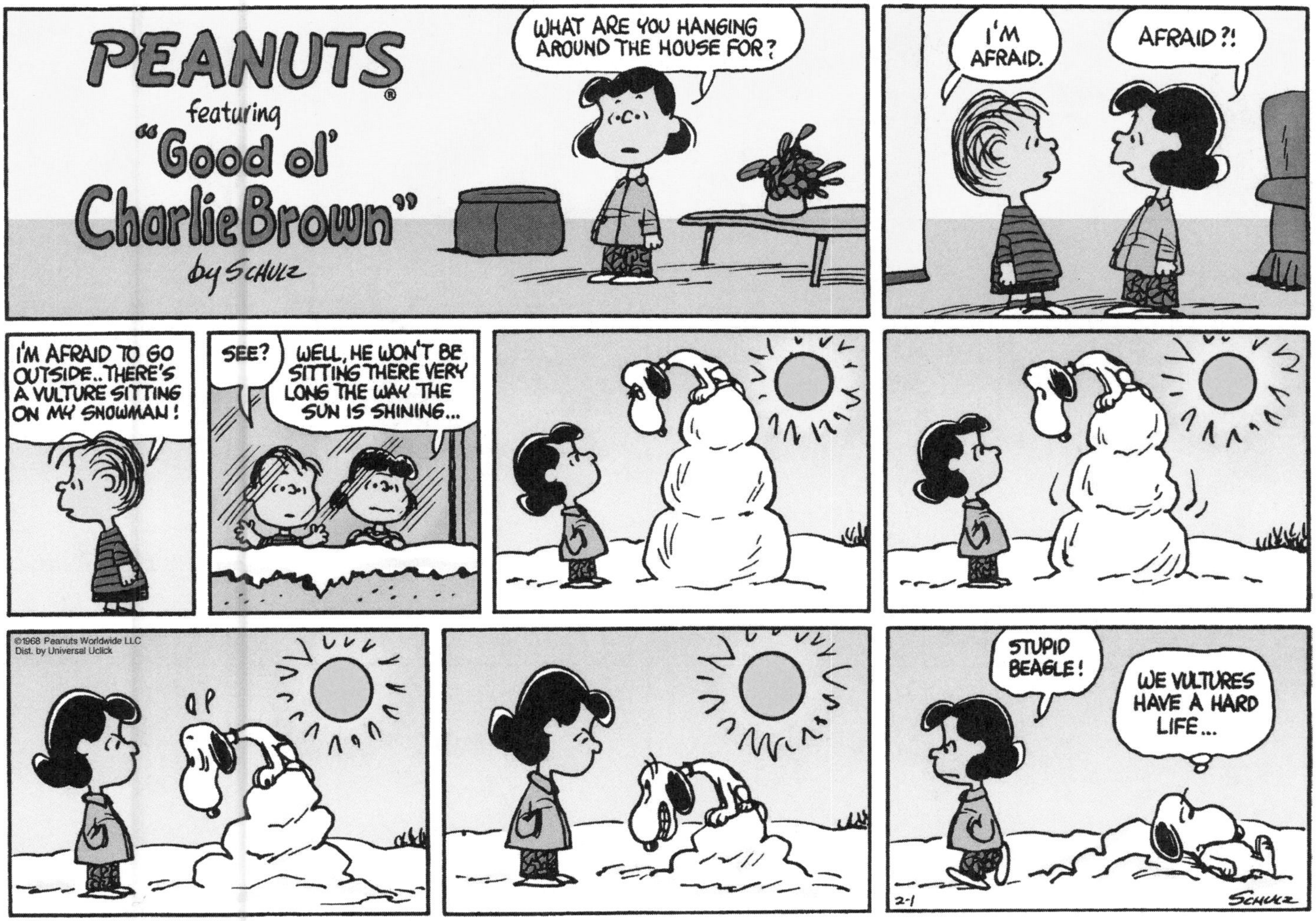
PEANUTS
featuring
"Good ol' Charlie Brown"
by SCHULZ
WHAT ARE YOU HANGING AROUND THE HOUSE FOR?
I'M AFRAID.
AFRAID?!
I'M AFRAID TO GO OUTSIDE.. THERE'S A VULTURE SITTING ON MY SNOWMAN!
SEE?
WELL, HE WON'T BE SITTING THERE VERY LONG THE WAY THE SUN IS SHINING...
©1968 Peanuts Worldwide LLC
Dist. by Universal Uclick
STUPID BEAGLE!
WE VULTURES HAVE A HARD LIFE...
2-1
SCHULZ

IF YOU HIT ME WITH THAT SNOWBALL, I'LL **CLOBBER** YOU WITH THIS ONE!
2-5
© 1968 Peanuts Worldwide LLC, Dist. by Universal Uclick
ARE YOU GOING TO LET HER BLUFF YOU THAT WAY?
www.snoopy.com
NEVER TRADE A HIT FOR A CLOBBER!
SCHULZ

YOU'RE A VERY BORING PERSON, CHARLIE BROWN
YAWN
2-7
© 1968 Peanuts Worldwide LLC, Dist. by Universal Uclick
EXCUSE ME...
www.snoopy.com
I GET BORED JUST TALKING ABOUT HOW BORING YOU ARE..
SCHULZ

MOM SAYS TO TURN OFF THE TV, AND GO TO BED
© 1965 Peanuts Worldwide LLC, Dist. by Universal Uclick
RATS!
www.snoopy.com
I ENJOY BEING THE BEARER OF BAD NEWS!
2-16
SCHULZ

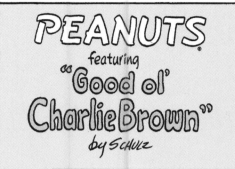

PEANUTS
featuring
"Good ol' Charlie Brown"
by Schulz

HAPPY VALENTINE'S DAY!

HERE, LITTLE RED-HAIRED GIRL...THIS IS FOR YOU.. IT'S A VALENTINE...

THIS IS A VALENTINE I MADE ESPECIALLY FOR YOU

HERE, LITTLE RED-HAIRED GIRL, THIS IS A VALENTINE I WANT YOU TO HAVE...

HERE, LITTLE RED-HAIRED GIRL...THIS IS A VALENTINE TO SHOW HOW MUCH I LIKE YOU...

HERE, THIS VALENTINE IS FOR YOU, SWEET LITTLE RED-HAIRED GIRL...

HERE, YOU LITTLE DOLL, YOU...THIS VALENTINE IS FOR YOU...

HERE, LITTLE RED-HAIRED GIRL, THIS VALENTINE IS FOR YOU, AND I HOPE YOU LIKE IT AS MUCH AS I LIKE YOU, AND...

SIGH

©1968 Peanuts Worldwide LLC
Dist. by Universal Uclick

US MAIL

HI, CHARLIE BROWN... DID YOU GIVE THAT LITTLE RED-HAIRED GIRL YOUR VALENTINE?

I COULDN'T DO IT..I MAILED IT ANONYMOUSLY...

GOOD OL' CHARLIE BROWN...HE'S THE CHARLIE BROWNIEST!

Schulz

2-8

23

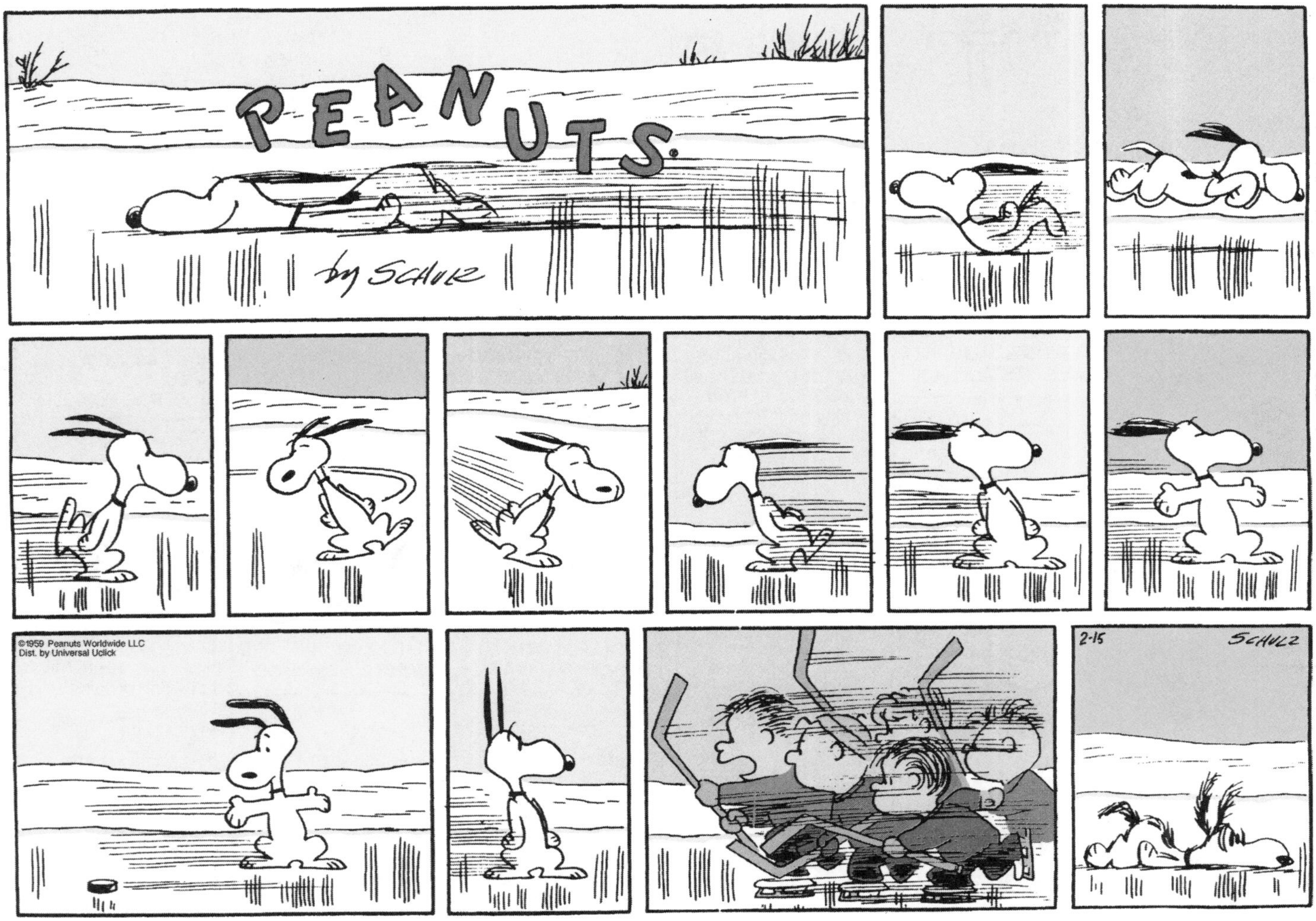
PEANUTS
by SCHULZ
©1959 Peanuts Worldwide LLC
Dist. by Universal Uclick
2-15
SCHULZ

WAITING FOR VALENTINES!
2-9
© 1968 Peanuts Worldwide LLC, Dist. by Universal Uclick
www.snoopy.com
SCHULZ

WAITING FOR VALENTINES...
OH.....WELL, GOOD LUCK..
THANK YOU
YOU'LL NEED IT!
YOU DIDN'T HAVE TO SAY THAT!!
2-10
© 1968 Peanuts Worldwide LLC, Dist. by Universal Uclick
www.snoopy.com
SCHULZ

SIGH
2-11
© 1968 Peanuts Worldwide LLC, Dist. by Universal Uclick
www.snoopy.com
SCHULZ

AND I GOT A VALENTINE FROM JOYCE AND I GOT ONE FROM PEGGY
AND I GOT ONE FROM ZELMA, AND JANELL, AND BOOTS, AND PAT, AND SYDNEY, AND WINNIE, AND JEAN, AND ROSEMARY, AND COURTNEY, AND FERN, AND MEREDITH ...
© 1968 Peanuts Worldwide LLC. Dist. by Universal Uclick
AND AMY, AND JILL, AND BETTY, AND MARGE, AND KAY, AND FRIEDA, AND ANNABELLE, AND SUE, AND EVA, AND JUDY, AND RUTH ...
2-12
www.snoopy.com
AND BARBARA, AND OL' HELEN, AND ANN, AND JANE, AND DOROTHY, AND MARGARET, AND...
I CAN'T STAND IT... I JUST CAN'T STAND IT...
SCHULZ

2-13
AND I GOT A VALENTINE FROM CLARA, AND I GOT ONE FROM VIRGINIA AND ONE FROM RUBY..
© 1968 Peanuts Worldwide LLC. Dist. by Universal Uclick
AND I GOT ONE FROM JOY, AND CÉCILE, AND JULIE, AND HEDY, AND JUNE, AND MARIE ...
www.snoopy.com
AND KATHLEEN, AND MAGGIE, AND DIANE, AND VIVIAN, AND CHARLOTTE, AND TEKLA, AND LILLIAN, AND...
GOOD GRIEF!
SCHULZ

AND EDNA, AND NAOMI, AND LILA, AND FRAN, AND..
YOU DIDN'T GET A VALENTINE FROM LILA!
I DIDN'T? DIDN'T LILA SEND ME A VALENTINE?
2-14
© 1968 Peanuts Worldwide LLC. Dist. by Universal Uclick
LILA DOESN'T LOVE ME ANY MORE!
www.snoopy.com
OH, WELL... AND CONNIE, AND CHIYO, AND MARILYN, AND AILEEN, AND..
I CAN'T STAND IT... I JUST CAN'T STAND IT....
SCHULZ

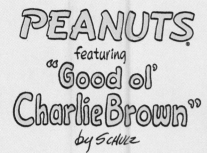

PEANUTS
featuring
"Good ol'
Charlie Brown"
by Schulz

HMM..

LET'S SEE..WE'LL HAVE TO HAVE A STATION WAGON, A TOWN CAR AND A SPORTS CAR...OUR HOME SHOULD BE IN AT LEAST THE ONE-HUNDRED-THOUSAND CLASS... DO PIANO PLAYERS MAKE A LOT OF MONEY?

I DON'T KNOW...I SUPPOSE IT DEPENDS ON HOW HARD THEY PRACTICE...

I SEE..

WELL, I'LL PROBABLY NEED A HALF DOZEN FUR COATS, AT LEAST THIRTY SKI OUTFITS AND ABOUT FIFTY FORMALS...I'LL NEEDS LOTS OF JEWELRY AND EXOTIC PERFUMES AND I'LL NEED ABOUT A HUNDRED PAIRS OF SHOES...

WE'LL HAVE TO HAVE A SWIMMING POOL, OLYMPIC SIZE, HEATED, AND RIDING HORSES, A TENNIS COURT AND A HUGE FORMAL GARDEN...WE WILL TRAVEL EXTENSIVELY, OF COURSE; ROUND-THE-WORLD CRUISES...THAT SORT OF THING...AND...

1-26

KEEP PRACTICING, KID!

TOMORROW IS VALENTINE'S DAY...
ARE YOU GOING TO GIVE ME A VALENTINE?
I NEVER HAVE... WHAT MAKES YOU THINK I'LL GIVE YOU ONE THIS YEAR?
HOPE!!
© 1965 Peanuts Worldwide LLC, Dist. by Universal Uclick
www.snoopy.com
2/13
SCHULZ

YOU KNOW, THERE ARE TIMES WHEN YOU REALLY BUG ME!
BUT I MUST ADMIT THERE ARE ALSO TIMES WHEN I FEEL LIKE GIVING YOU A HUG...
© 1968 Peanuts Worldwide LLC, Dist. by Universal Uclick
www.snoopy.com
THAT'S THE WAY I AM... BUGABLE AND HUGABLE!
2-4
SCHULZ

THIS IS THE SAME THING I HAD TO EAT YESTERDAY..
IN FACT, THIS IS THE SAME THING I HAD TO EAT EVERY DAY FOR THE PAST MONTH!
© 1968 Peanuts Worldwide LLC, Dist. by Universal Uclick
I THINK I'LL REGISTER A COMPLAINT...
www.snoopy.com
AFTER I'VE FINISHED EATING!
2-6
SCHULZ

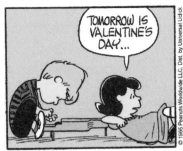

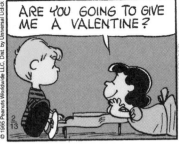

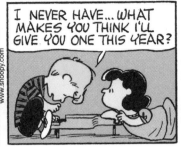

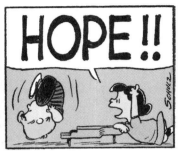

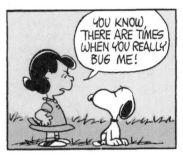

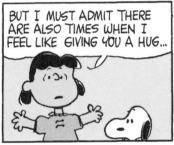

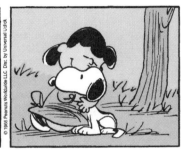

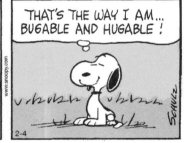

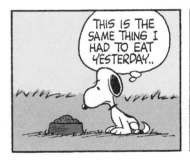

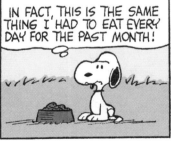

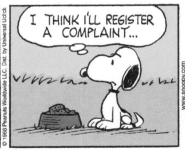

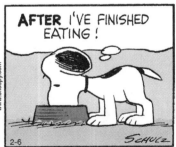

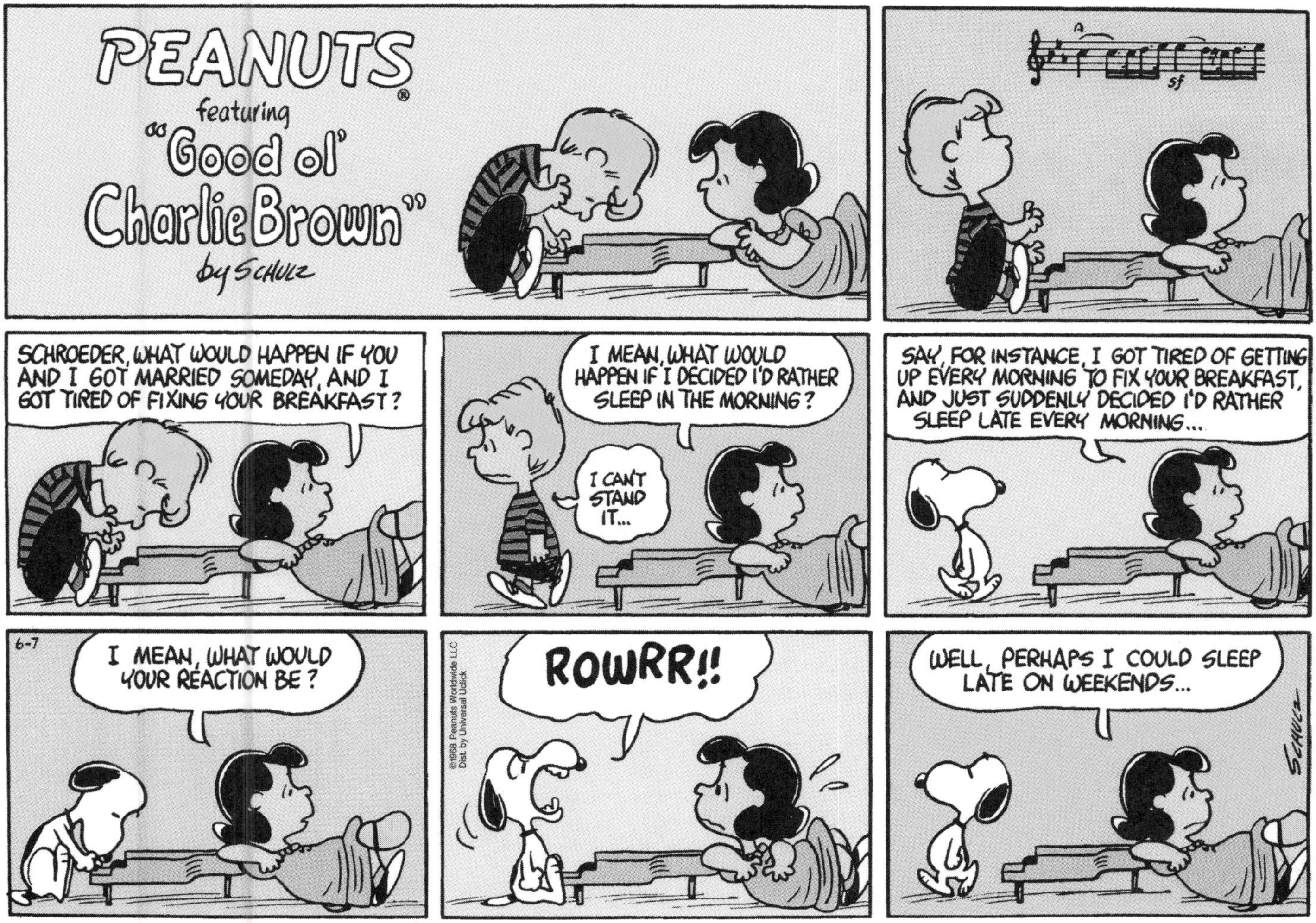
PEANUTS®
featuring
"Good ol' Charlie Brown"
by SCHULZ
SCHROEDER, WHAT WOULD HAPPEN IF YOU AND I GOT MARRIED SOMEDAY, AND I GOT TIRED OF FIXING YOUR BREAKFAST?
I MEAN, WHAT WOULD HAPPEN IF I DECIDED I'D RATHER SLEEP IN THE MORNING?
I CAN'T STAND IT...
SAY, FOR INSTANCE, I GOT TIRED OF GETTING UP EVERY MORNING TO FIX YOUR BREAKFAST, AND JUST SUDDENLY DECIDED I'D RATHER SLEEP LATE EVERY MORNING...
6-7
I MEAN, WHAT WOULD YOUR REACTION BE?
©1968 Peanuts Worldwide LLC
Dist. by Universal Uclick
ROWRR!!
WELL, PERHAPS I COULD SLEEP LATE ON WEEKENDS...
SCHULZ

2-11
LOOK AT THIS TINY LITTLE BUG
IT'S APPALLING HOW LITTLE HE KNOWS... HE'S NOT LIKE US...
HE DOESN'T KNOW ANYTHING ABOUT VOTING, OR DISEASE, OR EARTHQUAKES, OR LOVE OR MONDAY MORNINGS..
WHO'S BETTER OFF?
SCHULZ

THERE'S AN ARTICLE HERE IN THE PAPER ABOUT THIS DOG...
HIS OWNER IS BEING SUED BECAUSE THE DOG DUG UP THE NEIGHBOR'S FLOWER GARDEN
2-16
BOY, YOU DOGS SURE DO SOME STRANGE THINGS
I CANNOT BE RESPONSIBLE FOR THE ACTIONS OF MY COLLEAGUES!
SCHULZ

WHY DON'T TREES HAVE LEAVES IN THE WINTER?
BOY, YOU SURE ASK SOME STUPID QUESTIONS!
2-18
EVEN STUPID QUESTIONS HAVE ANSWERS!
SCHULZ

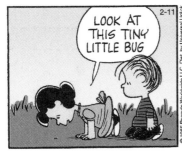

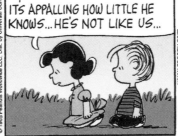

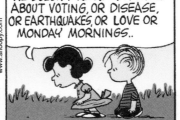

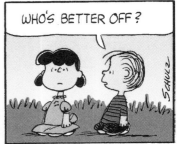

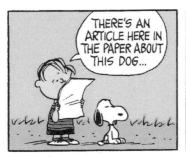

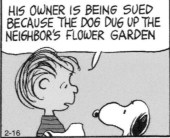

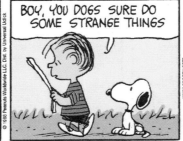

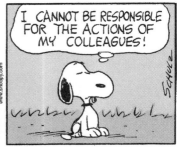

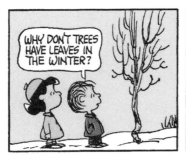

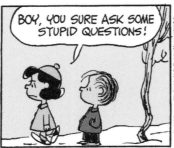

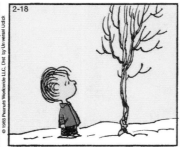

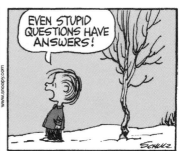

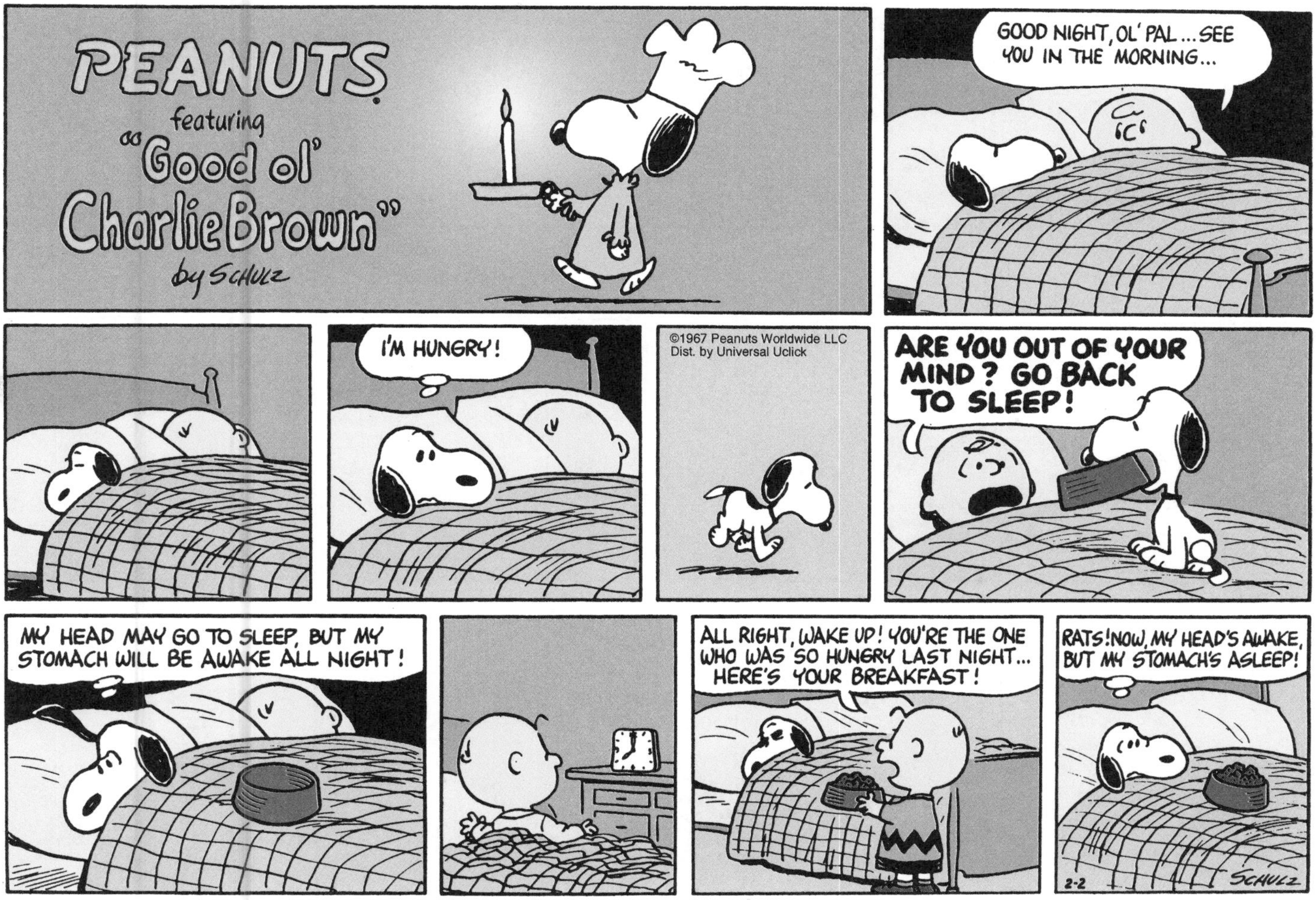
PEANUTS
featuring
"Good ol' CharlieBrown"
by SCHULZ
GOOD NIGHT, OL' PAL...SEE YOU IN THE MORNING...
I'M HUNGRY!
©1967 Peanuts Worldwide LLC
Dist. by Universal Uclick
ARE YOU OUT OF YOUR MIND? GO BACK TO SLEEP!
MY HEAD MAY GO TO SLEEP, BUT MY STOMACH WILL BE AWAKE ALL NIGHT!
ALL RIGHT, WAKE UP! YOU'RE THE ONE WHO WAS SO HUNGRY LAST NIGHT... HERE'S YOUR BREAKFAST!
RATS! NOW, MY HEAD'S AWAKE, BUT MY STOMACH'S ASLEEP!
2-2
SCHULZ

YOU'RE THE WORST KIND OF LITTLE BROTHER A GIRL COULD HAVE!
IF I COULD HAVE HAD MY CHOICE, YOU WOULD HAVE BEEN THE LAST ONE I WOULD HAVE CHOSEN!
THIRTY YEARS FROM NOW YOU'LL LOVE ME!
BIG SISTERS ALWAYS LOVE THEIR BROTHERS THIRTY YEARS LATER
2-17
SCHULZ
© 1965 Peanuts Worldwide LLC, Dist. by Universal Uclick
www.snoopy.com

YOU'RE A FINE ONE TO TALK!
YOU'RE ALWAYS SAYING I'M SUCH A TERRIBLE LITTLE BROTHER..
WELL, WHAT MAKES YOU THINK YOU'RE SUCH A WONDERFUL OLDER SISTER?
WAAH!
I STRUCK A NERVE!
2-18
SCHULZ
© 1965 Peanuts Worldwide LLC, Dist. by Universal Uclick
www.snoopy.com

HERE'S THE WORLD WAR I FLYING ACE STANDING BESIDE HIS SOPWITH CAMEL
A LIGHT SNOW IS FALLING... THERE'LL BE NO FLYING TODAY
FEELING FRISKY, THE FLYING ACE THROWS A SNOWBALL AT ONE OF HIS MECHANICS...
ACTUALLY, GENERAL PERSHING JUST HATES TO SEE US THROWING SNOWBALLS...
2-19
SCHULZ
© 1968 Peanuts Worldwide LLC, Dist. by Universal Uclick
www.snoopy.com

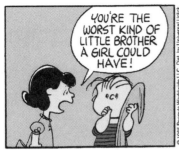

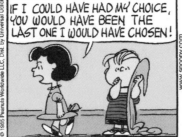

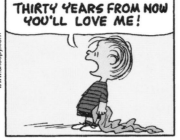

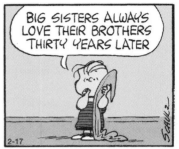

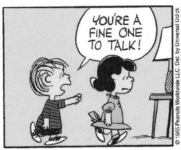

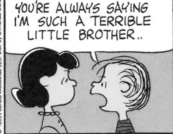

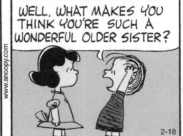

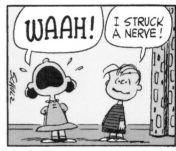

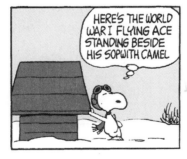

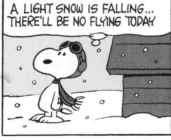

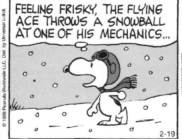

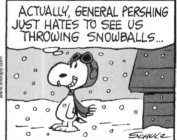

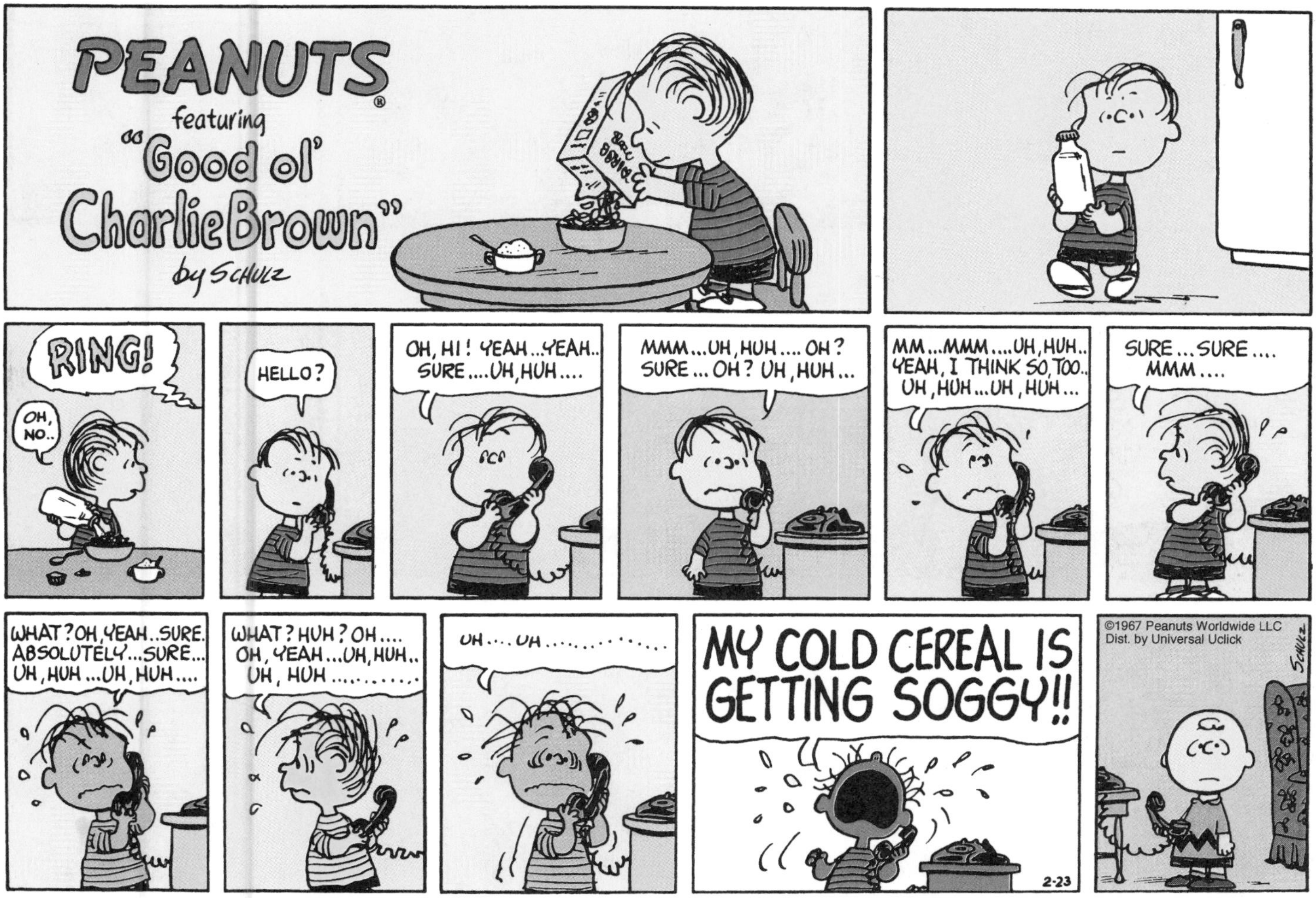
PEANUTS®
featuring
"Good ol' Charlie Brown"
by SCHULZ
RING!
OH, NO..
HELLO?
OH, HI! YEAH...YEAH.. SURE....UH, HUH....
MMM...UH, HUH.... OH? SURE... OH? UH, HUH...
MM...MMM....UH, HUH.. YEAH, I THINK SO, TOO.. UH, HUH...UH, HUH...
SURE... SURE.... MMM....
WHAT? OH, YEAH..SURE. ABSOLUTELY...SURE... UH, HUH...UH, HUH....
WHAT? HUH? OH.... OH, YEAH...UH, HUH.. UH, HUH ....
UH....UH...............
MY COLD CEREAL IS GETTING SOGGY!!
2-23
©1967 Peanuts Worldwide LLC Dist. by Universal Uclick
SCHULZ

YOU'RE CUTE, YOU KNOW THAT?
© 1965 Peanuts Worldwide LLC, Dist. by Universal Uclick
YOU'RE SO CUTE I THINK I'M GOING TO GIVE YOU A BIG HUG AND A KISS ON THE NOSE!
www.snoopy.com
2-20
THAT'S REAL CONCENTRATION
SCHULZ

I HAVE AN HISTORICAL QUESTION FOR YOU..
© 1965 Peanuts Worldwide LLC, Dist. by Universal Uclick
DID BEETHOVEN EVER HAVE ANY BEAUTIFUL GIRLS NEARBY WHILE HE WAS PRACTICING HIS PIANO?
2/22
www.snoopy.com
NO, I DON'T THINK BEETHOVEN EVER HAD ANY NUTTY FEMALES HANGING ON HIS PIANO WHILE HE WAS TRYING TO PRACTICE!
SCHULZ
THAT ISN'T QUITE WHAT I SAID

© 1968 Peanuts Worldwide LLC, Dist. by Universal Uclick
www.snoopy.com
I HATE WINDY DAYS!
SCHULZ
2-23

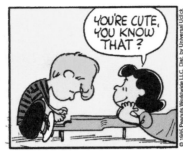

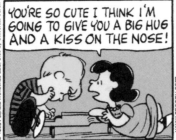

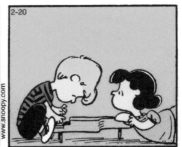

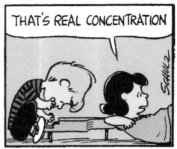

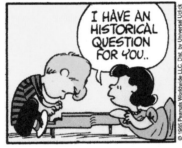

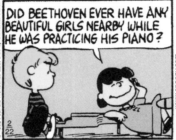

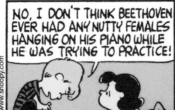

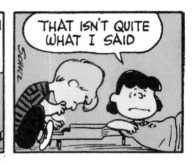

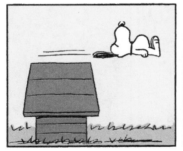

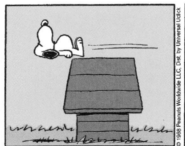

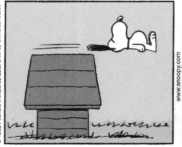

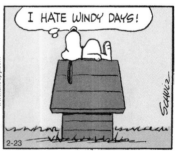

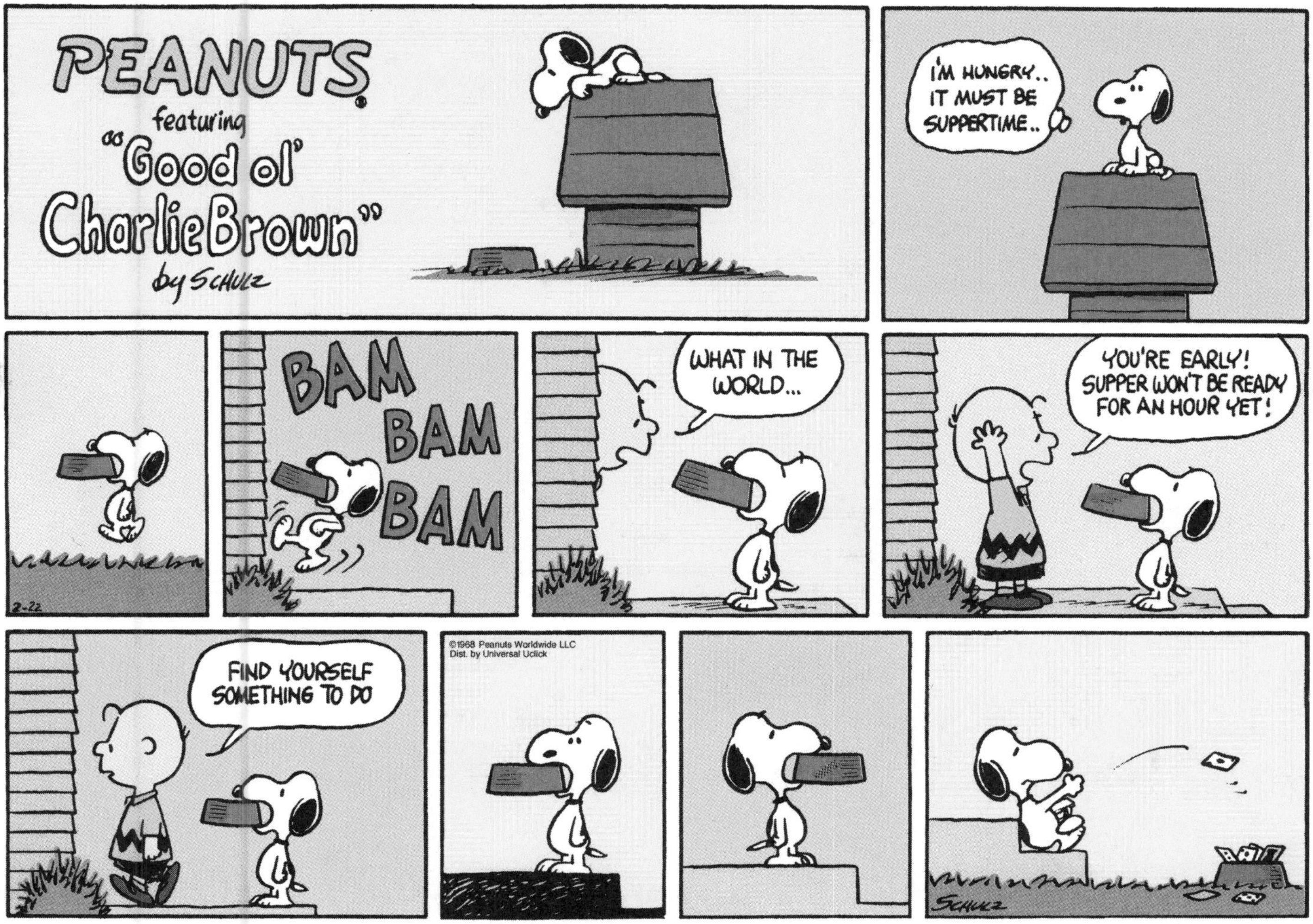
PEANUTS
featuring
"Good ol' Charlie Brown"
by SCHULZ
I'M HUNGRY.. IT MUST BE SUPPERTIME..
BAM BAM BAM
WHAT IN THE WORLD...
YOU'RE EARLY! SUPPER WON'T BE READY FOR AN HOUR YET!
FIND YOURSELF SOMETHING TO DO
©1968 Peanuts Worldwide LLC
Dist. by Universal Uclick
SCHULZ

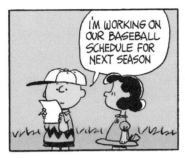

I'M WORKING ON OUR BASEBALL SCHEDULE FOR NEXT SEASON
GET US SOME GAMES WITH SOME REAL LITTLE KIDS, CHARLIE BROWN, SO WE CAN SLAUGHTER THEM...
2-20
© 1968 Peanuts Worldwide LLC. Dist. by Universal Uclick
AND THEN GET US SOME GAMES WITH SOME REAL OLD LADIES, AND WE'LL SLAUGHTER THEM, TOO!
www.snoopy.com
PLAN OUR SCHEDULE RIGHT, CHARLIE BROWN, AND WE'LL HAVE A GREAT SEASON!
SCHULZ

2-21
!
© 1968 Peanuts Worldwide LLC. Dist. by Universal Uclick
THAT'S THE LAST STRAW! IF HE WANTS ANY SUPPER, HE CAN COME AND GET IT HIMSELF!
www.snoopy.com
SERVANTS' ENTRANCE IN THE REAR →
SCHULZ

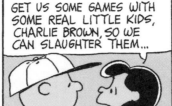

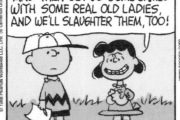

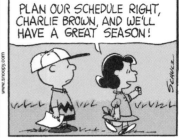

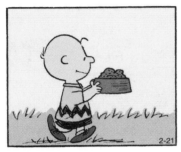

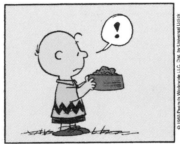

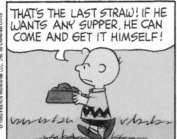

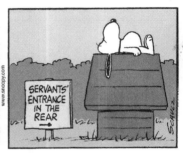

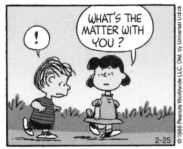

!
WHAT'S THE MATTER WITH YOU?
2-25
© 1966 Peanuts Worldwide LLC. Dist. by Universal Uclick
MY FEET HURT
www.snoopy.com
I THINK THESE NEW SHOES ARE TOO TIGHT
IT FEELS LIKE MY FEET ARE BEING MUGGED!
SCHULZ

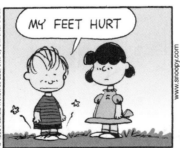

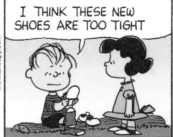

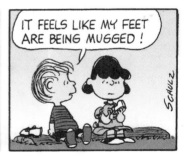

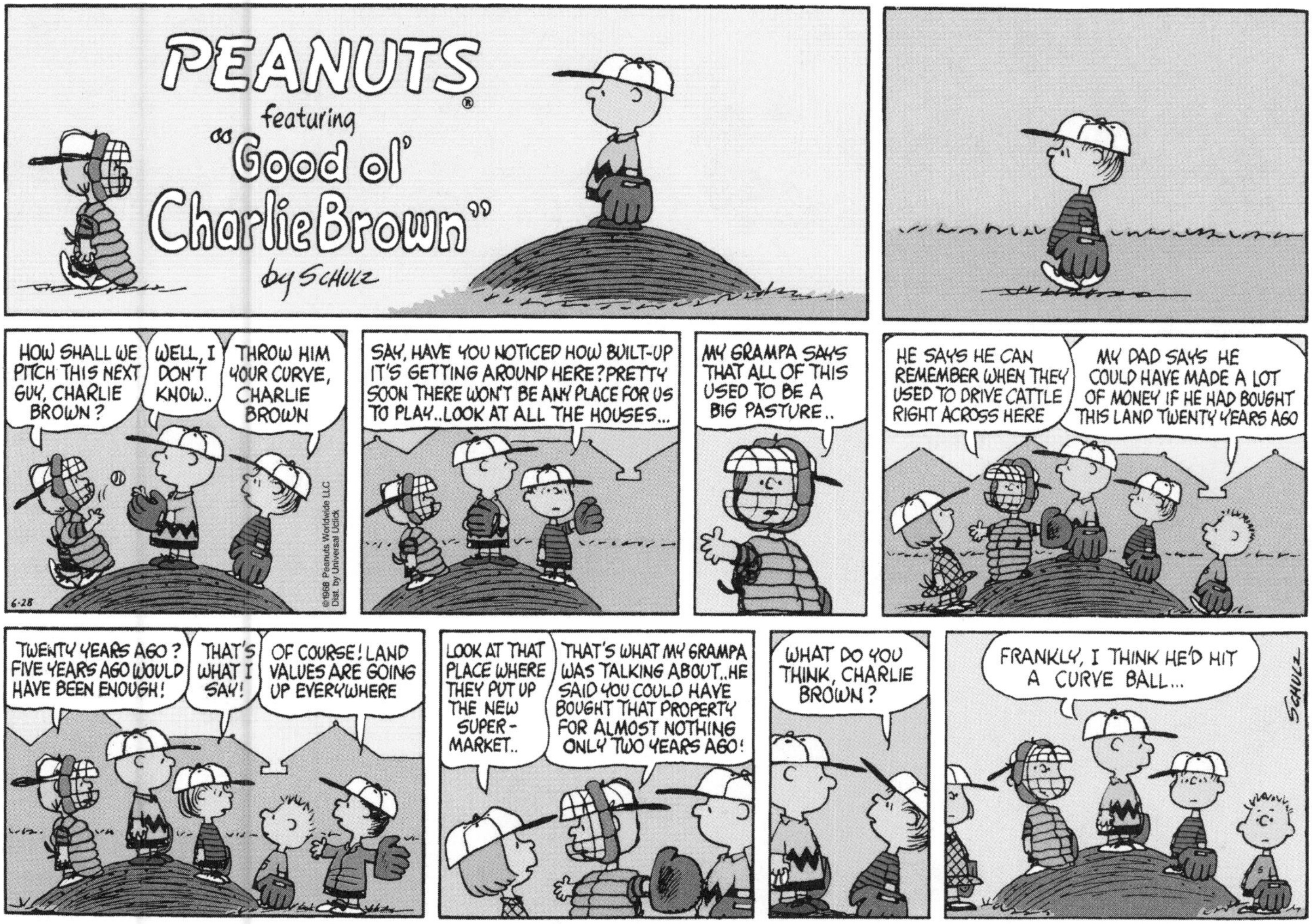
PEANUTS
featuring
"Good ol' Charlie Brown"
by SCHULZ
HOW SHALL WE PITCH THIS NEXT GUY, CHARLIE BROWN?
WELL, I DON'T KNOW..
THROW HIM YOUR CURVE, CHARLIE BROWN
6-28
©1968 Peanuts Worldwide LLC Dist. by Universal Uclick
SAY, HAVE YOU NOTICED HOW BUILT-UP IT'S GETTING AROUND HERE? PRETTY SOON THERE WON'T BE ANY PLACE FOR US TO PLAY..LOOK AT ALL THE HOUSES...
MY GRAMPA SAYS THAT ALL OF THIS USED TO BE A BIG PASTURE..
HE SAYS HE CAN REMEMBER WHEN THEY USED TO DRIVE CATTLE RIGHT ACROSS HERE
MY DAD SAYS HE COULD HAVE MADE A LOT OF MONEY IF HE HAD BOUGHT THIS LAND TWENTY YEARS AGO
TWENTY YEARS AGO? FIVE YEARS AGO WOULD HAVE BEEN ENOUGH!
THAT'S WHAT I SAY!
OF COURSE! LAND VALUES ARE GOING UP EVERYWHERE
LOOK AT THAT PLACE WHERE THEY PUT UP THE NEW SUPER-MARKET..
THAT'S WHAT MY GRAMPA WAS TALKING ABOUT..HE SAID YOU COULD HAVE BOUGHT THAT PROPERTY FOR ALMOST NOTHING ONLY TWO YEARS AGO!
WHAT DO YOU THINK, CHARLIE BROWN?
FRANKLY, I THINK HE'D HIT A CURVE BALL...
SCHULZ

MY STOMACH HURTS...

I THINK I WORRY ABOUT TOO MANY THINGS...

THE MORE I WORRY, THE MORE MY STOMACH HURTS...THE MORE MY STOMACH HURTS, THE MORE I WORRY....

MY STOMACH HATES ME!

SO HERE I AM ABOUT TO SEE THE SCHOOL NURSE..

SHE'LL PROBABLY JUST TAKE MY TEMPERATURE AND LOOK AT MY THROAT...

MAYBE SHE'LL TAKE A BLOOD TEST...I HOPE SHE DOESN'T TAKE A BLOOD TEST...MAYBE SHE'LL JUST WEIGH ME...

IF SHE MENTIONS EXPLORATORY SURGERY, I'LL SCREAM!

THE SCHOOL NURSE TOLD ME TO GO HOME UNTIL MY STOMACH FELT BETTER

I WISH IT WOULDN'T HURT ALL THE TIME...

OTHER PEOPLE'S STOMACHS DON'T HURT ALL THE TIME...

MAYBE I HAVE A CHEAP STOMACH!

38

PSYCHIATRIC HELP 5¢
THE DOCTOR IS IN
I HAD TO GO TO THE SCHOOL NURSE YESTERDAY BECAUSE MY STOMACH HURT...
YOU WORRY TOO MUCH, CHARLIE BROWN... NO WONDER YOUR STOMACH HURTS...YOU'VE GOT TO STOP ALL THIS SILLY WORRYING!
© 1968 Peanuts Worldwide LLC. Dist. by Universal Uclick
HOW DO I STOP?
THE DOCTOR IS IN
2-27
www.snoopy.com
THAT'S **YOUR** WORRY! FIVE CENTS, PLEASE!!
THE DOCTOR IS IN
SCHULZ

© 1966 Peanuts Worldwide LLC. Dist. by Universal Uclick
2-26
?
www.snoopy.com
DO THUMBS EVER SPOIL?
SCHULZ

MOM SAYS SHE WANTS TO WASH YOUR BLANKET..
© 1966 Peanuts Worldwide LLC. Dist. by Universal Uclick
OKAY... HERE, TAKE IT...
YOU MEAN YOU CAN GIVE IT UP JUST LIKE THAT?
www.snoopy.com
SURE, IT DOESN'T BOTHER ME A BIT...
2-27
ALL I HAVE TO DO IS SPEND THE DAY IN BED WITH AN ICE-BAG ON MY HEAD!
SCHULZ

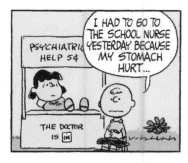

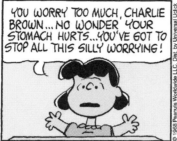

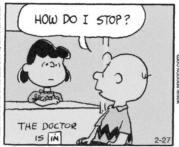

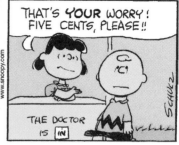

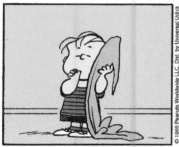

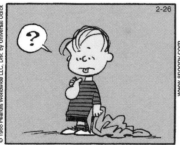

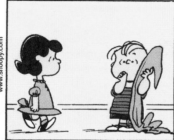

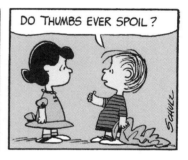

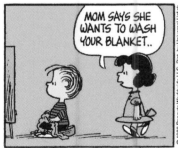

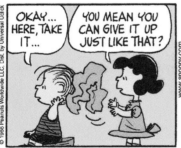

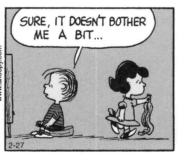

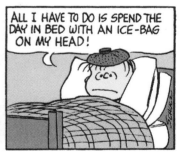

PEANUTS
featuring
"Good ol'
CharlieBrown"
by SCHULZ

DANGER!
Kite-eating
tree

HELLO, YOU DIRTY KITE-EATING TREE! HAVE YOU HAD A HARD WINTER? I'LL BET YOU'RE HUNGRY, AREN'T YOU?

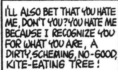

I'LL ALSO BET THAT YOU HATE ME, DON'T YOU? YOU HATE ME BECAUSE I RECOGNIZE YOU FOR WHAT YOU ARE, A DIRTY, SCHEMING, NO-GOOD, KITE-EATING TREE!

YOU ALSO HATE ME BECAUSE YOU NEED ME! I'M THE ONLY ONE AROUND HERE WHO FLIES KITES, AND WITHOUT ME, YOU'D GET PRETTY HUNGRY!

WHAT WOULD YOU DO IF I DECIDED NOT TO FLY ANY KITES THIS YEAR? WHAT WOULD YOU DO?

YOU'D STARVE TO DEATH, THAT'S WHAT YOU'D DO!

IT SORT OF SHAKES YOU UP, DOESN'T IT? WITHOUT ME, YOU'RE NOTHING!!

3-1

©1988 Peanuts Worldwide LLC
Dist. by Universal Uclick

EXCUSE ME, CHARLIE BROWN, BUT YOU LOOK SORT OF DIFFERENT... LIKE SOME CHANGE HAS COME OVER YOU...

I THINK MAYBE IT HAS...

FOR THE FIRST TIME IN MY LIFE I FEEL NEEDED!

40

SOMEDAY, I'D LIKE TO PUNCH A CAT IN THE NOSE!
2-28
I WONDER IF I'D EVER HAVE THE NERVE TO TRY IT...
© 1988 Peanuts Worldwide LLC. Dist. by Universal Uclick
PROBABLY NOT
www.snoopy.com
IT'S KIND OF FUN TO THINK ABOUT, THOUGH..
SCHULZ

DO THEY ALWAYS BRING THE COWS IN FROM THE PASTURE AT NIGHT?
© 1965 Peanuts Worldwide LLC. Dist. by Universal Uclick
OF COURSE, YOU BLOCKHEAD! IF THEY LEAVE THEM OUT OVER NIGHT, THEY GET PASTEURIZED!!
3-1
www.snoopy.com
I NEVER REALIZED THAT
I GUESS I'D MAKE A LOUSY FARMER!
SCHULZ

?
3-6
© 1965 Peanuts Worldwide LLC. Dist. by Universal Uclick
HMM...
www.snoopy.com
THERE'S A BUG ON THIS RUG...
THINK YOU'RE PRETTY SNUG, DON'T YOU?
SCHULZ

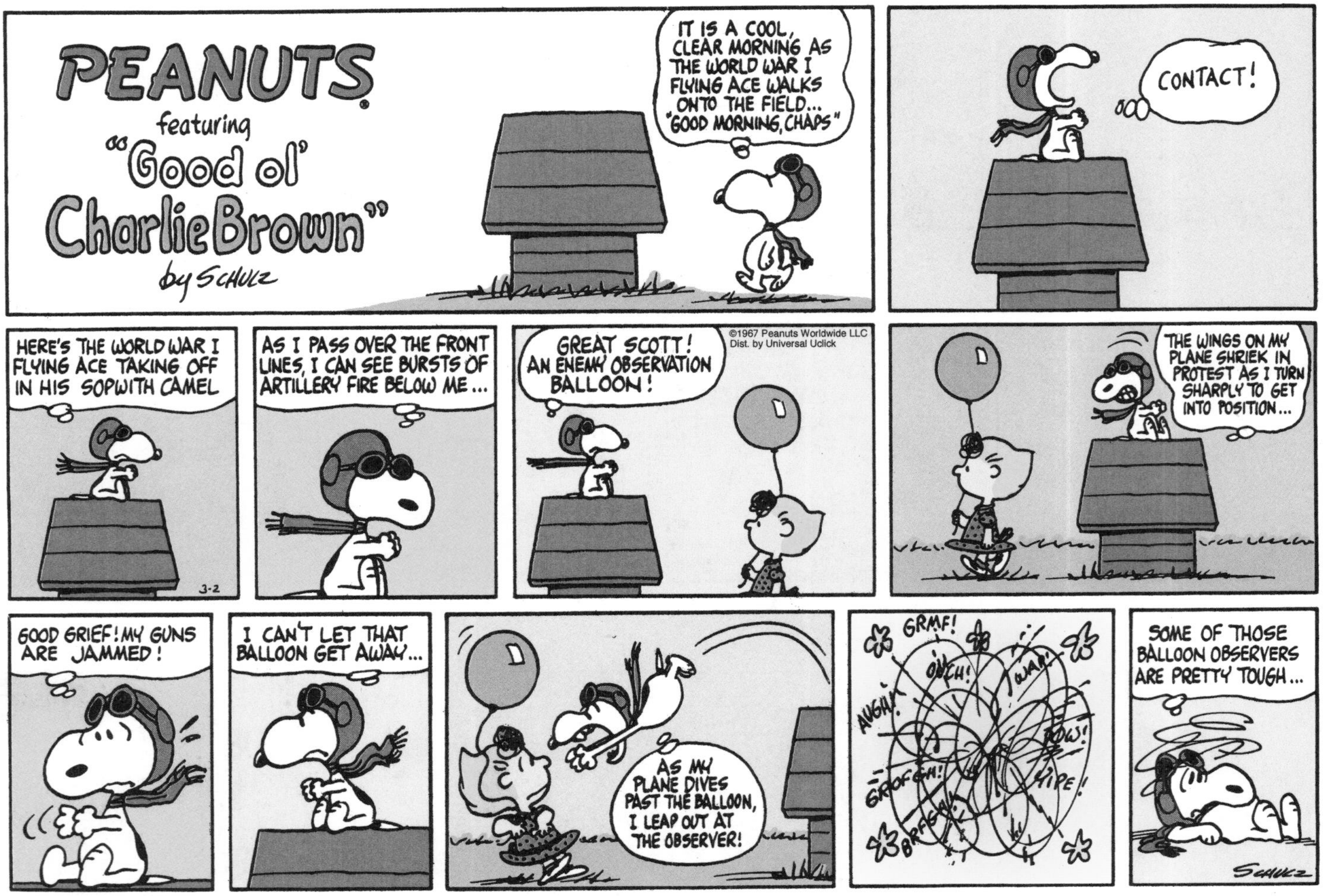
PEANUTS
featuring
"Good ol' Charlie Brown"
by SCHULZ
IT IS A COOL, CLEAR MORNING AS THE WORLD WAR I FLYING ACE WALKS ONTO THE FIELD... "GOOD MORNING, CHAPS"
CONTACT!
HERE'S THE WORLD WAR I FLYING ACE TAKING OFF IN HIS SOPWITH CAMEL
3-2
AS I PASS OVER THE FRONT LINES, I CAN SEE BURSTS OF ARTILLERY FIRE BELOW ME...
GREAT SCOTT! AN ENEMY OBSERVATION BALLOON!
©1967 Peanuts Worldwide LLC
Dist. by Universal Uclick
THE WINGS ON MY PLANE SHRIEK IN PROTEST AS I TURN SHARPLY TO GET INTO POSITION...
GOOD GRIEF! MY GUNS ARE JAMMED!
I CAN'T LET THAT BALLOON GET AWAY...
AS MY PLANE DIVES PAST THE BALLOON, I LEAP OUT AT THE OBSERVER!
GRMF!
OUCH!
WAP!
AUGH!
POW!
GROFGH!
YIPE!
SOME OF THOSE BALLOON OBSERVERS ARE PRETTY TOUGH...
SCHULZ

THIS YEAR WE'RE GOING TO STRESS PROPER CONDITIONING..
3-3
I WANT EACH PLAYER TO DO TWENTY PUSHUPS EVERY DAY!
© 1968 Peanuts Worldwide LLC, Dist. by Universal Uclick
HOW ABOUT ONE PUSHUP EVERY TWENTY DAYS?
www.snoopy.com
WHAT A CRABBY MANAGER..
SCHULZ

HEY, MANAGER, I CAN'T DO TWENTY PUSHUPS...
WELL, MAYBE YOU SHOULD START WITH JUST FIFTEEN OR MAYBE TEN...LET ME DEMONSTRATE...
© 1968 Peanuts Worldwide LLC, Dist. by Universal Uclick
PUSHUPS CAN BE VERY DIFFICULT IF YOU'RE OUT OF SHAPE..SOMETIMES IT'S BEST TO START WITH JUST...
www.snoopy.com
...ONE!
SCHULZ
3-4

I WAS WATCHING THIS BALL GAME ON TV LAST YEAR..
3-7
ONE OF THE PLAYERS GOT REAL MAD AT THE UMPIRE, AND KICKED DIRT ON HIM...
© 1968 Peanuts Worldwide LLC, Dist. by Universal Uclick
...LIKE THIS!
www.snoopy.com
YOU CAN LEARN A LOT WATCHING THOSE GAMES ON TV!
SCHULZ

NOW, LOOK HERE.. I DON'T THINK YOU'RE EVEN TRYING!
3-9
BLEAH!
© 1968 Peanuts Worldwide LLC, Dist. by Universal Uclick
COME BACK HERE!! YOU CAN'T QUIT THE TEAM BEFORE THE SEASON EVEN STARTS!
www.snoopy.com
I SHOULDN'T HAVE ACCUSED HIM OF NOT TRYING...BEAGLE-SHORTSTOPS ARE SO SENSITIVE...
SCHULZ

WHAT'LL WE DO? SNOOPY'S QUIT THE TEAM!
ALL I DID WAS BAWL HIM OUT A LITTLE..
DON'T BLAME YOURSELF, CHARLIE BROWN...
3-10
© 1968 Peanuts Worldwide LLC, Dist. by Universal Uclick
THAT'S THE TROUBLE WITH THAT STUPID DOG...HE'S ALWAYS CHANGING RAINBOWS!
www.snoopy.com
"CHANGING RAINBOWS"?!
SCHULZ

PLEASE COME BACK TO THE TEAM, SNOOPY...
IF YOU COME BACK, I'LL DO ANYTHING! I'LL RAISE YOUR FOOD ALLOWANCE... YOU CAN PLAY ANY POSITION YOU WANT.. YOU CAN EVEN BE MANAGER!
3-11
© 1968 Peanuts Worldwide LLC, Dist. by Universal Uclick
MANAGER?
www.snoopy.com
HERE'S THE WORLD FAMOUS BASEBALL MANAGER STANDING IN THE DUGOUT..
NOW WHAT HAVE I DONE?
SCHULZ

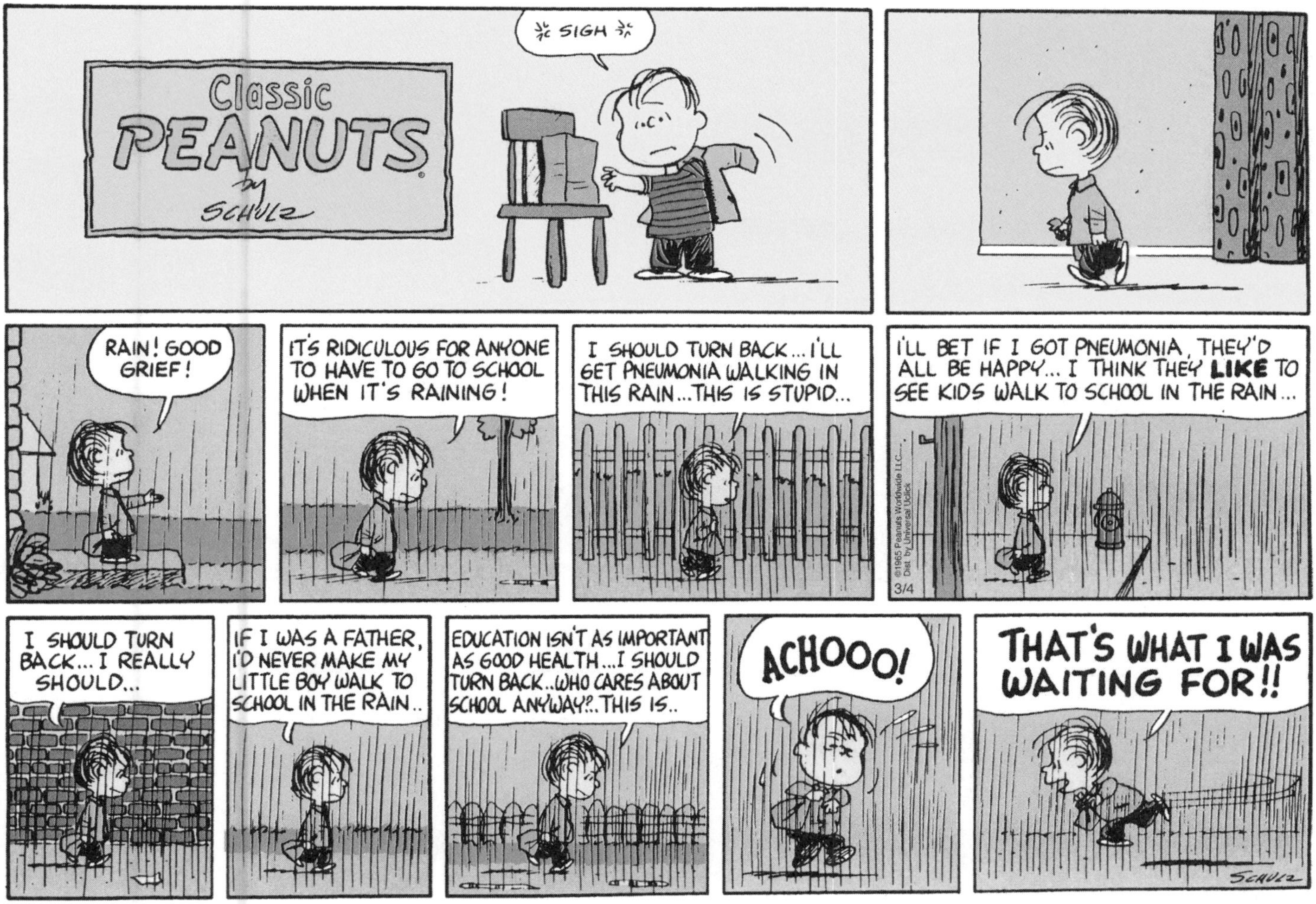
Classic PEANUTS by SCHULZ
SIGH
RAIN! GOOD GRIEF!
IT'S RIDICULOUS FOR ANYONE TO HAVE TO GO TO SCHOOL WHEN IT'S RAINING!
I SHOULD TURN BACK... I'LL GET PNEUMONIA WALKING IN THIS RAIN... THIS IS STUPID...
I'LL BET IF I GOT PNEUMONIA, THEY'D ALL BE HAPPY... I THINK THEY **LIKE** TO SEE KIDS WALK TO SCHOOL IN THE RAIN...
©1965 Peanuts Worldwide LLC. Dist. by Universal Uclick
3/4
I SHOULD TURN BACK... I REALLY SHOULD...
IF I WAS A FATHER, I'D NEVER MAKE MY LITTLE BOY WALK TO SCHOOL IN THE RAIN..
EDUCATION ISN'T AS IMPORTANT AS GOOD HEALTH... I SHOULD TURN BACK.. WHO CARES ABOUT SCHOOL ANYWAY?.. THIS IS..
ACHOOO!
THAT'S WHAT I WAS WAITING FOR!!
SCHULZ

MANAGER?
THAT STUPID BEAGLE IS GOING TO BE OUR NEW MANAGER? NOTHING DOING! I'LL...
© 1968 Peanuts Worldwide LLC. Dist. by Universal Uclick
3-12
BOOT!
www.snoopy.com
WE BASEBALL MANAGERS DON'T STAND FOR ANY BACK-TALK!
SCHULZ

STRIKE THREE!
3-13
© 1968 Peanuts Worldwide LLC. Dist. by Universal Uclick
BOOT!
www.snoopy.com
THIS NEW MANAGER IS GOING TO BE ROUGH TO PLAY FOR!
SCHULZ

KLUNK!
3-14
© 1968 Peanuts Worldwide LLC. Dist. by Universal Uclick
BOOT!
BOOT!
www.snoopy.com
SCHULZ

IT'S KIND OF NICE NOT BEING MANAGER..
ON THE NIGHT BEFORE OUR GAMES I ALWAYS USED TO LIE AWAKE WORRYING...
I WONDER IF OUR NEW MANAGER IS LYING AWAKE WORRYING...
Z
3-16
© 1968 Peanuts Worldwide LLC. Dist. by Universal Uclick
www.snoopy.com
SCHULZ

HERE WE GO... THE FIRST PITCH OF THE SEASON!
GOOD GRIEF! A HOME RUN!!
BOOT!
3-17
© 1968 Peanuts Worldwide LLC. Dist. by Universal Uclick
www.snoopy.com
SCHULZ

OH, OH! OUR NEW MANAGER IS GIVING ME THE SIGNAL TO STEAL SECOND..
"YOU'RE OUT!!"
BOOT!
3-18
© 1968 Peanuts Worldwide LLC. Dist. by Universal Uclick
www.snoopy.com
SCHULZ

WELL, WE LOST OUR FIRST GAME OF THE SEASON..
I WONDER HOW OUR NEW MANAGER WILL TAKE THIS DEFEAT ?
3-19
© 1968 Peanuts Worldwide LLC. Dist. by Universal Uclick
BOOT! BOOT! BOOT!
BOOT! BOOT! BOOT!
www.snoopy.com
I HATE LOSING!
SCHULZ

CHARLIE BROWN, WHEN A TEAM LOSES A GAME, IS IT THE FAULT OF THE PLAYERS OR THE MANAGER?
3-20
WELL, I DON'T KNOW...IT'S KIND OF HARD TO SAY, AND I...
© 1968 Peanuts Worldwide LLC. Dist. by Universal Uclick
WELL, I'M NOT AFRAID TO SAY! WHEN A TEAM LOSES A GAME, I THINK IT'S THE FAULT OF THE MANAGER!
www.snoopy.com
BOOT!
SCHULZ

ACTUALLY, RUNNING A BALL CLUB IS A VERY HARD JOB
IF YOU WANT, I'LL BE GLAD TO TAKE OVER AS MANAGER AGAIN.....
3-21
© 1968 Peanuts Worldwide LLC. Dist. by Universal Uclick
SMAK!
www.snoopy.com
A KISS ON THE NOSE, AND I'M OFF THE HOOK!

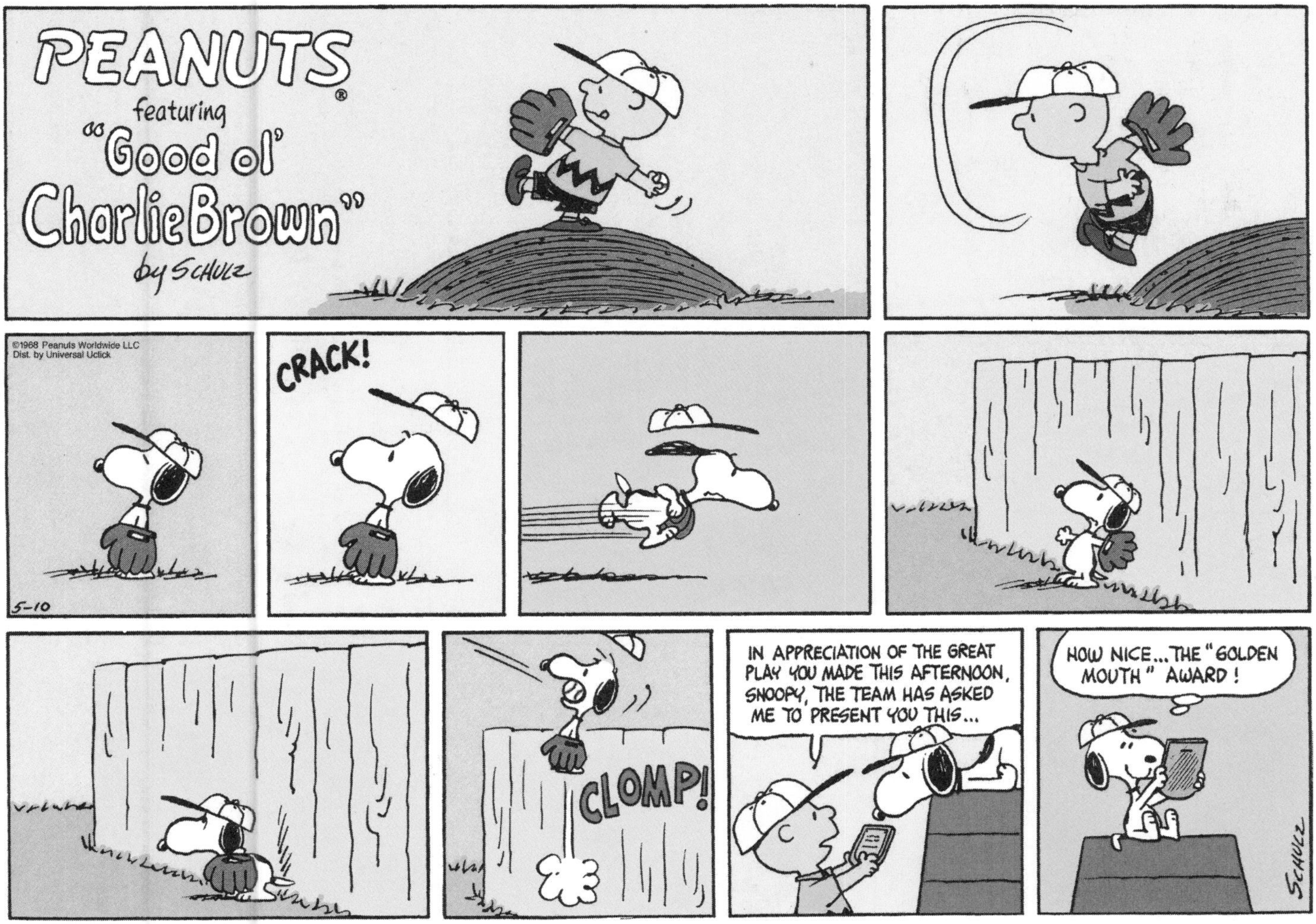
PEANUTS®
featuring
"Good ol' Charlie Brown"
by SCHULZ
©1968 Peanuts Worldwide LLC
Dist. by Universal Uclick
5-10
CRACK!
CLOMP!
IN APPRECIATION OF THE GREAT PLAY YOU MADE THIS AFTERNOON, SNOOPY, THE TEAM HAS ASKED ME TO PRESENT YOU THIS...
HOW NICE... THE "GOLDEN MOUTH" AWARD!
SCHULZ

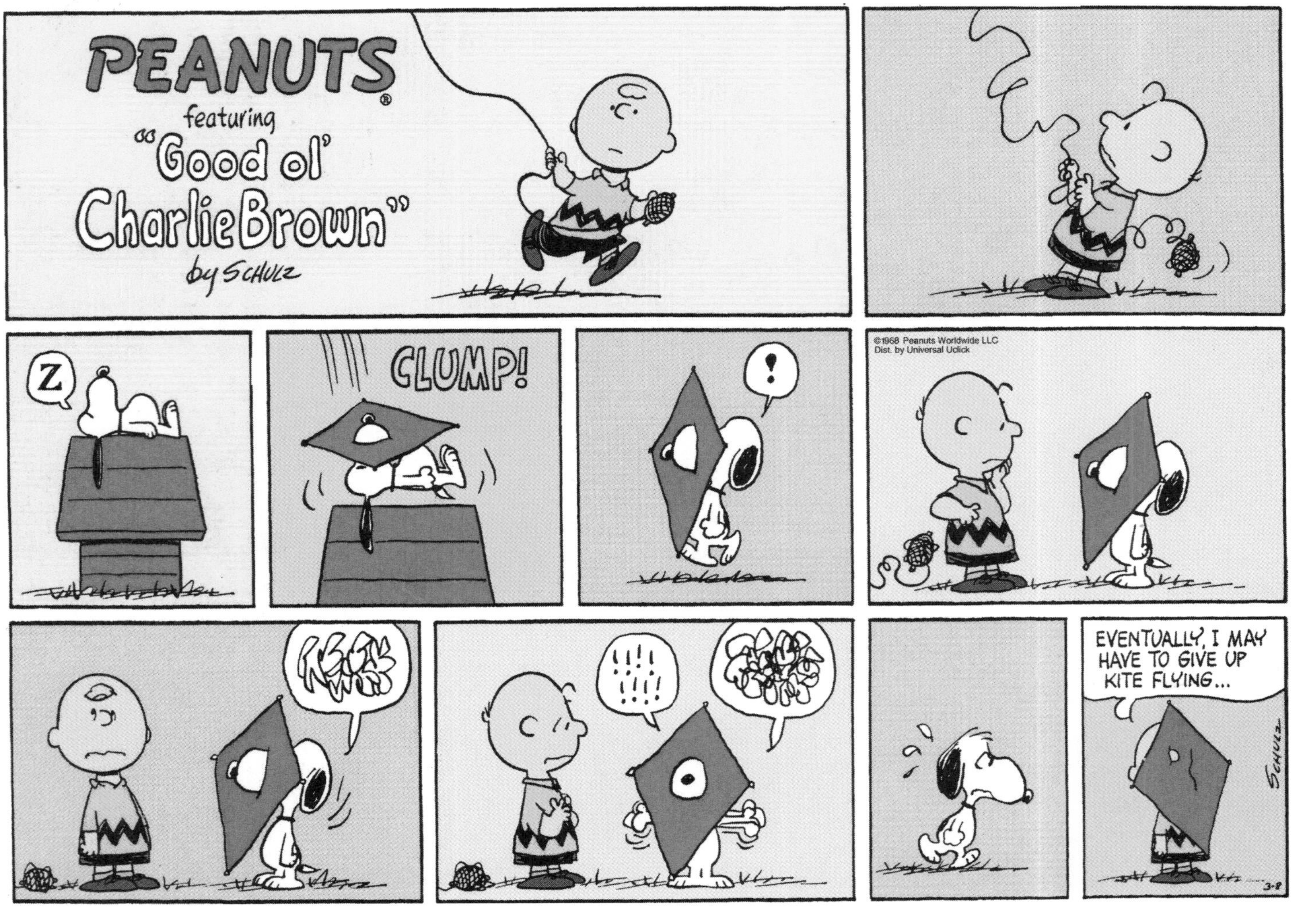
PEANUTS®
featuring
"Good ol' Charlie Brown"
by SCHULZ
Z
CLUMP!
!
©1968 Peanuts Worldwide LLC
Dist. by Universal Uclick
!!!!
!!!!
EVENTUALLY, I MAY HAVE TO GIVE UP KITE FLYING...
SCHULZ
3-8

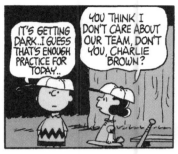

IT'S GETTING DARK..I GUESS THAT'S ENOUGH PRACTICE FOR TODAY..
YOU THINK I DON'T CARE ABOUT OUR TEAM, DON'T YOU, CHARLIE BROWN?
WELL, JUST TO SHOW YOU THAT I DO, I'VE FIGURED OUT A WAY FOR US TO PLAY NIGHT GAMES!
© 1968 Peanuts Worldwide LLC, Dist. by Universal Uclick
GO AHEAD... GO OUT ON THE PITCHER'S MOUND, AND SEE..
3-5
www.snoopy.com
SCHULZ

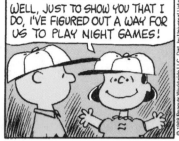

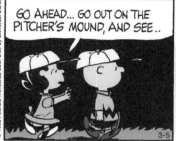

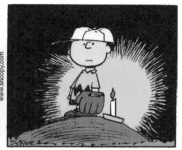

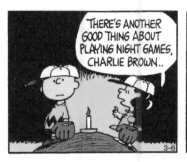

THERE'S ANOTHER GOOD THING ABOUT PLAYING NIGHT GAMES, CHARLIE BROWN..
3-6
SAY YOU'RE PITCHING A LOUSY GAME, SEE, AND WE WANT TO GET YOU OUT OF THERE...WELL, ALL WE HAVE TO DO IS COME OUT TO THE MOUND AND BLOW OUT YOUR CANDLE!
© 1968 Peanuts Worldwide LLC, Dist. by Universal Uclick
POOF!
SCHULZ
www.snoopy.com
I THINK WE'D BETTER STICK TO DAY GAMES!

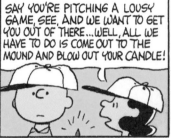

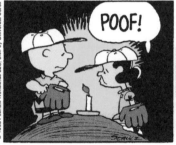

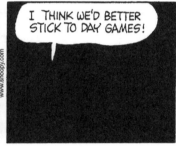

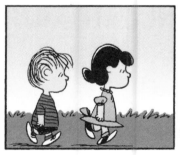

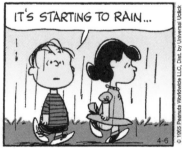

IT'S STARTING TO RAIN...
4-6
© 1965 Peanuts Worldwide LLC, Dist. by Universal Uclick
IT FIGURES...
www.snoopy.com
IT ALWAYS RAINS ON OUR GENERATION!
SCHULZ

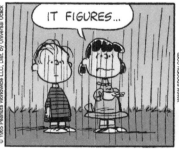

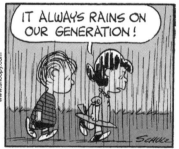

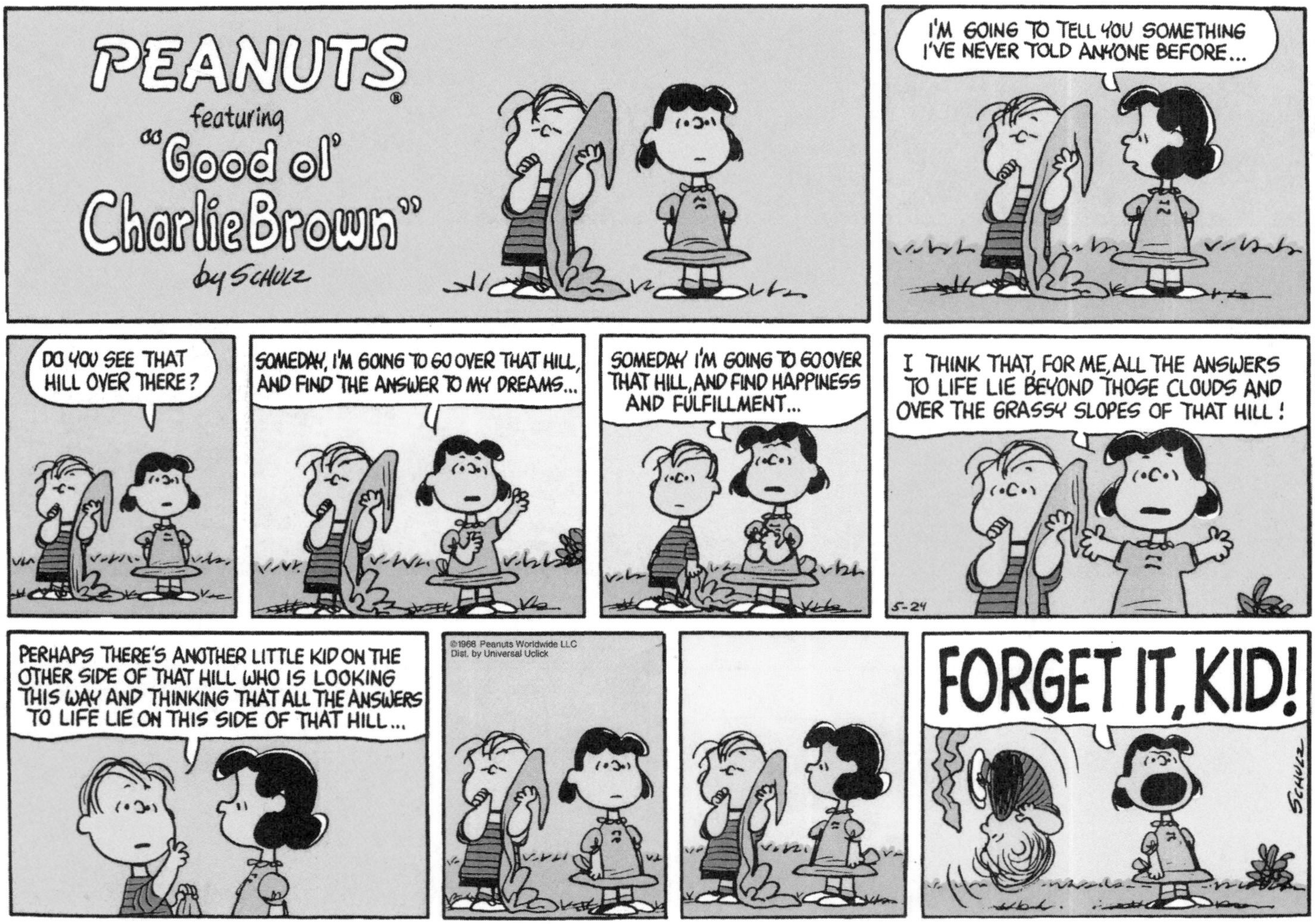
PEANUTS®
featuring "Good ol' Charlie Brown"
by SCHULZ
I'M GOING TO TELL YOU SOMETHING I'VE NEVER TOLD ANYONE BEFORE...
DO YOU SEE THAT HILL OVER THERE?
SOMEDAY, I'M GOING TO GO OVER THAT HILL, AND FIND THE ANSWER TO MY DREAMS...
SOMEDAY I'M GOING TO GO OVER THAT HILL, AND FIND HAPPINESS AND FULFILLMENT...
I THINK THAT, FOR ME, ALL THE ANSWERS TO LIFE LIE BEYOND THOSE CLOUDS AND OVER THE GRASSY SLOPES OF THAT HILL!
5-24
PERHAPS THERE'S ANOTHER LITTLE KID ON THE OTHER SIDE OF THAT HILL WHO IS LOOKING THIS WAY AND THINKING THAT ALL THE ANSWERS TO LIFE LIE ON THIS SIDE OF THAT HILL...
©1968 Peanuts Worldwide LLC
Dist. by Universal Uclick
FORGET IT, KID!
SCHULZ

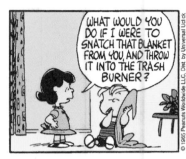

WHAT WOULD YOU DO IF I WERE TO SNATCH THAT BLANKET FROM YOU, AND THROW IT INTO THE TRASH BURNER?
© 1965 Peanuts Worldwide LLC, Dist. by Universal Uclick
I'D COLLAPSE RIGHT ON THE SPOT...THEY'D HAVE TO HAUL ME AWAY IN AN AMBULANCE, AND PLACE ME IN AN OXYGEN TENT!
3-8
www.snoopy.com
HOW DO I THINK OF THINGS LIKE THAT?
SCHULZ

3-10
© 1965 Peanuts Worldwide LLC, Dist. by Universal Uclick
www.snoopy.com
AAUGH!
THIS STUPID BLANKET **HATES** ME!
SCHULZ

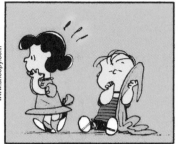

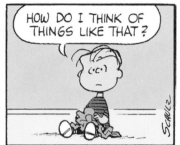

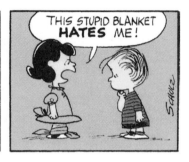

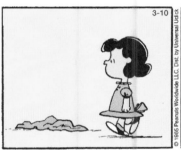

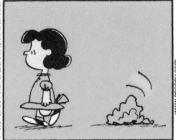

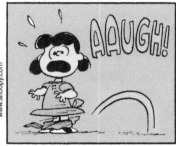

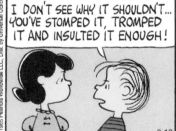

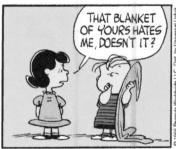

THAT BLANKET OF YOURS HATES ME, DOESN'T IT?
© 1965 Peanuts Worldwide LLC, Dist. by Universal Uclick
I DON'T SEE WHY IT SHOULDN'T... YOU'VE STOMPED IT, TROMPED IT AND INSULTED IT ENOUGH!
3-12
www.snoopy.com
BUT A COUPLE OF DAYS AGO IT EVEN ATTACKED ME! IT GRABBED ME AROUND THE LEGS, AND TRIED TO THROW ME!
WHAT DO YOU WANT ME TO DO, KEEP IT ON A LEASH?
SCHULZ

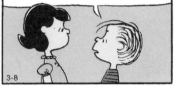

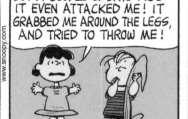

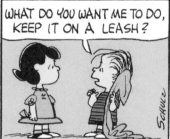

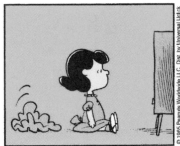

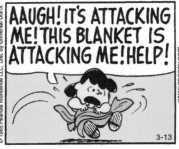

© 1965 Peanuts Worldwide LLC, Dist. by Universal Uclick
AAUGH! IT'S ATTACKING ME! THIS BLANKET IS ATTACKING ME! HELP!
www.snoopy.com
3-13
DOWN! DOWN, BOY! DOWN!
GASP I'M THE ONLY PERSON I KNOW WHO'S EVER BEEN ATTACKED BY A BLANKET!
SCHULZ

NOW, LOOK HERE...
© 1965 Peanuts Worldwide LLC, Dist. by Universal Uclick
WHEN YOU'RE NOT AROUND, YOU KEEP THAT BLANKET LOCKED UP IN YOUR ROOM, DO YOU HEAR? IT'S A MENACE! IT HATES ME!
3-14
www.snoopy.com
OKAY... HOW'S THAT?
SCHULZ

3-15
© 1965 Peanuts Worldwide LLC, Dist. by Universal Uclick
AUGH!
www.snoopy.com
AAUGH! AUGH! AUGH!
GOOD GRIEF! WHAT AM I GOING TO DO WITH YOU? AND STOP GIGGLING!
SCHULZ

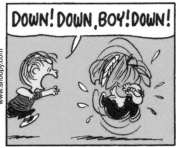

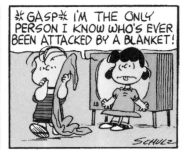

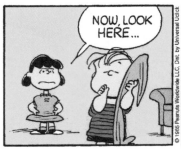

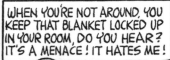

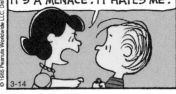

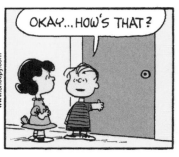

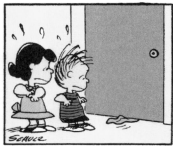

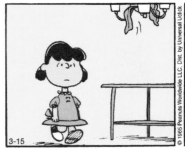

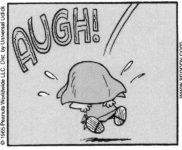

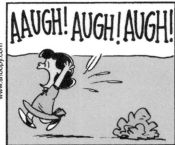

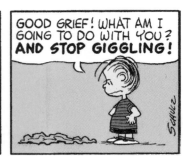

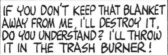

I'M WARNING YOU, LINUS!
IF YOU DON'T KEEP THAT BLANKET AWAY FROM ME, I'LL DESTROY IT, DO YOU UNDERSTAND? I'LL THROW IT IN THE TRASH BURNER!
3-16
WHAT'S IT DOING NOW?! KEEP IT AWAY FROM ME! WHAT'S IT DOING?!
IT WANTS TO MAKE UP...IT WANTS TO SHAKE HANDS..
I'M NOT SHAKING HANDS WITH ANY STUPID BLANKET!
© 1965 Peanuts Worldwide LLC. Dist. by Universal Uclick
www.snoopy.com

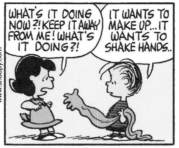

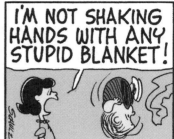

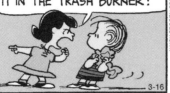

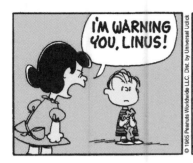

YOU'RE NOT BEING FAIR, LUCY..
3-17
MY BLANKET WANTS A TRUCE... IT'S WILLING TO MAKE UP...WHY DON'T YOU SHAKE HANDS?
ALL RIGHT... ANYTHING TO KEEP FROM BEING LEAPED ON... I'LL FORGIVE AND FORGET...SHAKE!
AAUGH!
© 1965 Peanuts Worldwide LLC. Dist. by Universal Uclick
www.snoopy.com

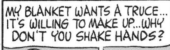

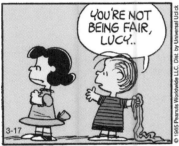

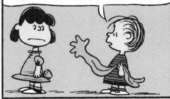

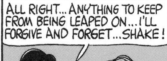

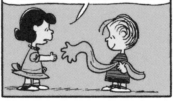

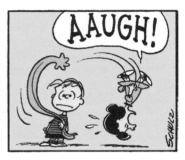

MOM? ARE YOU HOME? MOM? DAD? ANYBODY HOME?
LINUS? ARE YOU HOME?! ISN'T ANYBODY HOME? WHERE IS EVERYBODY?
3-19
DON'T TELL ME I'M ALL ALONE IN THIS HOUSE WITH THAT.....
BLANKET!
© 1965 Peanuts Worldwide LLC. Dist. by Universal Uclick
www.snoopy.com

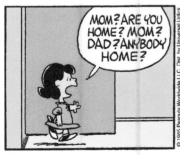

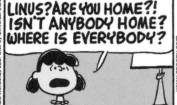

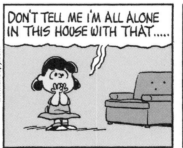

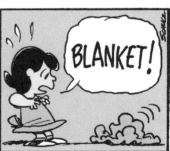

3-9
© 1965 Peanuts Worldwide LLC. Dist. by Universal Uclick
www.snoopy.com
AAUGH!
WHAT'S THE MATTER?
IT HISSED AT ME!
SCHULZ

I HATE THAT BLANKET, AND IT HATES ME!
© 1965 Peanuts Worldwide LLC. Dist. by Universal Uclick
IF I GET JUST HALF A CHANCE, I'M GOING TO THROW THAT THING IN THE TRASH BURNER!
3-22
www.snoopy.com
AAUGH!
GET IT OFF ME! GET IT OFF ME!
DOWN, BOY! DOWN!
SCHULZ

© 1968 Peanuts Worldwide LLC. Dist. by Universal Uclick
3-28
www.snoopy.com
BEETHOVEN LIKED GIRLS!
SCHULZ

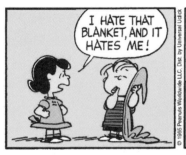

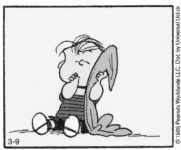

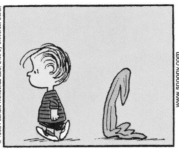

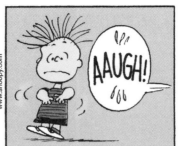

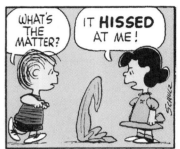

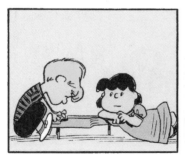

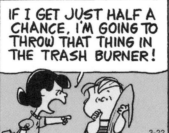

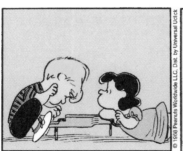

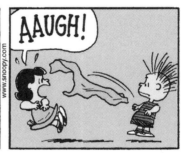

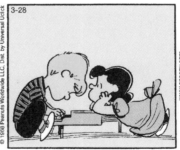

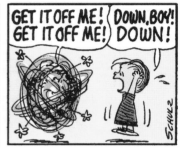

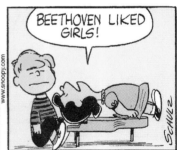

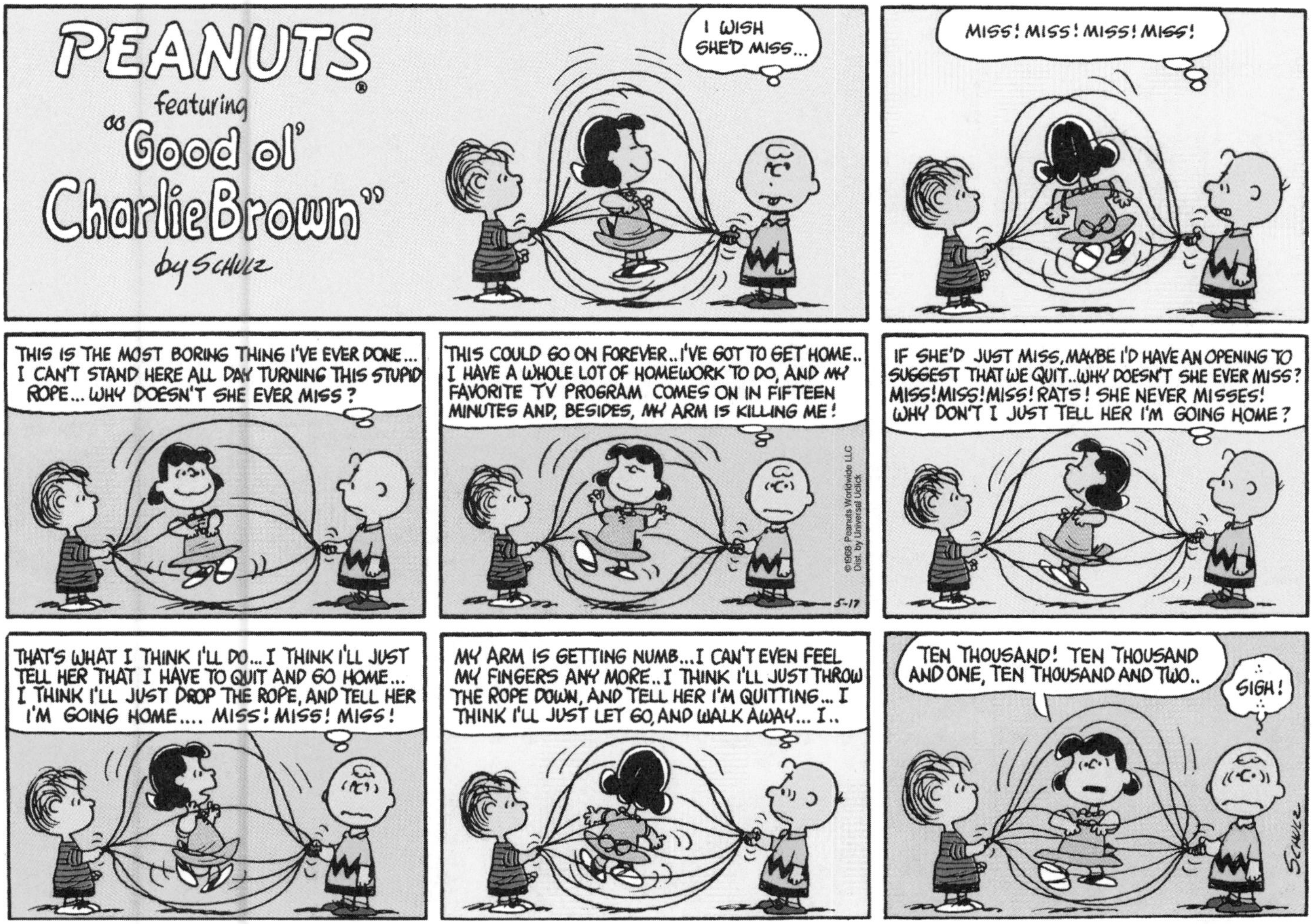
PEANUTS®
featuring
"Good ol' CharlieBrown"
by SCHULZ
I WISH SHE'D MISS...
MISS! MISS! MISS! MISS!
THIS IS THE MOST BORING THING I'VE EVER DONE... I CAN'T STAND HERE ALL DAY TURNING THIS STUPID ROPE... WHY DOESN'T SHE EVER MISS?
THIS COULD GO ON FOREVER.. I'VE GOT TO GET HOME.. I HAVE A WHOLE LOT OF HOMEWORK TO DO, AND MY FAVORITE TV PROGRAM COMES ON IN FIFTEEN MINUTES AND, BESIDES, MY ARM IS KILLING ME!
©1968 Peanuts Worldwide LLC
Dist. by Universal Uclick
5-17
IF SHE'D JUST MISS, MAYBE I'D HAVE AN OPENING TO SUGGEST THAT WE QUIT.. WHY DOESN'T SHE EVER MISS? MISS! MISS! MISS! RATS! SHE NEVER MISSES! WHY DON'T I JUST TELL HER I'M GOING HOME?
THAT'S WHAT I THINK I'LL DO... I THINK I'LL JUST TELL HER THAT I HAVE TO QUIT AND GO HOME... I THINK I'LL JUST DROP THE ROPE, AND TELL HER I'M GOING HOME.... MISS! MISS! MISS!
MY ARM IS GETTING NUMB... I CAN'T EVEN FEEL MY FINGERS ANY MORE.. I THINK I'LL JUST THROW THE ROPE DOWN, AND TELL HER I'M QUITTING... I THINK I'LL JUST LET GO, AND WALK AWAY... I..
TEN THOUSAND! TEN THOUSAND AND ONE, TEN THOUSAND AND TWO..
SIGH!
SCHULZ

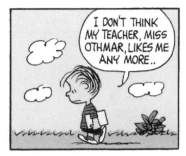

I DON'T THINK MY TEACHER, MISS OTHMAR, LIKES ME ANY MORE..
SHE DOESN'T LOOK AT ME THE WAY SHE USED TO... SHE DOESN'T EVEN LOOK AT ME AT ALL...
3-23
© 1968 Peanuts Worldwide LLC, Dist. by Universal Uclick
IT'S A TERRIBLE THING TO DISCOVER THAT YOUR TEACHER DOESN'T LIKE YOU ANY MORE...
www.snoopy.com
IT'S LIKE HAVING A SUBSCRIPTION RUN OUT..
SCHULZ

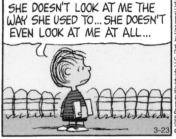

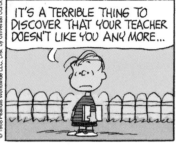

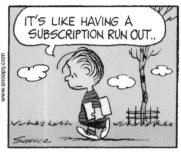

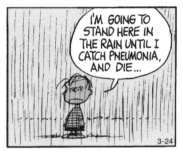

I'M GOING TO STAND HERE IN THE RAIN UNTIL I CATCH PNEUMONIA, AND DIE...
3-24
IF MISS OTHMAR DOESN'T LIKE ME ANY MORE, I HAVE NOTHING TO LIVE FOR!
© 1968 Peanuts Worldwide LLC, Dist. by Universal Uclick
www.snoopy.com
I WONDER IF YOU CAN CATCH PNEUMONIA WITHOUT GETTING SO WET?
SCHULZ

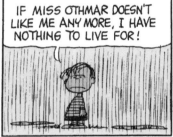

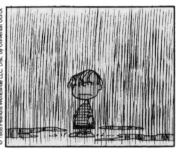

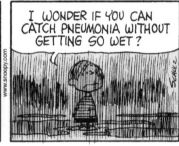

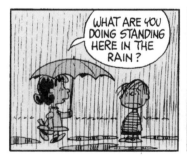

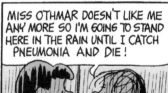

WHAT ARE YOU DOING STANDING HERE IN THE RAIN?
MISS OTHMAR DOESN'T LIKE ME ANY MORE SO I'M GOING TO STAND HERE IN THE RAIN UNTIL I CATCH PNEUMONIA AND DIE!
© 1968 Peanuts Worldwide LLC, Dist. by Universal Uclick
HOW DO YOU KNOW MISS OTHMAR DOESN'T LIKE YOU ANY MORE?
SHE DOESN'T LOOK AT ME THE WAY SHE USED TO...
3-25
www.snoopy.com
PLEASE MOVE YOUR UMBRELLA.. YOU'RE THROWING ME OFF SCHEDULE!
SCHULZ

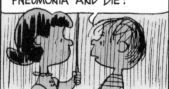

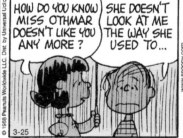

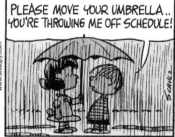

I RAISED MY HAND, AND MISS OTHMAR LOOKED RIGHT THROUGH ME..

NOBODY CAN LOOK RIGHT THROUGH YOU BETTER THAN A TEACHER CAN LOOK RIGHT THROUGH YOU

3-26

WHEN A TEACHER LOOKS RIGHT THROUGH YOU, YOU KNOW YOU'VE BEEN LOOKED RIGHT THROUGH!

WHY DOES MISS OTHMAR LOOK RIGHT THROUGH ME?

MISS OTHMAR STILL LIKES ME! IT WAS ALL A MISUNDERSTANDING!

I THOUGHT SHE WASN'T LOOKING AT ME THE WAY SHE USED TO, AND I WAS RIGHT! SHE NEEDED **GLASSES**! HOW ABOUT THAT?

3-27

WHAT APPEARED TO BE A STRAIN IN "TEACHER-PUPIL" RELATIONS, TURNED OUT TO BE UNCORRECTED MYOPIA! MISS OTHMAR STILL LIKES ME

WHAT ARE YOU DOING NOW?

I'M WRITING A NOTE OF APPRECIATION TO HER OPHTHALMOLOGIST!

OUR GENERATION HAS BEEN GIVEN THE WORKS..

ALL OF THE WORLD'S PROBLEMS ARE BEING SHOVED AT US...

4-7

WHAT DO YOU THINK WE SHOULD DO?

STICK THE NEXT GENERATION

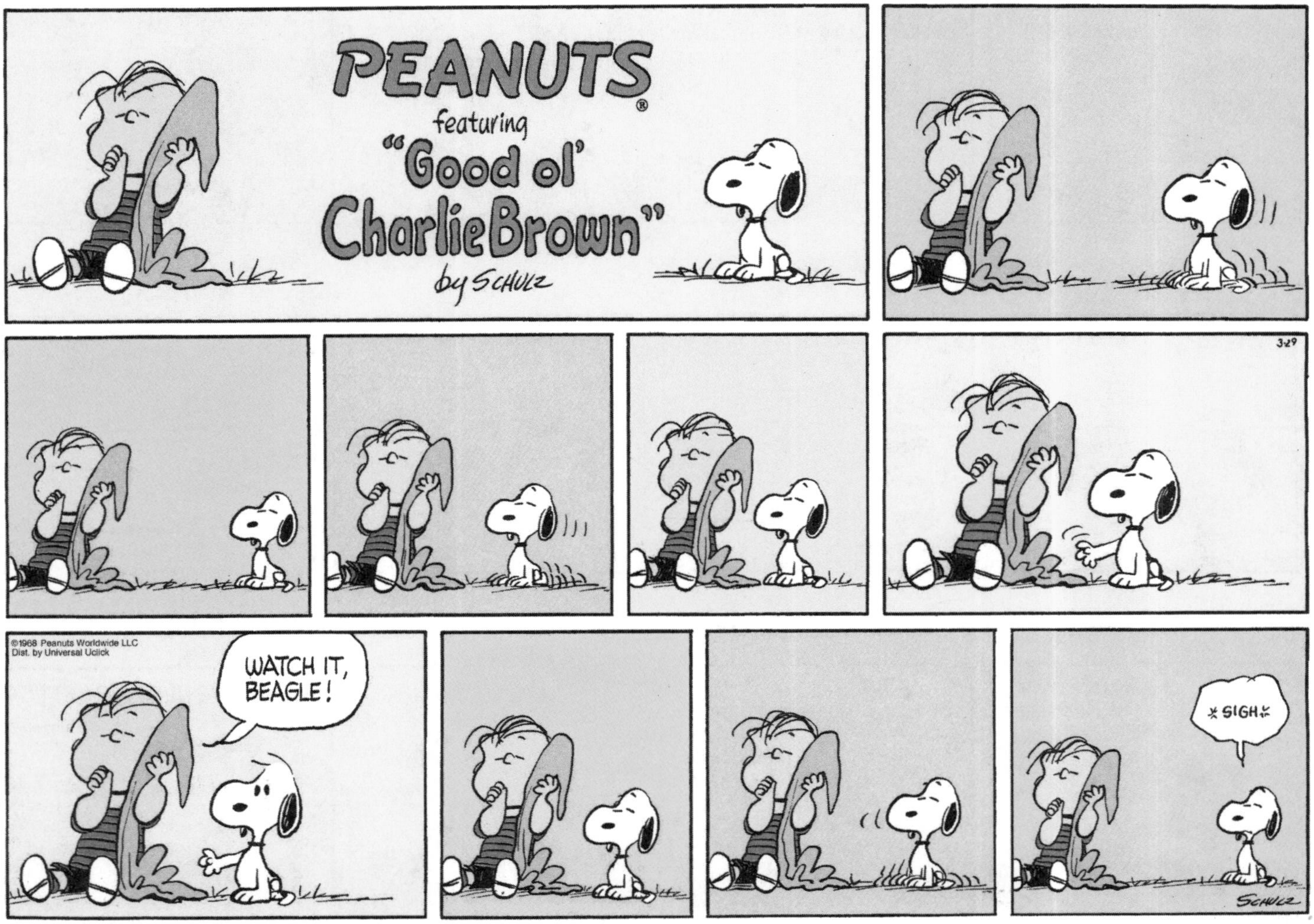
PEANUTS®
featuring
"Good ol' CharlieBrown"
by SCHULZ
3-29
©1968 Peanuts Worldwide LLC
Dist. by Universal Uclick
WATCH IT, BEAGLE!
SIGH
SCHULZ

WELL, HOW DO YOU LIKE THE HOT CHOCOLATE I MADE FOR YOU?
IT'S TERRIBLE! IT'S TOO WEAK! IT TASTES LIKE SOME WARM WATER THAT HAS HAD A BROWN CRAYON DIPPED IN IT!
4-3
© 1966 Peanuts Worldwide LLC. Dist. by Universal Uclick
YOU'RE RIGHT..
www.snoopy.com
I'LL GO PUT IN ANOTHER CRAYON!
SCHULZ

LOOK, IF YOU'RE GOING TO MAKE US SOME HOT CHOCOLATE, MAKE IT RIGHT!
WELL, I WAS GOING TO USE THIS BOX OF CHOCOLATE-MIX HERE, BUT I CHANGED MY MIND..
4-4
© 1966 Peanuts Worldwide LLC. Dist. by Universal Uclick
I DIDN'T WANT TO USE THIS AFTER WHAT I READ ON THE SIDE..
WHAT DOES IT SAY ON THE SIDE?
www.snoopy.com
IT'S FULL OF INGREDIENTS!
SCHULZ

BOY, LOOK AT IT RAIN...WHAT IF IT FLOODS THE WHOLE WORLD?
4-10
IT WILL NEVER DO THAT..IN THE NINTH CHAPTER OF GENESIS, GOD PROMISED NOAH THAT WOULD NEVER HAPPEN AGAIN, AND THE SIGN OF THE PROMISE IS THE RAINBOW..
© 1965 Peanuts Worldwide LLC. Dist. by Universal Uclick
YOU'VE TAKEN A GREAT LOAD OFF MY MIND...
www.snoopy.com
SOUND THEOLOGY HAS A WAY OF DOING THAT!
SCHULZ

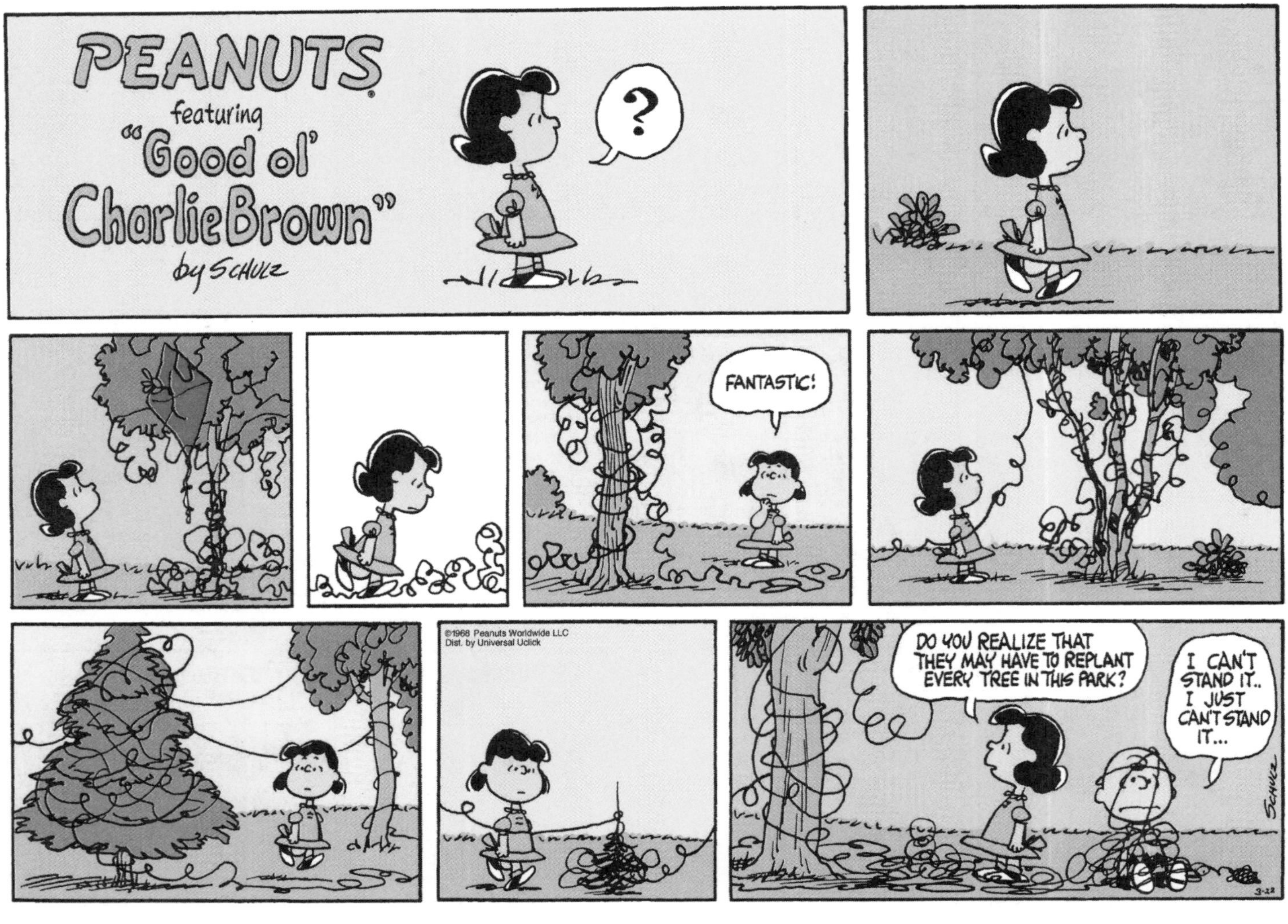
PEANUTS
featuring
"Good ol' CharlieBrown"
by SCHULZ
?
FANTASTIC!
©1968 Peanuts Worldwide LLC
Dist. by Universal Uclick
DO YOU REALIZE THAT THEY MAY HAVE TO REPLANT EVERY TREE IN THIS PARK?
I CAN'T STAND IT.. I JUST CAN'T STAND IT...
SCHULZ

DEAR EDITOR OF "LETTERS TO THE EDITOR", HOW HAVE YOU BEEN?
"HOW HAVE YOU BEEN?" WHAT SORT OF LETTER IS THAT TO WRITE TO AN EDITOR?
© 1966 Peanuts Worldwide LLC, Dist. by Universal Uclick
I JUST THOUGHT HE MIGHT APPRECIATE HAVING SOMEONE INQUIRE ABOUT THE STATE OF HIS HEALTH
www.snoopy.com
EDITORS ARE SORT OF HUMAN, TOO, YOU KNOW!
4-8
SCHULZ

WHY DON'T YOU BE A GOOD BROTHER, AND MAKE ME AN ICE CREAM CONE?
4-16
KOFF KOFF
© 1966 Peanuts Worldwide LLC, Dist. by Universal Uclick
Vanilla
www.snoopy.com
SCHULZ
I KNOW YOU HAVE A COLD SO I PUT A MENTHOL COUGH DROP ON TOP

THIS "SNOW WHITE" HAS BEEN HAVING TROUBLE SLEEPING, SEE?
WELL, SHE GOES TO THIS WITCH WHO GIVES HER AN APPLE TO EAT WHICH PUTS HER TO SLEEP..
© 1965 Peanuts Worldwide LLC, Dist. by Universal Uclick
JUST AS SHE'S BEGINNING TO SLEEP REAL WELL..YOU KNOW, FOR THE FIRST TIME IN WEEKS...THIS STUPID PRINCE COMES ALONG, AND KISSES HER, AND WAKES HER UP!
www.snoopy.com
I ADMIRE THE WONDERFUL WAY YOU HAVE OF GETTING THE REAL MEANING OUT OF A STORY..
SCHULZ
4-16

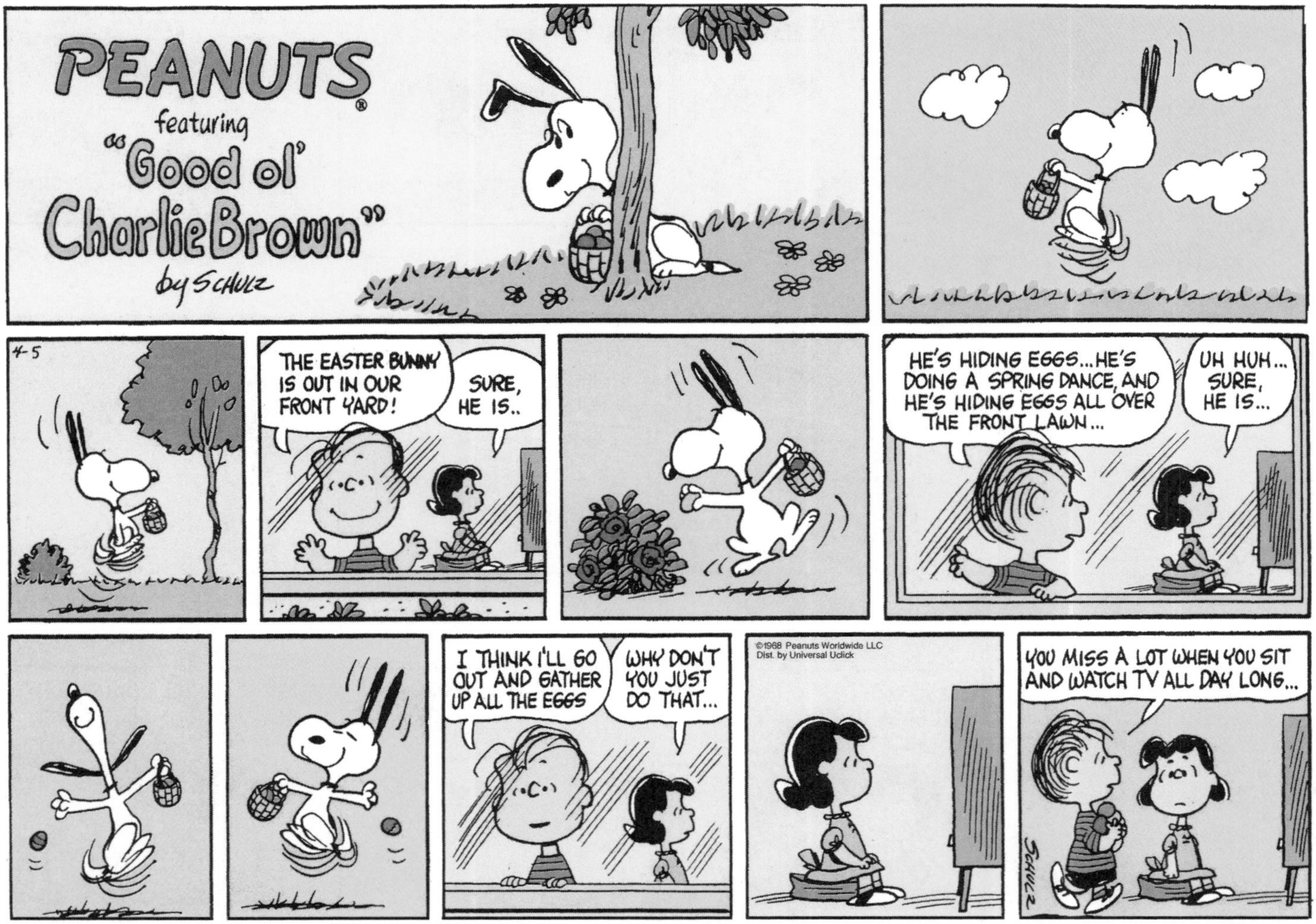
PEANUTS®
featuring
"Good ol' CharlieBrown"
by SCHULZ
4-5
THE EASTER BUNNY IS OUT IN OUR FRONT YARD!
SURE, HE IS..
HE'S HIDING EGGS...HE'S DOING A SPRING DANCE, AND HE'S HIDING EGGS ALL OVER THE FRONT LAWN...
UH HUH... SURE, HE IS...
I THINK I'LL GO OUT AND GATHER UP ALL THE EGGS
WHY DON'T YOU JUST DO THAT...
©1968 Peanuts Worldwide LLC
Dist. by Universal Uclick
SCHULZ
YOU MISS A LOT WHEN YOU SIT AND WATCH TV ALL DAY LONG...

THAT'S PECULIAR...
© 1965 Peanuts Worldwide LLC, Dist. by Universal Uclick
4-17
www.snoopy.com
MY TEETH KEEP DRAGGING ON MY FINGERPRINTS!
SCHULZ

YOU? A DOCTOR?
HA! THAT'S A LAUGH!
© 1966 Peanuts Worldwide LLC, Dist. by Universal Uclick
I FEEL SORRY FOR THE PATIENT WHO LOOKS UP FROM THE OPERATING TABLE, AND SEES YOU HOLDING THAT BLANKET
4-27
www.snoopy.com
YOU THINK I CAN'T PERFORM SURGERY WITH ONE HAND?
SCHULZ

I DREAD GETTING OLD...
DON'T WORRY ABOUT IT...YOU HAVE A LONG WAY TO GO...
4-24
© 1966 Peanuts Worldwide LLC, Dist. by Universal Uclick
I DON'T WANT TO HAVE TO WEAR BIFOCAL TEETH!
YOU MEAN FALSE TEETH
www.snoopy.com
SCHULZ
SEE? I'M GETTING OLD ALREADY.. I'M LOSING MY MEMORY!

PEANUTS.
featuring
"Good ol'
Charlie Brown"
by Schulz

CLOMP!

ALL RIGHT, I SAW THAT! BUT I'M GOING TO PRETEND THAT IT NEVER HAPPENED!

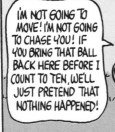

I'M NOT GOING TO MOVE! I'M NOT GOING TO CHASE YOU! IF YOU BRING THAT BALL BACK HERE BEFORE I COUNT TO TEN, WE'LL JUST PRETEND THAT NOTHING HAPPENED!

©1967 Peanuts Worldwide LLC
Dist. by Universal Uclick

4-6

ONE, TWO, THREE, FOUR, FIVE, SIX, SEVEN, EIGHT, NINE...

PFFT!

THANK YOU... THAT WAS A VERY WISE DECISION!

SIGH

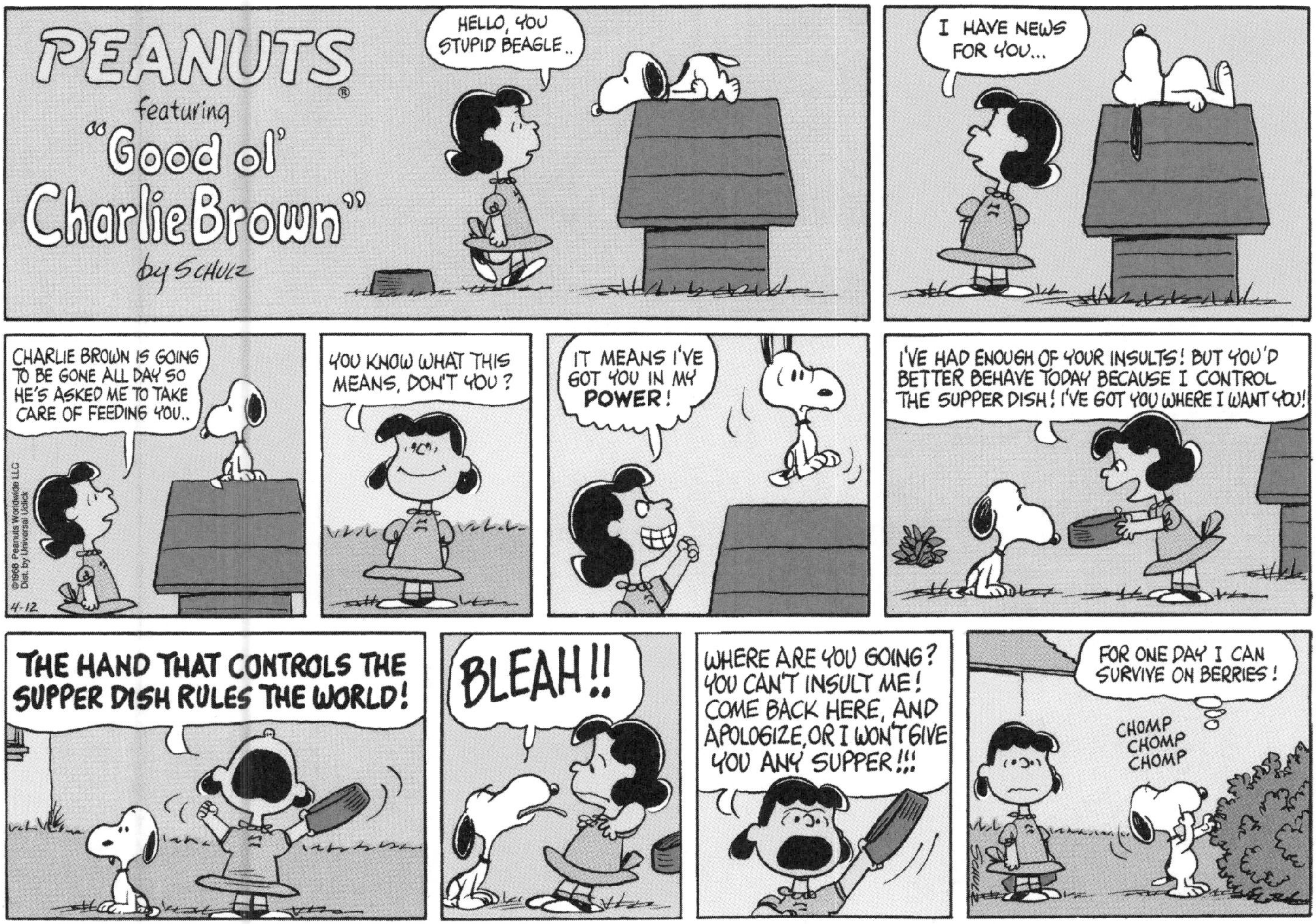
PEANUTS®
featuring "Good ol' Charlie Brown"
by SCHULZ
HELLO, YOU STUPID BEAGLE..
I HAVE NEWS FOR YOU...
CHARLIE BROWN IS GOING TO BE GONE ALL DAY SO HE'S ASKED ME TO TAKE CARE OF FEEDING YOU..
©1968 Peanuts Worldwide LLC
Dist. by Universal Udick
4-12
YOU KNOW WHAT THIS MEANS, DON'T YOU?
IT MEANS I'VE GOT YOU IN MY POWER!
I'VE HAD ENOUGH OF YOUR INSULTS! BUT YOU'D BETTER BEHAVE TODAY BECAUSE I CONTROL THE SUPPER DISH! I'VE GOT YOU WHERE I WANT YOU!
THE HAND THAT CONTROLS THE SUPPER DISH RULES THE WORLD!
BLEAH!!
WHERE ARE YOU GOING? YOU CAN'T INSULT ME! COME BACK HERE, AND APOLOGIZE, OR I WON'T GIVE YOU ANY SUPPER!!!
FOR ONE DAY I CAN SURVIVE ON BERRIES!
CHOMP CHOMP CHOMP
SCHULZ

YOU GOT A "C" IN HISTORY? THAT'S ONLY AVERAGE!
SO WHAT? I'M AN AVERAGE STUDENT IN AN AVERAGE SCHOOL IN AN AVERAGE COMMUNITY....
WHAT'S WRONG WITH BEING AVERAGE?
BECAUSE YOU'RE CAPABLE OF DOING MUCH BETTER..
THAT'S THE AVERAGE ANSWER!
© 1965 Peanuts Worldwide LLC, Dist. by Universal Uclick
4-20
www.snoopy.com
SCHULZ

4-21
YOU THINK BEING AVERAGE IS ENOUGH, DON'T YOU?
WELL, IT **ISN'T**!
WHAT SHAPE WOULD THE WORLD BE IN TODAY IF EVERYONE SETTLED FOR BEING AVERAGE?
WHAT SHAPE **IS** THE WORLD IN TODAY?
© 1965 Peanuts Worldwide LLC, Dist. by Universal Uclick
www.snoopy.com
SCHULZ

MISS OTHMAR?
SLURP
SLURP
I WAS WONDERING IF YOU'D CARE TO RECONCILE OUR FAILURE TO SAY "GRACE" BEFORE DRINKING MILK WITH THE STORY OF DANIEL IN THE SIXTH CHAPTER OF THAT BOOK
4-27
OH...
MISS OTHMAR IS NEVER MUCH FOR RECONCILING...
SLURP
SLURP
© 1965 Peanuts Worldwide LLC, Dist. by Universal Uclick
www.snoopy.com
SCHULZ

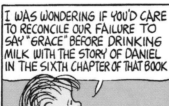

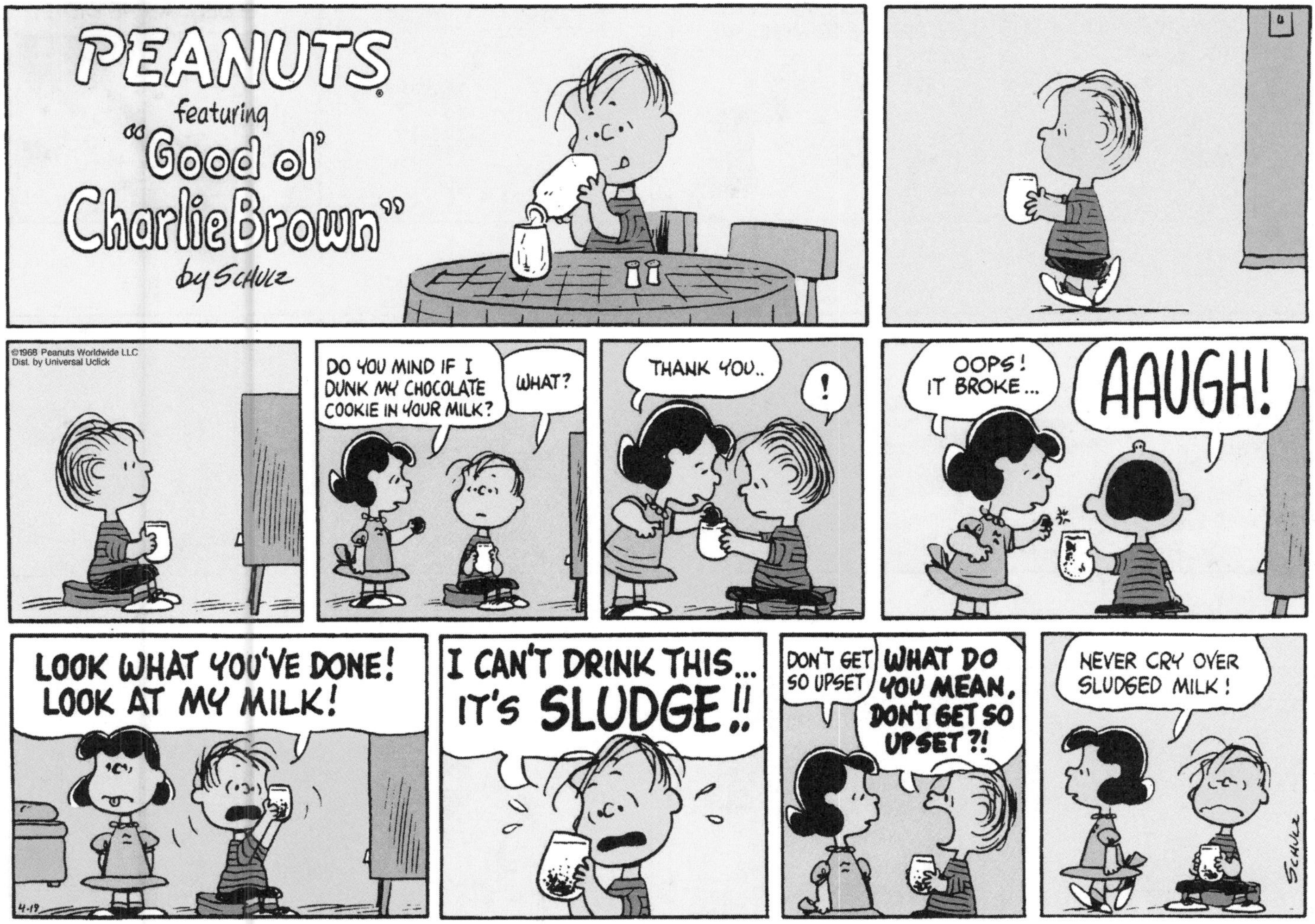
PEANUTS
featuring
"Good ol' CharlieBrown"
by SCHULZ
©1968 Peanuts Worldwide LLC
Dist. by Universal Uclick
DO YOU MIND IF I DUNK MY CHOCOLATE COOKIE IN YOUR MILK?
WHAT?
THANK YOU..
!
OOPS! IT BROKE...
AAUGH!
LOOK WHAT YOU'VE DONE! LOOK AT MY MILK!
I CAN'T DRINK THIS... IT'S SLUDGE!!
DON'T GET SO UPSET
WHAT DO YOU MEAN, DON'T GET SO UPSET?!
NEVER CRY OVER SLUDGED MILK!
SCHULZ

BEETHOVEN HAD A LOT OF PROBLEMS, DIDN'T HE?
I SUPPOSE IN THOSE DAYS THERE WERE NO SYNDICATED ADVICE COLUMNS FROM WHICH HE COULD GET HELP...
8/25
www.snoopy.com
NO, I DON'T SUPPOSE THERE WERE...
© 1964 Peanuts Worldwide LLC. Dist. by Universal Uclick
IT'S AMAZING THAT HE DID AS WELL AS HE DID!

2-17
© 1968 Peanuts Worldwide LLC. Dist. by Universal Uclick
www.snoopy.com
THUMB À LA MODE!
SCHULZ

!
5-6
TRY TO STAY CALM.... I HAVE TERRIBLE NEWS!
© 1968 Peanuts Worldwide LLC. Dist. by Universal Uclick
DAD'S BEEN TRANSFERRED! WE'RE MOVING TO A NEW CITY!
www.snoopy.com
AAUGH!
SCHULZ

WHAT WOULD YOU SAY IF I TOLD YOU THAT I WAS MOVING AWAY?
WOULD YOU MISS MY SMILING FACE?
© 1966 Peanuts Worldwide LLC. Dist. by Universal Uclick
I COULD STAND IT
OH, I KNOW YOU COULD STAND IT
5-8
www.snoopy.com
BUT WOULD YOU MISS MY SMILING FACE?!
SCHULZ

IT'S JUST NO USE! I CAN'T PRACTICE WITH YOU HANGING AROUND!
THE TRUTH IS YOU'RE EMBARRASSED BY A PRETTY FACE! THAT'S IT, ISN'T IT?
© 1965 Peanuts Worldwide LLC. Dist. by Universal Uclick
5-15
A PRETTY FACE MAKES YOU UNEASY, DOESN'T IT? HUH? DOESN'T IT?!
www.snoopy.com
HE SHOULDN'T FEEL THAT WAY... LOTS OF PEOPLE GET EMBARRASSED IN THE PRESENCE OF A PRETTY FACE...
SCHULZ

© 1966 Peanuts Worldwide LLC. Dist. by Universal Uclick
www.snoopy.com
DON'T TELL ME I'VE GROWN ACCUSTOMED TO THAT FACE!
5-15
SCHULZ

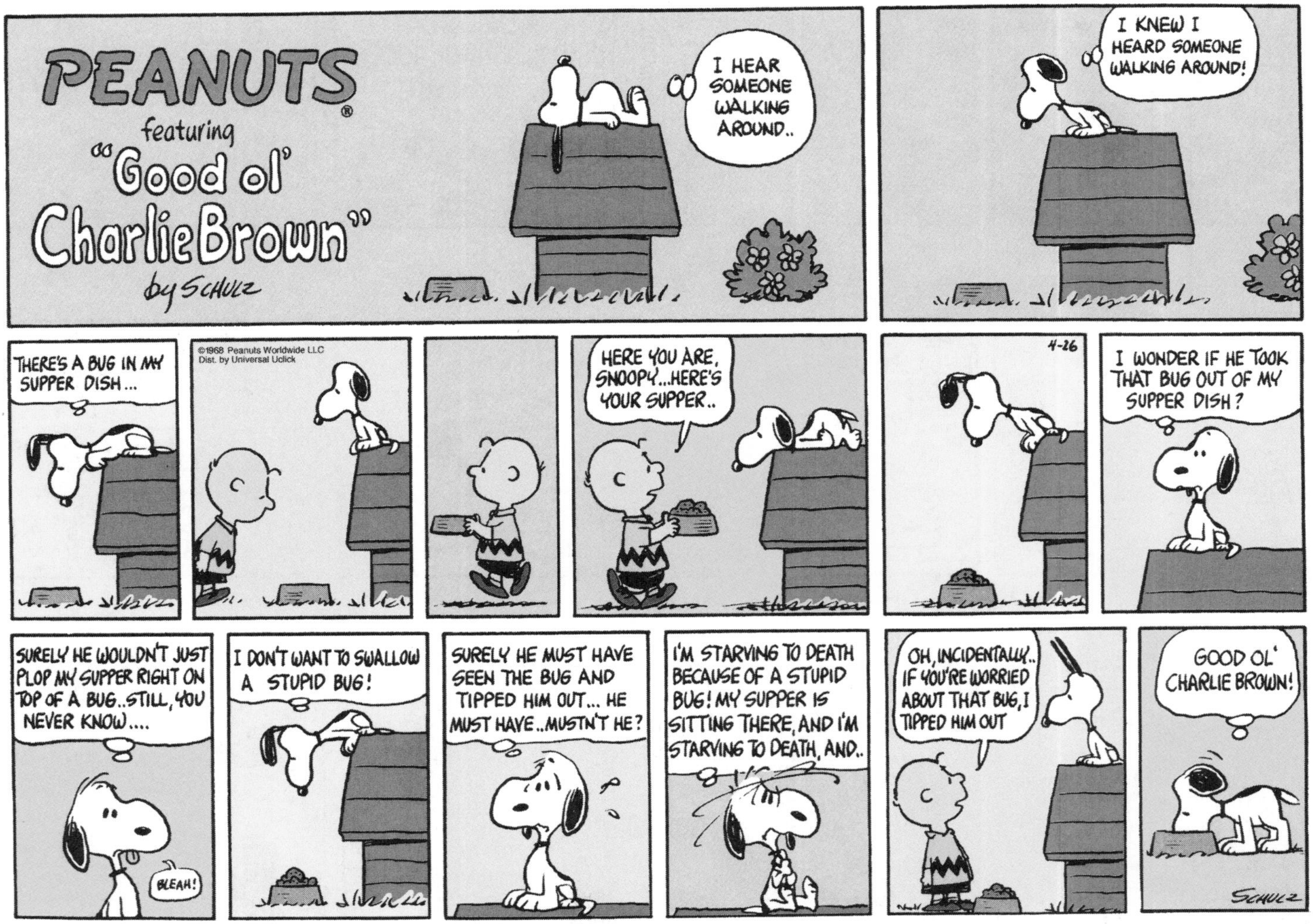
PEANUTS®
featuring
"Good ol' CharlieBrown"
by SCHULZ
I HEAR SOMEONE WALKING AROUND..
I KNEW I HEARD SOMEONE WALKING AROUND!
THERE'S A BUG IN MY SUPPER DISH...
©1968 Peanuts Worldwide LLC
Dist. by Universal Uclick
HERE YOU ARE, SNOOPY...HERE'S YOUR SUPPER..
4-26
I WONDER IF HE TOOK THAT BUG OUT OF MY SUPPER DISH?
SURELY HE WOULDN'T JUST PLOP MY SUPPER RIGHT ON TOP OF A BUG..STILL, YOU NEVER KNOW....
BLEAH!
I DON'T WANT TO SWALLOW A STUPID BUG!
SURELY HE MUST HAVE SEEN THE BUG AND TIPPED HIM OUT... HE MUST HAVE..MUSTN'T HE?
I'M STARVING TO DEATH BECAUSE OF A STUPID BUG! MY SUPPER IS SITTING THERE, AND I'M STARVING TO DEATH, AND..
OH, INCIDENTALLY.. IF YOU'RE WORRIED ABOUT THAT BUG, I TIPPED HIM OUT
GOOD OL' CHARLIE BROWN!
SCHULZ

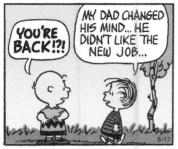

YOU'RE BACK!?!
MY DAD CHANGED HIS MIND... HE DIDN'T LIKE THE NEW JOB...
5-17
WHAT KIND OF A NEIGHBORHOOD IS THIS? IT DIDN'T CHANGE A BIT WHILE WE WERE GONE!
© 1966 Peanuts Worldwide LLC. Dist. by Universal Uclick
DON'T PEOPLE EVER PROGRESS AROUND HERE? WHAT A STUPID NEIGHBORHOOD!!
www.snoopy.com
SHE'S BACK, TOO...
SCHULZ

5-18
© 1966 Peanuts Worldwide LLC. Dist. by Universal Uclick
www.snoopy.com
YOUR SWEETIE IS BACK!
SCHULZ

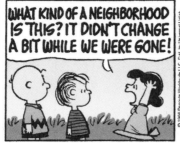

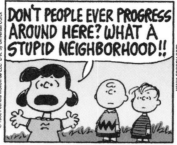

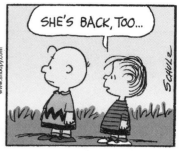

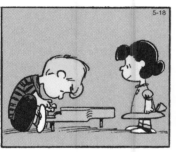

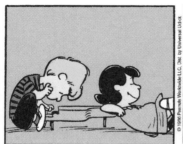

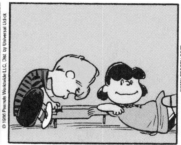

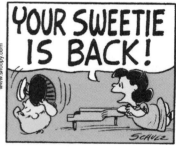

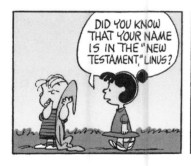

DID YOU KNOW THAT YOUR NAME IS IN THE "NEW TESTAMENT," LINUS?
YES, IN SECOND TIMOTHY, THE FOURTH CHAPTER AND THE TWENTY-FIRST VERSE, "DO YOUR BEST TO COME BEFORE WINTER. EUBULUS SENDS GREETINGS TO YOU, AS DO PUDENS AND LINUS AND CLAUDIA AND ALL THE BRETHREN."
5-29
© 1966 Peanuts Worldwide LLC. Dist. by Universal Uclick
www.snoopy.com
YOU DRIVE ME CRAZY!
SCHULZ

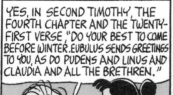

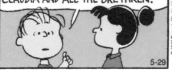

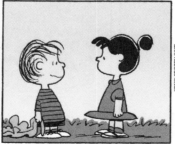

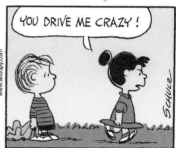

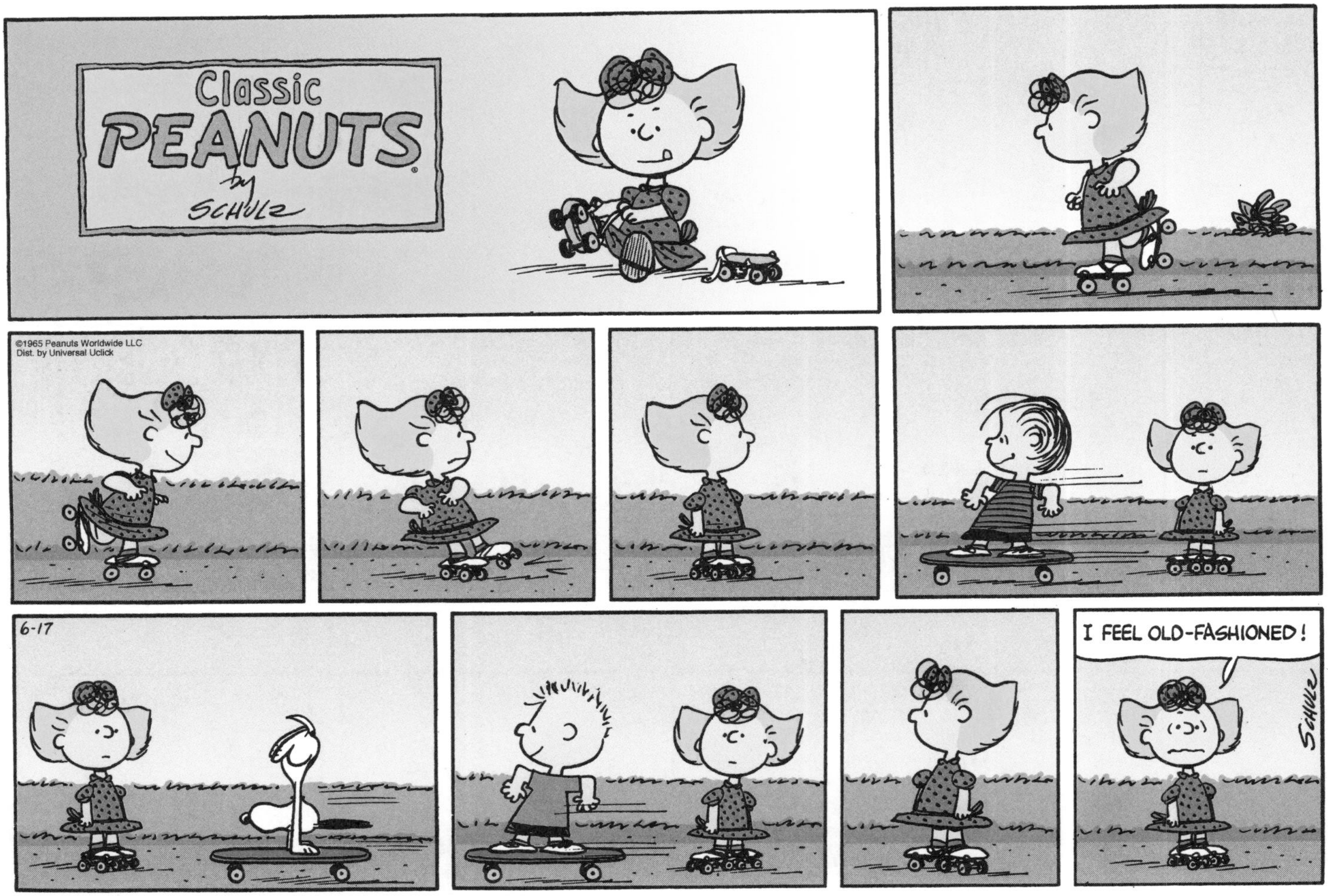
Classic
PEANUTS
by
SCHULZ
©1965 Peanuts Worldwide LLC
Dist. by Universal Uclick
6-17
I FEEL OLD-FASHIONED!
SCHULZ

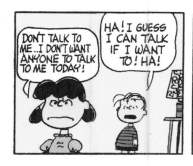

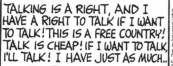

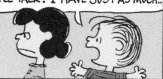

DON'T TALK TO ME...I DON'T WANT ANYONE TO TALK TO ME TODAY!
HA! I GUESS I CAN TALK IF I WANT TO! HA!
TALKING IS A RIGHT, AND I HAVE A RIGHT TO TALK IF I WANT TO TALK! THIS IS A FREE COUNTRY! TALK IS CHEAP! IF I WANT TO TALK, I'LL TALK! I HAVE JUST AS MUCH..
I SAID, 'DON'T TALK TO ME!'
SO WHO'S TALKING?
© 1966 Peanuts Worldwide LLC. Dist. by Universal Uclick
www.snoopy.com
6-8
SCHULZ

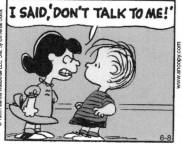

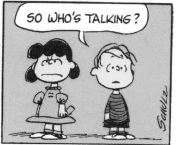

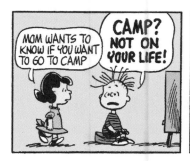

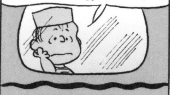

MOM WANTS TO KNOW IF YOU WANT TO GO TO CAMP
CAMP? NOT ON YOUR LIFE!
THOSE CAMPS ARE ALWAYS OUT IN THE WOODS SOME PLACE, AND THOSE WOODS ARE FULL OF QUEEN SNAKES! HAVE YOU EVER BEEN CHOMPED BY A QUEEN SNAKE?
BOY, YOU GET CHOMPED BY A QUEEN SNAKE, AND YOU'VE HAD IT! YOU WON'T GET ME NEAR ANY WOODS FULL OF QUEEN SNAKES! NO, SIR, NOT ME! I'LL JUST...
I'LL TELL HER YOU'LL BE VERY HAPPY TO GO!
AUGH!
© 1966 Peanuts Worldwide LLC. Dist. by Universal Uclick
www.snoopy.com
6-10
SCHULZ

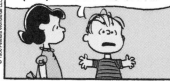

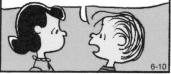

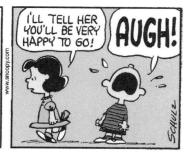

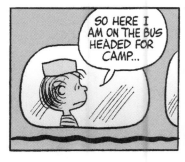

SO HERE I AM ON THE BUS HEADED FOR CAMP...
I'LL PROBABLY NO SOONER STEP OFF THE BUS WHEN I'LL GET CHOMPED BY A QUEEN SNAKE..
WHY DO THEY SEND LITTLE KIDS TO CAMP WHO DON'T WANT TO GO?
I'M DOOMED!
© 1966 Peanuts Worldwide LLC. Dist. by Universal Uclick
www.snoopy.com
6-13
SCHULZ

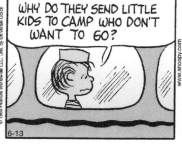

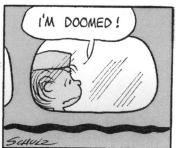

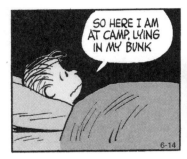

SO HERE I AM AT CAMP, LYING IN MY BUNK
6-14
I HOPE NO QUEEN SNAKES CRAWL IN HERE DURING THE NIGHT...
© 1966 Peanuts Worldwide LLC. Dist. by Universal Uclick
www.snoopy.com
WHAT IF MY MOTHER AND DAD MOVE AWAY WHILE I'M GONE, AND DON'T TELL ME?
SCHULZ

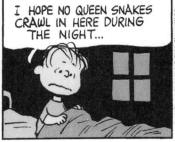

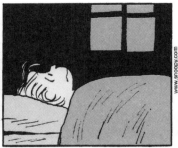

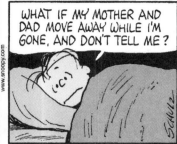

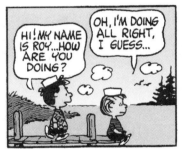

HI! MY NAME IS ROY...HOW ARE YOU DOING?
OH, I'M DOING ALL RIGHT, I GUESS...
YOU'LL GET TO LIKE THIS CAMP AFTER A FEW DAYS...I WAS HERE LAST YEAR, AND I THOUGHT I'D NEVER MAKE IT, BUT I DID...
OH?
6-17
© 1966 Peanuts Worldwide LLC. Dist. by Universal Uclick
YOU KNOW WHAT HAPPENED? I MET THIS FUNNY ROUND-HEADED KID...I CAN'T REMEMBER HIS NAME.. HE SURE WAS A FUNNY KID...
www.snoopy.com
HE WAS ALWAYS TALKING ABOUT THIS PECULIAR DOG HE HAD BACK HOME, AND SOME NUTTY FRIEND OF HIS WHO DRAGGED A BLANKET AROUND
SCHULZ

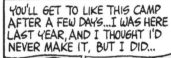

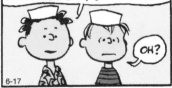

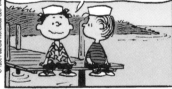

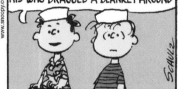

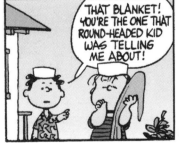

THAT BLANKET! YOU'RE THE ONE THAT ROUND-HEADED KID WAS TELLING ME ABOUT!
BOY, YOU'D BETTER PUT THAT BLANKET AWAY...IF THE OTHER KIDS SEE IT, THEY'LL TEASE YOU RIGHT OUT OF CAMP!
6-18
© 1966 Peanuts Worldwide LLC. Dist. by Universal Uclick
CRACK!
www.snoopy.com
THEY WON'T TEASE ME MORE THAN ONCE...
SCHULZ

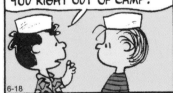

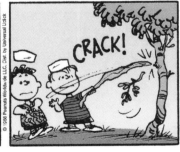

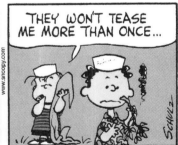

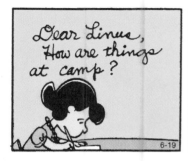

Dear Linus,
How are things at camp?
6-19
I almost made you some cookies today, but then I thought, "Why bother?"
© 1966 Peanuts Worldwide LLC. Dist. by Universal Uclick
Instead, I went out and bought some, but they looked so good I ate them all myself.
www.snoopy.com
Have a nice time at camp.
Your sister,
Lucy
SCHULZ

C'MON, LINUS, EACH OF US IS SUPPOSED TO SAY A FEW WORDS AROUND THE CAMPFIRE TONIGHT...
AS I STAND HERE TONIGHT FAR FROM HOME, I AM REMINDED OF THE WORDS FROM JEREMIAH, "KEEP YOUR VOICE FROM WEEPING, AND YOUR EYES FROM TEARS;
6-20
© 1966 Peanuts Worldwide LLC. Dist. by Universal Uclick
FOR YOUR WORK SHALL BE REWARDED, SAYS THE LORD, AND THEY SHALL COME BACK FROM THE LAND OF THE ENEMY. THERE IS HOPE FOR THE FUTURE, SAYS THE LORD, AND YOUR CHILDREN SHALL COME BACK TO THEIR OWN COUNTRY."
www.snoopy.com
INCIDENTALLY, HAVE ANY OF YOU EVER BEEN TOLD ABOUT "THE GREAT PUMPKIN"?
SCHULZ

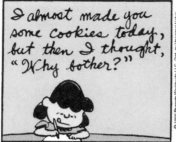

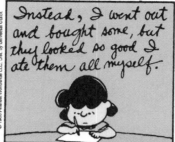

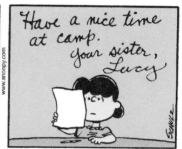

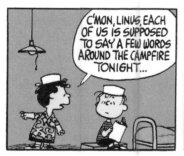

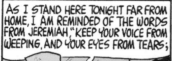

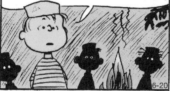

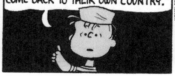

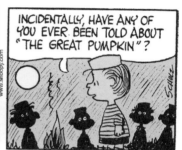

YOU'VE NEVER GONE FISHING? WELL, COME ON... YOU CAN WATCH ME...
THIS IS A ROD AND REEL, SEE?
© 1966 Peanuts Worldwide LLC. Dist. by Universal Uclick
WHAT I'M DOING NOW IS CALLED "CASTING"
www.snoopy.com
AND THAT'S WHAT IS KNOWN AS A "SNARL"
6-25
SCHULZ

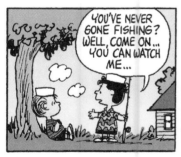

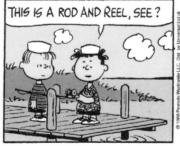

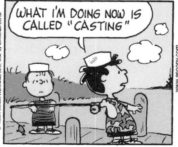

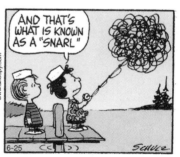

"MAIL CALL," LINUS! YOU GOT A BOX FROM HOME...
6-27
IT'S FROM MY SISTER, LUCY
MAYBE SHE MADE YOU SOME COOKIES OR SOMETHING...
WELL, I'LL BE! HOW ABOUT THAT?
A BOX OF JELLY-BREAD SANDWICHES!
SCHULZ

SO LONG, LINUS
SO LONG, ROY... IT'S BEEN NICE KNOWING YOU..
WELL, HERE I AM ON THE BUS GOING HOME FROM CAMP...
IT'LL BE GOOD TO SEE LUCY AGAIN, AND SCHROEDER, AND SNOOPY AND....
6-28
...AND THAT ROUND-HEADED KID...WHAT WAS HIS NAME?
SCHULZ

PSYCHIA HELP
I HAVE A STRANGE PROBLEM SO I'VE COME TO YOU FOR HELP..
THE DOCTOR IS IN
I CONSIDER MY BROTHER AS BEING A COMPLETE BLOCKHEAD...YET NOW THAT HE'S GONE OFF TO CAMP, I MISS HIM...WHAT'S WRONG WITH ME?
6-24
PSYCHIATRIC HELP 5¢
YOU'RE CRACKING UP!
THE DOCTOR IS IN
THAT'S WHAT I WAS AFRAID OF..
THE DOCTOR IS IN
SCHULZ

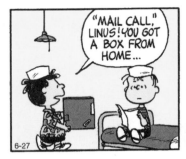

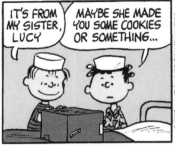

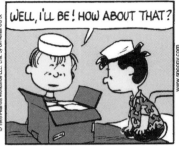

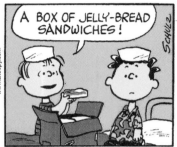

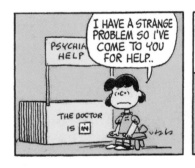

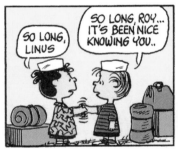

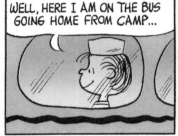

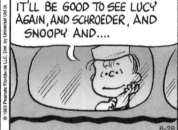

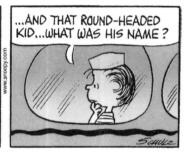

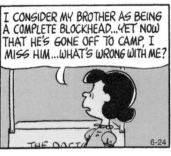

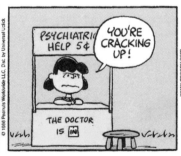

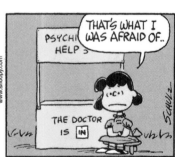

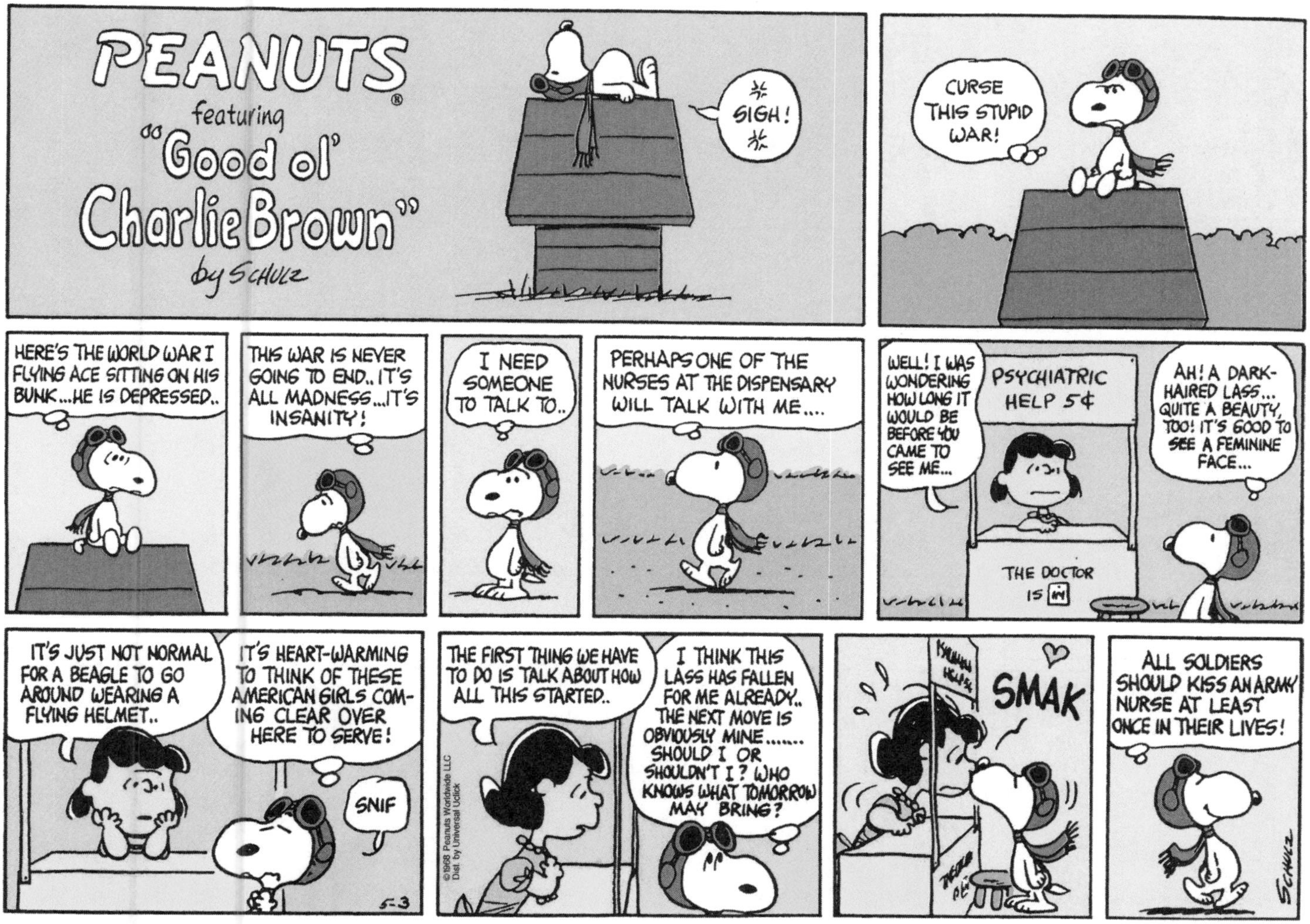
PEANUTS®
featuring "Good ol' Charlie Brown"
by SCHULZ
SIGH!
CURSE THIS STUPID WAR!
HERE'S THE WORLD WAR I FLYING ACE SITTING ON HIS BUNK...HE IS DEPRESSED..
THIS WAR IS NEVER GOING TO END.. IT'S ALL MADNESS...IT'S INSANITY!
I NEED SOMEONE TO TALK TO..
PERHAPS ONE OF THE NURSES AT THE DISPENSARY WILL TALK WITH ME....
WELL! I WAS WONDERING HOW LONG IT WOULD BE BEFORE YOU CAME TO SEE ME...
PSYCHIATRIC HELP 5¢
THE DOCTOR IS IN
AH! A DARK-HAIRED LASS... QUITE A BEAUTY, TOO! IT'S GOOD TO SEE A FEMININE FACE...
IT'S JUST NOT NORMAL FOR A BEAGLE TO GO AROUND WEARING A FLYING HELMET..
IT'S HEART-WARMING TO THINK OF THESE AMERICAN GIRLS COMING CLEAR OVER HERE TO SERVE!
SNIF
5-3
© 1968 Peanuts Worldwide LLC
Dist. by Universal Uclick
THE FIRST THING WE HAVE TO DO IS TALK ABOUT HOW ALL THIS STARTED..
I THINK THIS LASS HAS FALLEN FOR ME ALREADY.. THE NEXT MOVE IS OBVIOUSLY MINE....... SHOULD I OR SHOULDN'T I? WHO KNOWS WHAT TOMORROW MAY BRING?
SMAK
ALL SOLDIERS SHOULD KISS AN ARMY NURSE AT LEAST ONCE IN THEIR LIVES!
SCHULZ

I'M HOME!
WHO CARES? STOP MAKING SO MUCH NOISE!
6-29
HOW CAN I WATCH MY FAVORITE PROGRAM WHEN YOU'RE MAKING ALL THAT STUPID NOISE?!
I WAS RIGHT... I **AM** HOME!
SCHULZ
© 1966 Peanuts Worldwide LLC, Dist. by Universal Uclick
www.snoopy.com

PSYCHIATRIC HELP 5¢
THE DOCTOR IS IN
AND THEN HE WROTE THE GREAT NINTH SYMPHONY..
BUT HE WAS DEAF! HE NEVER HAD A CHANCE TO HEAR IT PERFORMED! ISN'T THAT TERRIBLE? THAT REALLY DEPRESSES ME...
TRY NOT TO THINK ABOUT IT.... FIVE CENTS, PLEASE!
THE DOCTOR IS IN
6-19
SOME CASES ARE RELATIVELY SIMPLE..
THE DOCTOR IS IN
SCHULZ
© 1965 Peanuts Worldwide LLC, Dist. by Universal Uclick
www.snoopy.com

PSYCHIATRIC HELP 5¢
THE DOCTOR IS IN
IF YOU'D LISTEN TO ME, YOU WOULDN'T NEED THAT THUMB AND BLANKET..
YEARS FROM NOW WHEN YOUR KIND HAS PASSED FROM THE SCENE, THUMBS AND BLANKETS WILL STILL BE AROUND!
POW!
DOCTORS ALWAYS TELL YOU TO SAY WHAT'S ON YOUR MIND, BUT THEY DON'T REALLY MEAN IT..
SCHULZ
6-21
© 1965 Peanuts Worldwide LLC, Dist. by Universal Uclick
www.snoopy.com

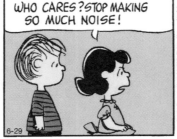

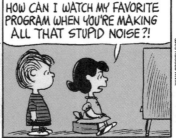

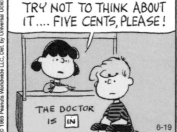

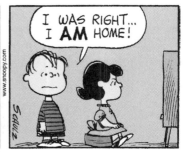

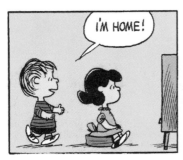

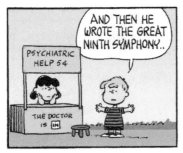

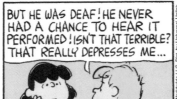

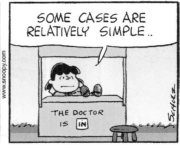

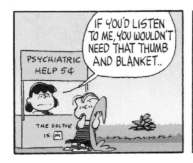

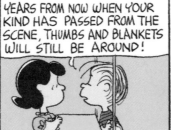

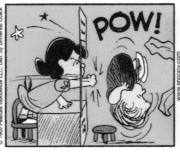

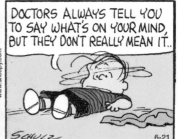

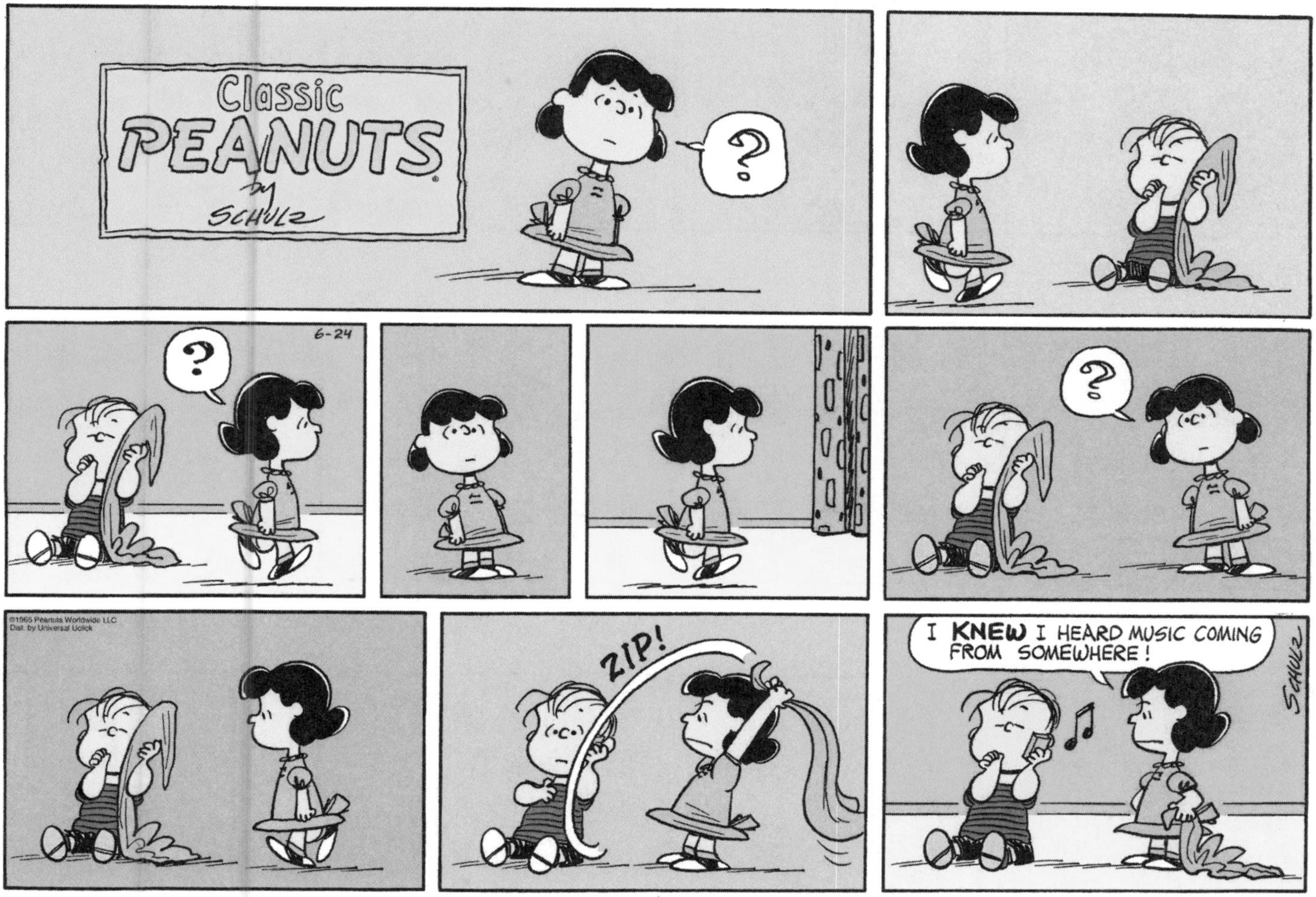

Classic
PEANUTS
by
SCHULZ
?
6-24
?
?
©1965 Peanuts Worldwide LLC
Dist. by Universal Uclick
ZIP!
I KNEW I HEARD MUSIC COMING FROM SOMEWHERE!
SCHULZ

7-3
WELL, I LEARNED SOMETHING ABOUT JUMPING ROPE IN THE RAIN....
SOME JUMP ROPES **SHRINK** !
SCHULZ
© 1966 Peanuts Worldwide LLC. Dist. by Universal Uclick
www.snoopy.com

ARE YOU GOING TO HANG ONTO THAT BLANKET FOR THE REST OF YOUR LIFE?
DON'T BE RIDICULOUS..SOMEDAY I'LL JUST TOSS IT AWAY LIKE THAT...
SOMEDAY!
7-5
SCHULZ
© 1966 Peanuts Worldwide LLC. Dist. by Universal Uclick
www.snoopy.com

WHERE'S THE TV?
IT'S GONE! MOM SAID WE FOUGHT SO MUCH OVER WHAT PROGRAMS WE WERE GOING TO WATCH, SHE DECIDED TO PUT IT AWAY..
NO TV?
NO TV AT ALL? **NONE?** NONE AT ALL?!?
7-8
I'LL DIE!!!
SCHULZ
© 1966 Peanuts Worldwide LLC. Dist. by Universal Uclick
www.snoopy.com

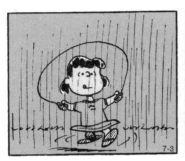

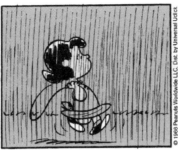

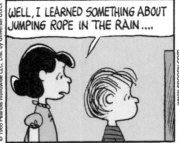

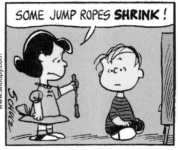

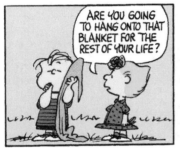

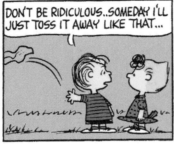

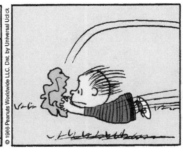

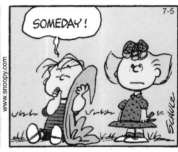

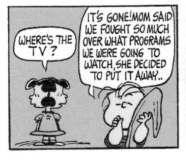

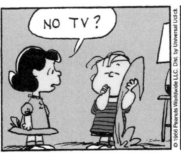

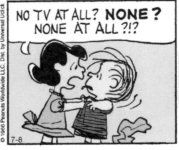

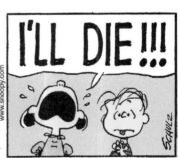

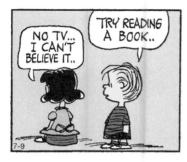

NO TV... I CAN'T BELIEVE IT..
TRY READING A BOOK..
7-9
A WHAT?
OR RADIO...TRY LISTENING TO THE RADIO...
© 1966 Peanuts Worldwide LLC, Dist. by Universal Uclick
TO THE WHAT?
OR PUT SOME RECORDS ON... LISTEN TO THE RECORD PLAYER...
www.snoopy.com
THE RECORD WHAT? READ WHAT? HUH? WHAT? WHAT? LISTEN TO WHAT? WHAT?
SCHULZ

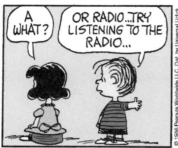

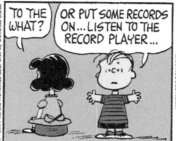

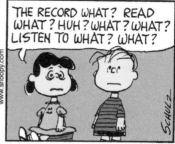

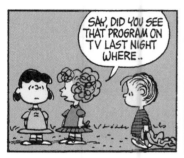

SAY, DID YOU SEE THAT PROGRAM ON TV LAST NIGHT WHERE..
WE DON'T HAVE A TV IN OUR HOUSE... MOM TOOK IT OUT BECAUSE ME AND MY..
7-10
© 1966 Peanuts Worldwide LLC, Dist. by Universal Uclick
STUPID BROTHER
www.snoopy.com
..WERE ALWAYS FIGHTING OVER IT!
SCHULZ

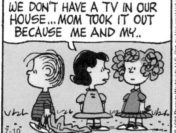

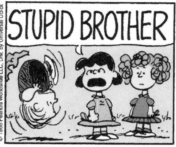

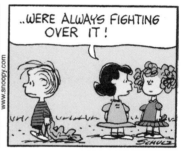

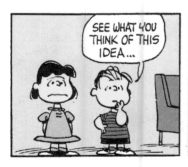

SEE WHAT YOU THINK OF THIS IDEA...
WHY DON'T WE TELL MOM THAT WE'RE SORRY ABOUT ARGUING OVER THE TV ALL THE TIME, AND PROMISE NEVER TO DO IT AGAIN?...THAT WAY, MAYBE SHE'LL FORGIVE US, AND BRING THE TV BACK INTO THE HOUSE..
7-12
© 1966 Peanuts Worldwide LLC, Dist. by Universal Uclick
YOU MEAN, COMPROMISE?
www.snoopy.com
NEVER!
I THINK I'M STUCK WITH A BAD ALLIANCE!
SCHULZ

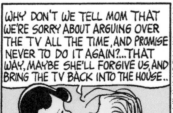

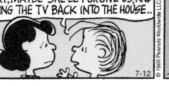

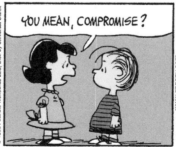

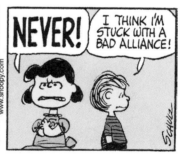

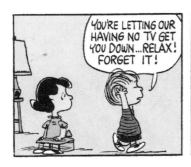

YOU'RE LETTING OUR HAVING NO TV GET YOU DOWN...RELAX! FORGET IT!
HE'S TAKING THIS WHOLE BUSINESS FAR TOO CALMLY...I WONDER IF HE'S SNEAKING OVER TO SOMEONE ELSE'S HOUSE TO WATCH TV....
© 1966 Peanuts Worldwide LLC, Dist. by Universal Uclick
7-13
www.snoopy.com
AH, HA!
!
SCHULZ

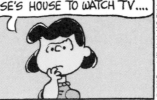

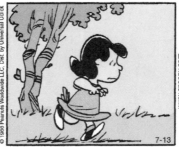

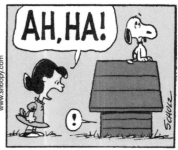

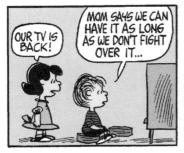

OUR TV IS BACK!
MOM SAYS WE CAN HAVE IT AS LONG AS WE DON'T FIGHT OVER IT...
IS THIS A GOOD PROGRAM YOU'RE WATCHING? THERE'S SOME CARTOONS ON THE OTHER CHANNEL...YOU LIKE CARTOONS, DON'T YOU? WHY DON'T WE WATCH SOME CARTOONS? WHY DON'T I JUST TURN THIS KNOB...
7-15
© 1966 Peanuts Worldwide LLC, Dist. by Universal Uclick
MOM!!
www.snoopy.com
READ ANY GOOD BOOKS LATELY?
SCHULZ

RRRRRR
THAT VACUUM CLEANER SURE MAKES A LOT OF NOISE...
RRRRR
© 1966 Peanuts Worldwide LLC, Dist. by Universal Uclick
7-18
RRRRRRRRRRR
www.snoopy.com
YOU'D MAKE A LOT OF NOISE TOO IF SOMEONE WERE PUSHING YOU ACROSS A CARPET ON YOUR FACE!
SCHULZ

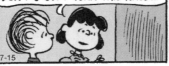

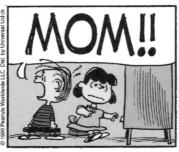

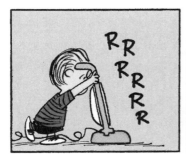

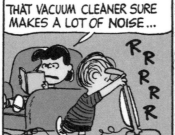

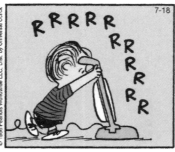

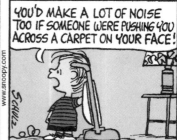

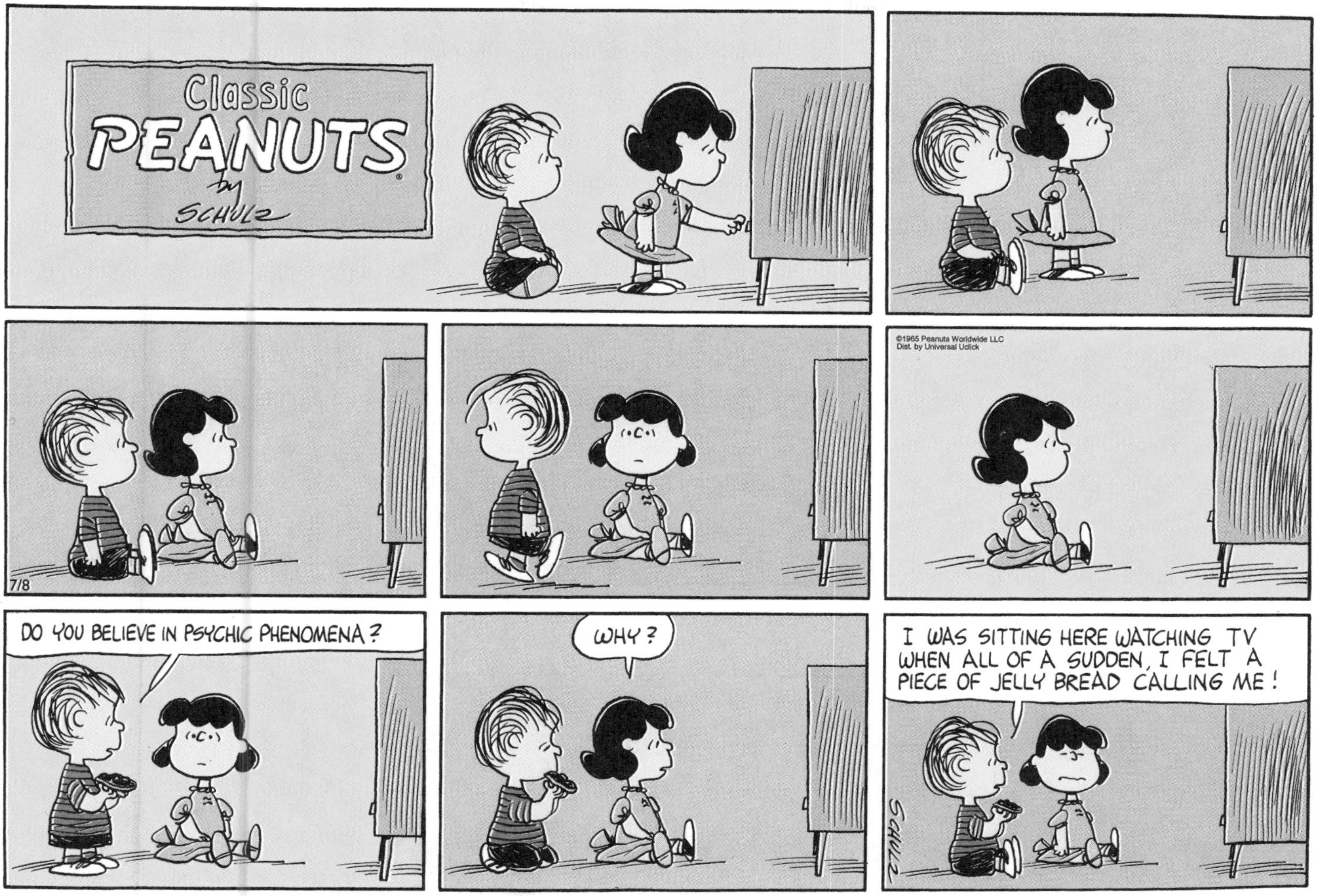
Classic
PEANUTS
by
SCHULZ
©1965 Peanuts Worldwide LLC
Dist. by Universal Uclick
7/8
DO YOU BELIEVE IN PSYCHIC PHENOMENA?
WHY?
I WAS SITTING HERE WATCHING TV WHEN ALL OF A SUDDEN, I FELT A PIECE OF JELLY BREAD CALLING ME!
SCHULZ

WHY DON'T YOU BE A GOOD LITTLE BROTHER, AND GO MAKE ME A JELLY-BREAD SANDWICH?
IF YOU DON'T, I'M GOING TO LEAP ON YOU, AND POUND YOU RIGHT THROUGH THE FLOOR!
© 1966 Peanuts Worldwide LLC. Dist. by Universal Uclick
SO WHY DON'T YOU MAKE ME THAT JELLY-BREAD SANDWICH, HUH? PLEASE, DEAR BROTHER?
www.snoopy.com
WHEN SOMEONE ASKS YOU THAT NICELY, HOW CAN YOU REFUSE?
7-26
SCHULZ

I CAN'T UNDERSTAND WHY YOU DON'T LIKE ME..
I HAVE NICE HAIR, A VERY PLEASANT SMILE, A CHEERFUL PERSONALITY, A KIND FACE AND A HEART FULL OF LOVE!
© 1964 Peanuts Worldwide LLC. Dist. by Universal Uclick
IF YOU ADD UP ALL MY FEATURES, I THINK YOU GET A PRETTY ATTRACTIVE ANSWER
www.snoopy.com
MAYBE YOU ADDED WRONG!
8/3
SCHULZ

I DON'T THINK YOU MUSICIANS KNOW WHAT LOVE IS!
ALL YOU EVER THINK ABOUT IS YOUR STUPID MUSIC! ALL YOU THINK ABOUT IS YOUR MUSIC AND YOURSELVES!
© 1964 Peanuts Worldwide LLC. Dist. by Universal Uclick
YOU DON'T CARE ANYTHING ABOUT OTHER PEOPLE! YOU DON'T CARE ABOUT LOVE OR TENDERNESS OR..
8-4
www.snoopy.com
SCHULZ

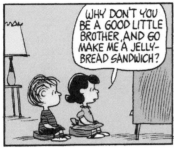

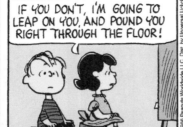

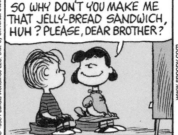

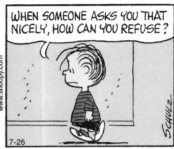

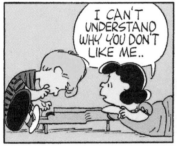

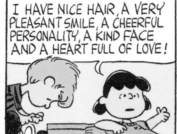

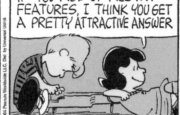

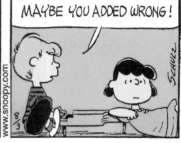

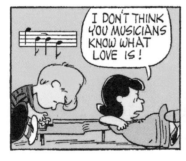

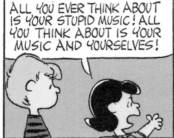

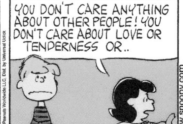

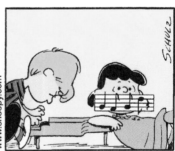

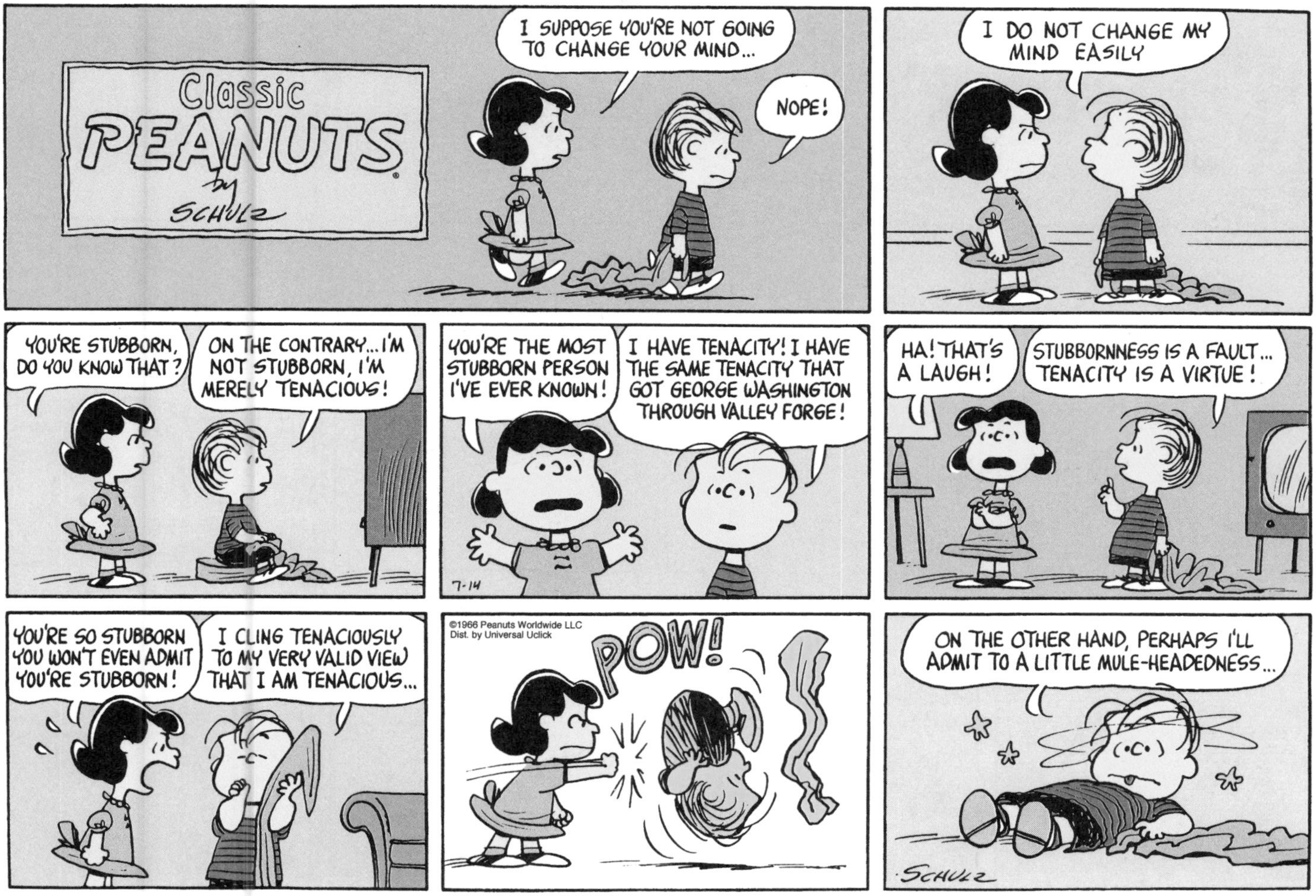
Classic PEANUTS by SCHULZ
I SUPPOSE YOU'RE NOT GOING TO CHANGE YOUR MIND...
NOPE!
I DO NOT CHANGE MY MIND EASILY
YOU'RE STUBBORN, DO YOU KNOW THAT?
ON THE CONTRARY... I'M NOT STUBBORN, I'M MERELY TENACIOUS!
YOU'RE THE MOST STUBBORN PERSON I'VE EVER KNOWN!
I HAVE TENACITY! I HAVE THE SAME TENACITY THAT GOT GEORGE WASHINGTON THROUGH VALLEY FORGE!
7-14
HA! THAT'S A LAUGH!
STUBBORNNESS IS A FAULT... TENACITY IS A VIRTUE!
YOU'RE SO STUBBORN YOU WON'T EVEN ADMIT YOU'RE STUBBORN!
I CLING TENACIOUSLY TO MY VERY VALID VIEW THAT I AM TENACIOUS...
©1966 Peanuts Worldwide LLC
Dist. by Universal Uclick
POW!
ON THE OTHER HAND, PERHAPS I'LL ADMIT TO A LITTLE MULE-HEADEDNESS...
SCHULZ

8-16
© 1965 Peanuts Worldwide LLC. Dist. by Universal Uclick
www.snoopy.com
YOU'RE NOT HAPPY, ARE YOU?
SCHULZ

YOU THINK BEETHOVEN WAS GREAT...
WELL, WHAT ABOUT CHOPIN, BACH, MOZART, BLOCH, BARTOK, BERLIOZ, BIZET, BRAHMS, DELIUS, DEBUSSY AND DVORAK?
© 1965 Peanuts Worldwide LLC. Dist. by Universal Uclick
WHAT ABOUT ELGAR, FRANCK, GLINKA, GRIEG, HANDEL, HAYDN, HUMPERDINCK, LISZT, MAHLER, MENDELSSOHN, RAVEL, RACHMANINOFF, SCHUBERT, SIBELIUS, TSCHAIKOWSKY AND VIVALDI?
8-17
www.snoopy.com
THEY WERE GREAT, TOO..
RATS! FOR ONE BRIEF MOMENT I THOUGHT I HAD HIM!
SCHULZ

YOU'RE THINKING OF KICKING OVER MY SAND CASTLE, AREN'T YOU?
WELL, WAIT JUST A MOMENT, WILL YOU, PLEASE, WHILE I STAND UP?
8-17
© 1965 Peanuts Worldwide LLC. Dist. by Universal Uclick
THIS WILL GIVE ME A CHANCE TO..
www.snoopy.com
BEAT YOU TO IT!!!
SCHULZ

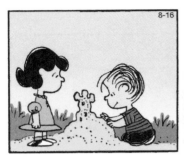

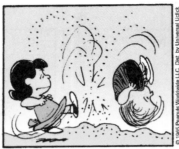

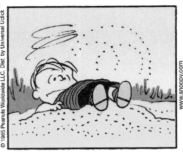

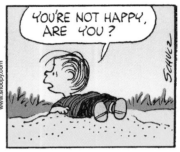

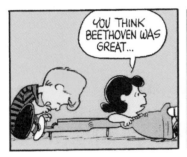

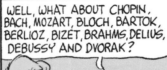

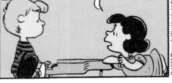

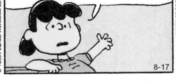

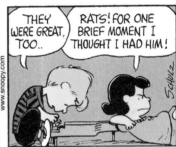

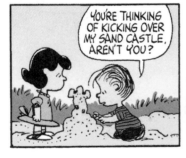

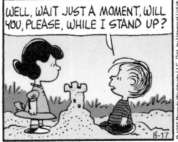

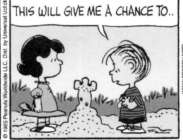

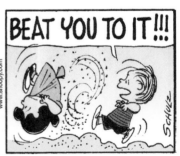

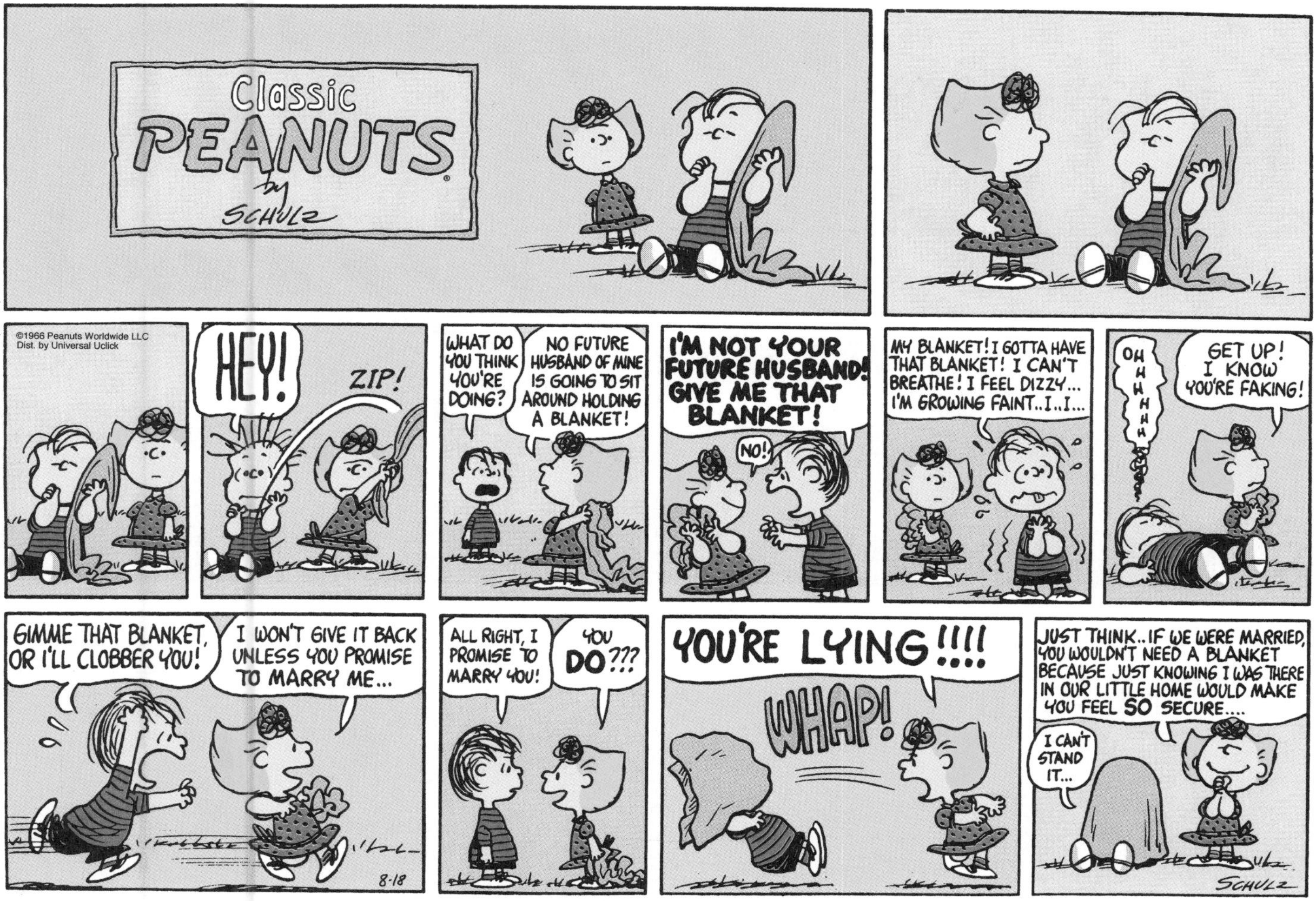
Classic PEANUTS by SCHULZ
©1966 Peanuts Worldwide LLC Dist. by Universal Uclick
HEY!
ZIP!
WHAT DO YOU THINK YOU'RE DOING?
NO FUTURE HUSBAND OF MINE IS GOING TO SIT AROUND HOLDING A BLANKET!
I'M NOT YOUR FUTURE HUSBAND! GIVE ME THAT BLANKET!
NO!
MY BLANKET! I GOTTA HAVE THAT BLANKET! I CAN'T BREATHE! I FEEL DIZZY... I'M GROWING FAINT..I..I...
OHHHHHH
GET UP! I KNOW YOU'RE FAKING!
GIMME THAT BLANKET, OR I'LL CLOBBER YOU!
I WON'T GIVE IT BACK UNLESS YOU PROMISE TO MARRY ME...
8-18
ALL RIGHT, I PROMISE TO MARRY YOU!
YOU DO???
YOU'RE LYING!!!!
WHAP!
JUST THINK..IF WE WERE MARRIED, YOU WOULDN'T NEED A BLANKET BECAUSE JUST KNOWING I WAS THERE IN OUR LITTLE HOME WOULD MAKE YOU FEEL SO SECURE....
I CAN'T STAND IT...
SCHULZ

HI, ROY... WHO YOU WRITIN' TO?

I'M WRITING TO A LITTLE KID NAMED LINUS THAT I MET AT CAMP SEVERAL WEEKS AGO

IS HE CUTE? IF HE IS, TELL HIM YOUR VERY GOOD FRIEND, "PEPPERMINT" PATTY SAYS, "HELLO"

TELL HIM WHAT A REAL SWINGER I AM...

PUT IN A GOOD WORD FOR ME, ROY, AND THE NEXT TIME WE INDIAN WRESTLE I'LL TRY NOT TO CLOBBER YOU!

YOU SAY YOU MET THIS LINUS KID AT CAMP?

YES, AND THE YEAR BEFORE I MET A FRIEND OF HIS NAMED CHARLIE BROWN..

HE WAS A STRANGE ROUND-HEADED KID WHO NEVER TALKED ABOUT ANYTHING EXCEPT BASEBALL AND THIS AWFUL TEAM OF HIS THAT ALWAYS LOSES...

I LOVE BASEBALL! GET ON THE PHONE, QUICK! TELL HIM YOUR FRIEND, "PEPPERMINT" PATTY, HAS VOLUNTEERED TO HELP!

I REALLY LOVE BASEBALL! I'LL TAKE OVER THIS KID'S TEAM, AND SHOW HIM HOW TO **WIN**!!

IT'S A GOOD THUMB, BUT NOT A GREAT THUMB!

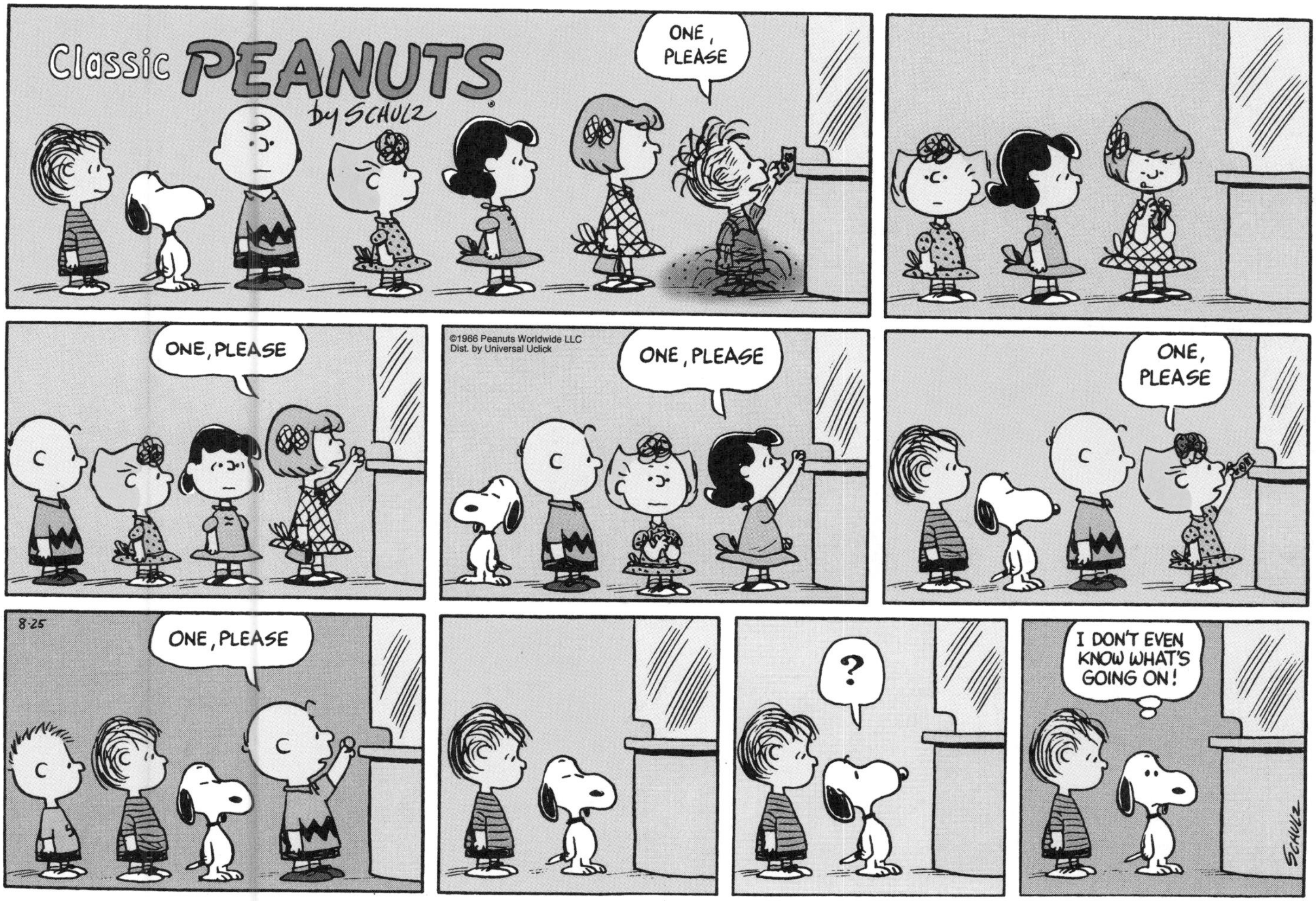
Classic PEANUTS
by SCHULZ
ONE, PLEASE
ONE, PLEASE
©1966 Peanuts Worldwide LLC
Dist. by Universal Uclick
ONE, PLEASE
ONE, PLEASE
8-25
ONE, PLEASE
?
I DON'T EVEN KNOW WHAT'S GOING ON!
SCHULZ

DO YOU THINK PATIENCE IS A VIRTUE?
OH, YES...AND I'M PROUD TO SAY THAT IT IS A VIRTUE WHICH I POSSESS
www.snoopy.com
YOU REALLY WOULD CONSIDER PATIENCE AS BEING A VIRTUE, THEN?
8-23
© 1964 Peanuts Worldwide LLC. Dist. by Universal Uclick
I SAID SO, DIDN'T I?!!
SCHULZ

YOU KNOW WHAT'S THE MATTER WITH YOU?
www.snoopy.com
YOU TALK TOO MUCH
9-3
POW
© 1964 Peanuts Worldwide LLC. Dist. by Universal Uclick
DO YOU REALLY THINK SO?
SCHULZ

SCHROEDER, DO YOU THINK I'M BEAUTIFUL?
I THINK YOU'RE THE MOST BEAUTIFUL GIRL THE WORLD HAS EVER KNOWN...
© 1965 Peanuts Worldwide LLC. Dist. by Universal Uclick
9-4
www.snoopy.com
YOU HATE ME, DON'T YOU?
SCHULZ

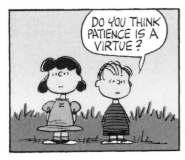

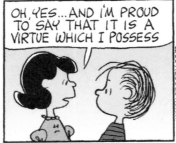

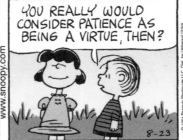

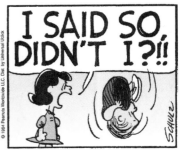

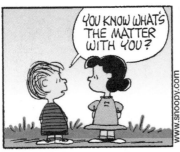

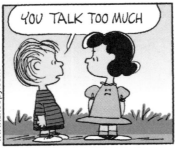

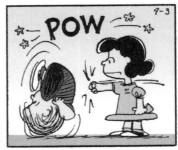

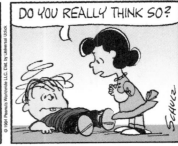

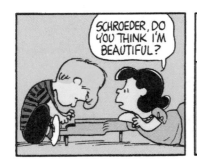

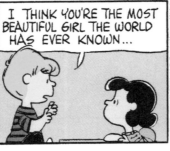

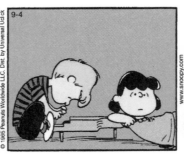

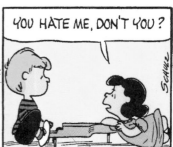

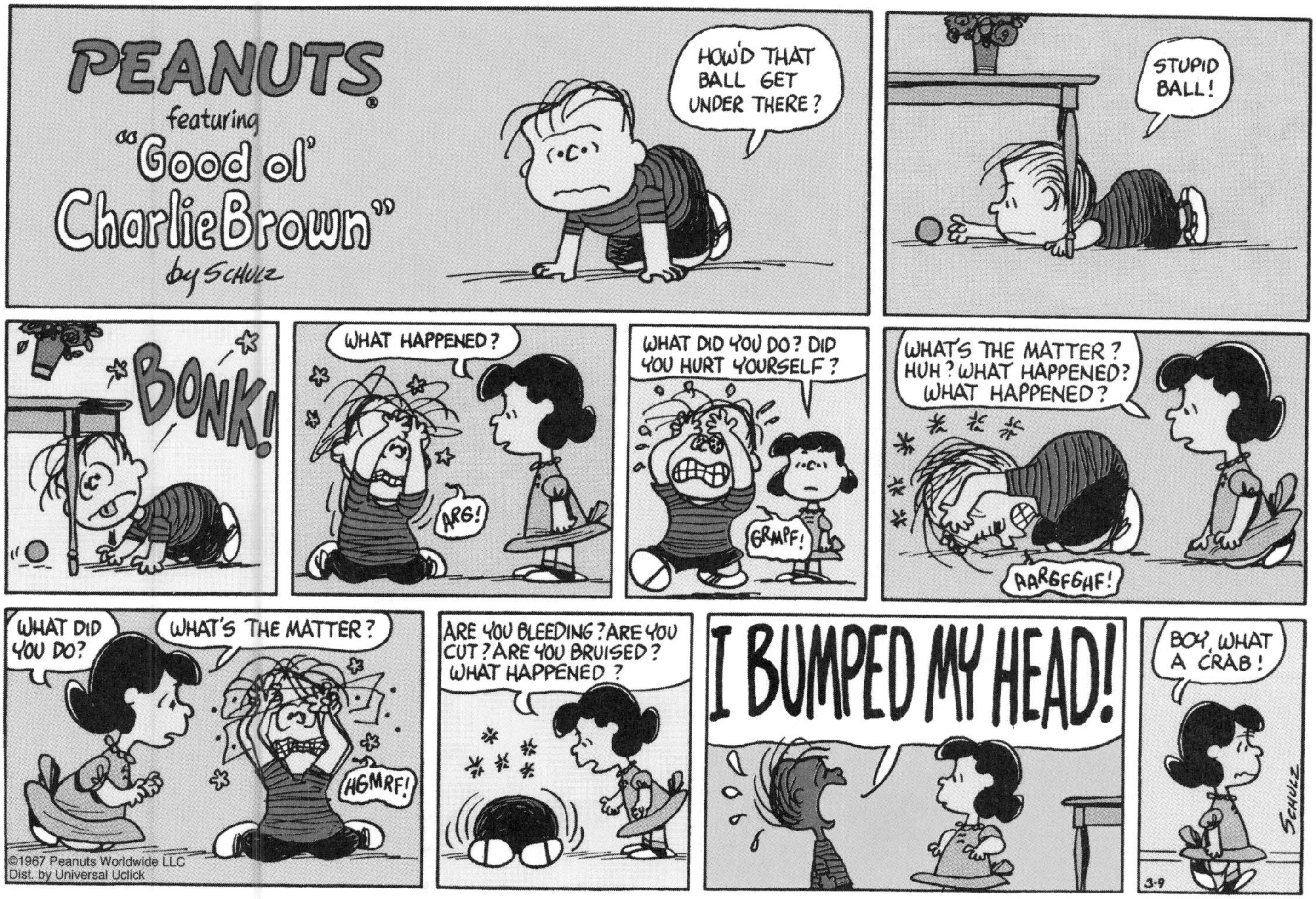
PEANUTS
featuring "Good ol' CharlieBrown"
by SCHULZ
HOW'D THAT BALL GET UNDER THERE?
STUPID BALL!
BONK!
WHAT HAPPENED?
ARG!
WHAT DID YOU DO? DID YOU HURT YOURSELF?
GRMPF!
WHAT'S THE MATTER? HUH? WHAT HAPPENED? WHAT HAPPENED?
AARGFGHF!
WHAT DID YOU DO?
WHAT'S THE MATTER?
HGMRF!
ARE YOU BLEEDING? ARE YOU CUT? ARE YOU BRUISED? WHAT HAPPENED?
I BUMPED MY HEAD!
BOY, WHAT A CRAB!
SCHULZ
3-9
©1967 Peanuts Worldwide LLC
Dist. by Universal Uclick

I'M GOING TO COLOR THE SKY BLUE AND THE GRASS GREEN
DON'T FORGET THAT "GRASS GREEN" IS AN ELUSIVE TERM ... THE COLOR OF GRASS CAN BE CHANGED BY THE TURNING OF THE BLADES AS THEY ARE BLOWN BY THE WIND...
9-7
© 1965 Peanuts Worldwide LLC, Dist. by Universal Uclick
THE IDEAL LOCATION TO OBSERVE A "GRASS GREEN" WOULD BE IN A TEMPERATURE ZONE AT A PLACE NOT LOWER THAN 36 DEGREES LATITUDE AT A DISTANCE OF FROM ONE TO TEN YARDS DURING MIDDAY, AND..
www.snoopy.com
SCHULZ

IS YOUR MOM PUTTING NOTES IN YOUR LUNCH AGAIN?
YES, THIS IS THE FIRST ONE THIS YEAR
"DEAR SON, I WILL BE AWAY WHEN YOU GET HOME FROM SCHOOL TODAY.. I HAVE BEEN INVITED TO A BRIDGE PARTY... I WILL LEAVE A SANDWICH AND SOME MILK IN THE REFRIGERATOR..."
© 1966 Peanuts Worldwide LLC, Dist. by Universal Uclick
"STUDY HARD TODAY.. MAKE US PROUD OF YOU.. THE FUTURE IS IN THE HANDS OF YOUR GENERATION.. I SUPPOSE IN MANY WAYS OUR GENERATION HAS FAILED YOURS, BUT WE DID TRY... PLEASE JUDGE US WITH MERCY.."
9-10
www.snoopy.com
MOM GETS CARRIED AWAY!
SCHULZ

I FEEL KIND OF DIZZY...
9-11
MAYBE YOU SHOULDN'T GO TO SCHOOL ... MAYBE YOU SHOULD STAY HOME
I CAN'T
© 1966 Peanuts Worldwide LLC, Dist. by Universal Uclick
HOW CAN MISSING ONE DAY HURT YOU?
www.snoopy.com
I MIGHT NOT GET TO GO TO THE COLLEGE OF MY CHOICE!
SCHULZ

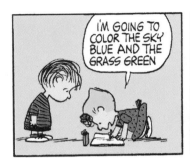

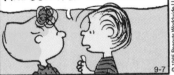

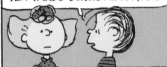

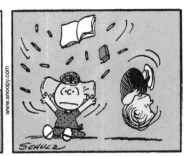

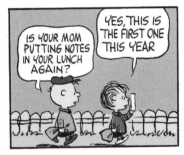

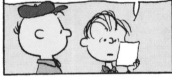

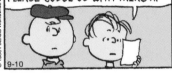

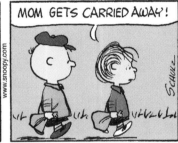

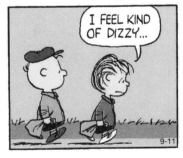

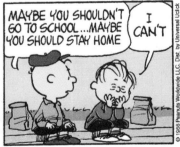

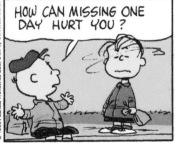

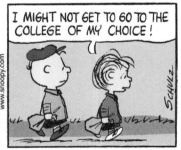

YOU CAN HAVE THESE THREE CRAYONS..I'LL TAKE THE REST...
I CAN'T COLOR A PICTURE WITH ONLY THREE CRAYONS
I WANT MORE
WHAT?
I FEEL LIKE OLIVER TWIST ASKING FOR MORE GRUEL!
9-12

9-13
THIS IS ONE OF THOSE ONE-MINUTE COMMERCIALS THAT SEEMS TWO MINUTES TOO LONG!

LOOK AT THAT BUG, WILL YOU?
HE THINKS HE'S BETTER THAN THAT OTHER BUG...
WHAT MAKES YOU THINK YOU'RE SO GREAT?!
I ENJOY PUTTING HIS KIND IN THEIR PLACE!
9-14

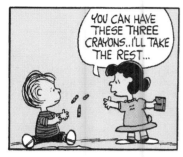

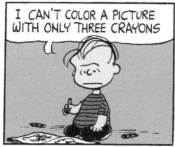

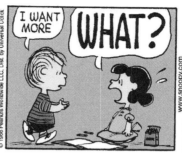

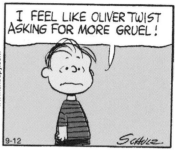

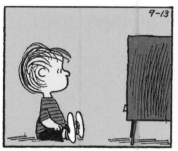

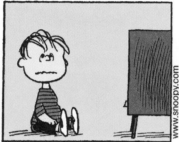

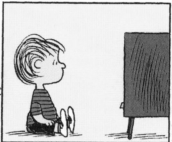

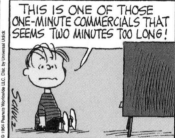

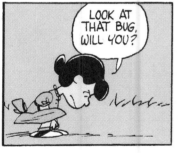

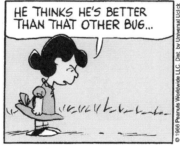

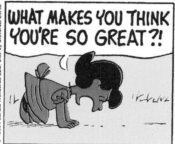

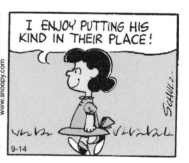

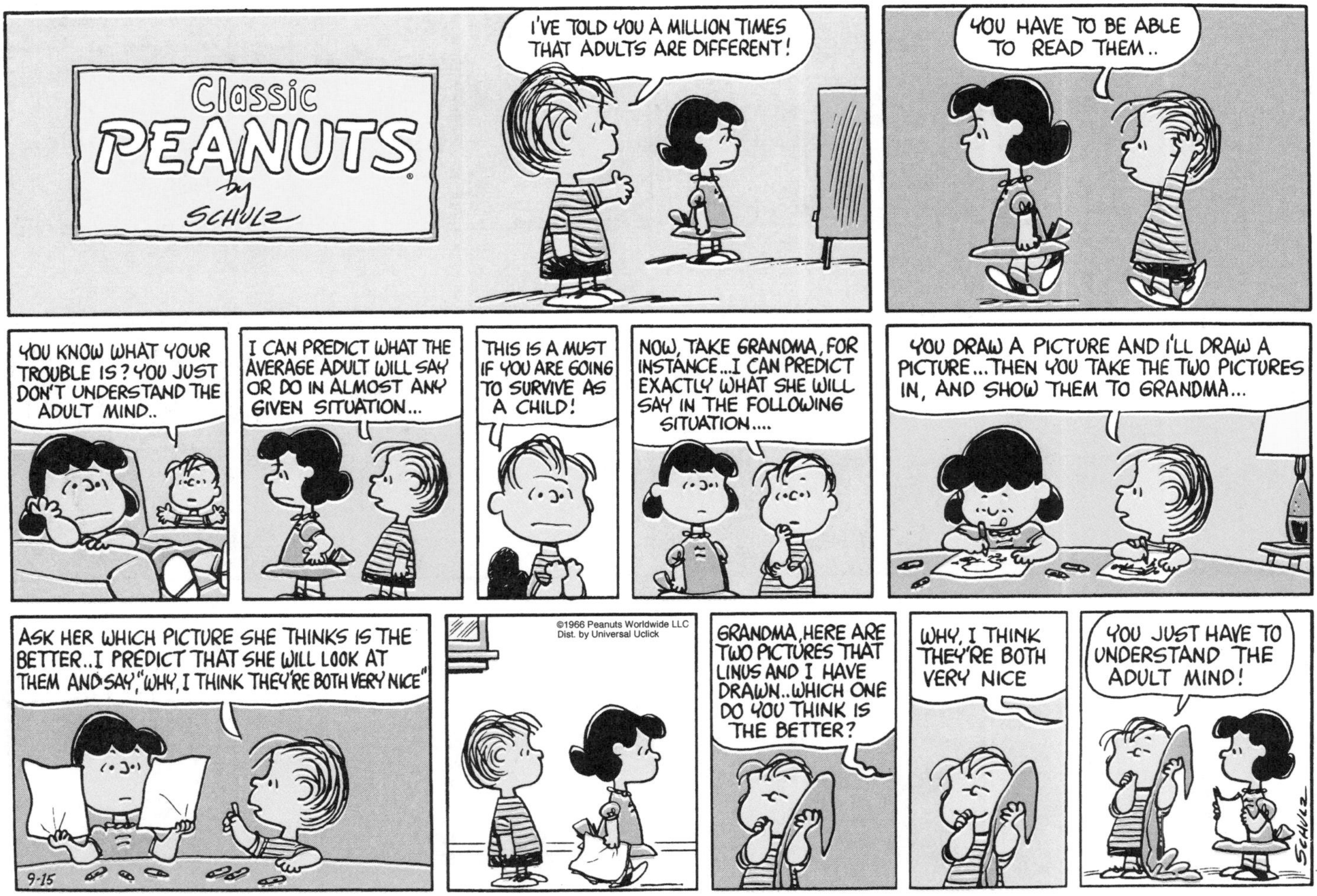
Classic PEANUTS by SCHULZ
I'VE TOLD YOU A MILLION TIMES THAT ADULTS ARE DIFFERENT!
YOU HAVE TO BE ABLE TO READ THEM..
YOU KNOW WHAT YOUR TROUBLE IS? YOU JUST DON'T UNDERSTAND THE ADULT MIND..
I CAN PREDICT WHAT THE AVERAGE ADULT WILL SAY OR DO IN ALMOST ANY GIVEN SITUATION...
THIS IS A MUST IF YOU ARE GOING TO SURVIVE AS A CHILD!
NOW, TAKE GRANDMA, FOR INSTANCE...I CAN PREDICT EXACTLY WHAT SHE WILL SAY IN THE FOLLOWING SITUATION....
YOU DRAW A PICTURE AND I'LL DRAW A PICTURE...THEN YOU TAKE THE TWO PICTURES IN, AND SHOW THEM TO GRANDMA...
ASK HER WHICH PICTURE SHE THINKS IS THE BETTER..I PREDICT THAT SHE WILL LOOK AT THEM AND SAY, "WHY, I THINK THEY'RE BOTH VERY NICE"
9-15
©1966 Peanuts Worldwide LLC
Dist. by Universal Uclick
GRANDMA, HERE ARE TWO PICTURES THAT LINUS AND I HAVE DRAWN..WHICH ONE DO YOU THINK IS THE BETTER?
WHY, I THINK THEY'RE BOTH VERY NICE
YOU JUST HAVE TO UNDERSTAND THE ADULT MIND!
SCHULZ

I'VE DECIDED TO TRY TO BE A BETTER PERSON
I'VE BEEN TRYING TO IMPROVE A LITTLE EACH DAY...
YOU DON'T LOOK ANY BETTER TO ME NOW THAN YOU DID LAST WEEK
I'M A SLOW STARTER!
www.snoopy.com
© 1964 Peanuts Worldwide LLC. Dist. by Universal Uclick
9-28
SCHULZ

YOU SEE ALL THESE LEAVES FALLING?
THIS HAPPENS EVERY YEAR...THIS IS ONE OF THE CYCLES OF NATURE
THERE IS A REAL LESSON TO BE LEARNED FROM THIS... DO YOU KNOW WHAT IT IS?
DON'T BE A LEAF...BE A TREE!
www.snoopy.com
9-29
© 1964 Peanuts Worldwide LLC. Dist. by Universal Uclick
SCHULZ

"SETS."... "ONE TO ONE MATCHING."
"EQUIVALENT SETS."... "NON-EQUIVALENT SETS."... "SETS OF ONE"..."SETS OF TWO".
"RENAMING TWO"..."SUBSETS"... "JOINING SETS"..."NUMBER SENTENCES"..."PLACEHOLDERS"...
ALL I WANT TO KNOW IS, HOW MUCH IS TWO AND TWO?
10-2
© 1965 Peanuts Worldwide LLC. Dist. by Universal Uclick
www.snoopy.com
SCHULZ

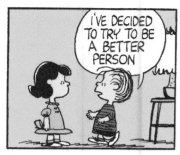

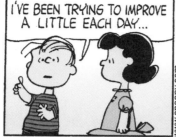

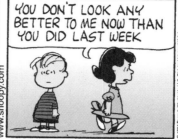

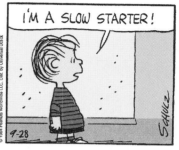

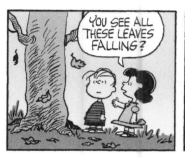

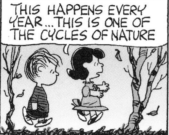

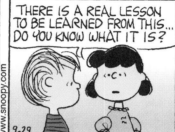

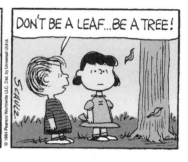

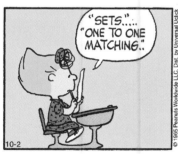

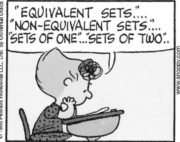

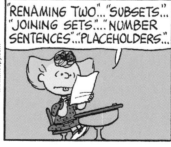

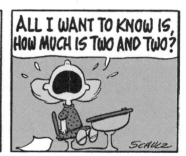

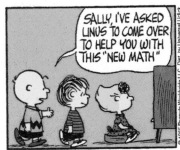

SALLY, I'VE ASKED LINUS TO COME OVER TO HELP YOU WITH THIS "NEW MATH"
© 1965 Peanuts Worldwide LLC, Dist. by Universal Uclick
I COULDN'T BE LESS INTERESTED! WHAT DO I CARE ABOUT "NEW MATH"? I'M ONLY GOING TO BE A HOUSEWIFE!
www.snoopy.com
THAT'S THE WRONG ATTITUDE...MATH CAN BE A VERY REWARDING SUBJECT...
HA!
10-3
I NEVER KNOW HOW TO ANSWER THAT..
SCHULZ

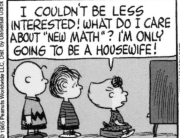

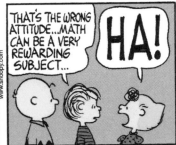

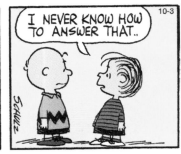

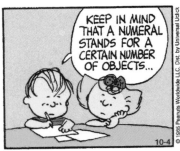

KEEP IN MIND THAT A NUMERAL STANDS FOR A CERTAIN NUMBER OF OBJECTS...
10-4
© 1965 Peanuts Worldwide LLC, Dist. by Universal Uclick
NOW, WHEN YOU COUNT, WHAT YOU ARE DOING IS MATCHING ELEMENTS ONE-TO-ONE WITH A SET OF COUNTING NUMBERS...
www.snoopy.com
IN A SET OF NUMBERS, THE LAST NUMERAL MATCHED TO THAT SET IS THE CARDINAL NUMBER..
THERE'S A GOOD PROGRAM ON TV TONIGHT AT SEVEN O'CLOCK
SCHULZ

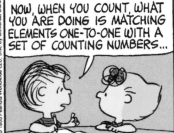

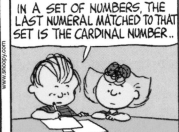

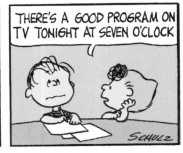

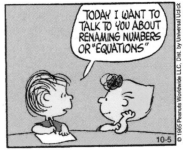

TODAY I WANT TO TALK TO YOU ABOUT RENAMING NUMBERS OR "EQUATIONS"
10-5
© 1965 Peanuts Worldwide LLC, Dist. by Universal Uclick
THIS IS A CONCEPT WHICH WILL BE CARRIED OVER WHEN YOU BEGIN TO STUDY ALGEBRA..
ALGEBRA?
www.snoopy.com
DON'T TALK TO ME ABOUT ALGEBRA! I DON'T EVEN UNDERSTAND MATH! YOU'LL DRIVE ME CRAZY!
I'M LOSING MY MIND AND NOBODY CARES!!
SCHULZ

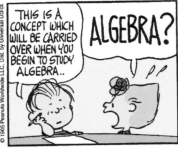

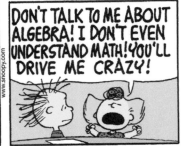

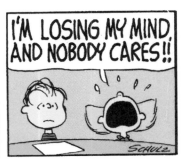

HERE..MOM JUST TOOK SOME OF YOUR SOCKS OUT OF THE DRYER..
10-4
SHE SAID FOR YOU TO PUT THEM IN YOUR DRESSER
© 1966 Peanuts Worldwide LLC, Dist. by Universal Uclick
www.snoopy.com
SECURITY IS HAVING A DRAWER-FULL OF WARM SOCKS!
SCHULZ

THE TITLE OF MY THEME IS, "EXPERIENCES AT SUMMER CAMP"
"AS I GOT OFF THE CAMP BUS THAT DAY, I SENSED THAT THE WOODS WERE FULL OF QUEEN SNAKES! QUEEN SNAKES TO THE LEFT OF ME.... QUEEN SNAKES TO THE RIGHT OF ME... QUEEN SNAKES ALL AROUND ME! I.."
© 1966 Peanuts Worldwide LLC, Dist. by Universal Uclick
KLUNK
!
www.snoopy.com
POOR MISS OTHMAR...I KEEP FORGETTING SHE HAS A THING ABOUT QUEEN SNAKES!
10-7
SCHULZ

I will not talk in class.
I will not talk in class.
10-10
© 1965 Peanuts Worldwide LLC, Dist. by Universal Uclick
I will not talk in class.
I will not talk in class.
I will not talk in class.
www.snoopy.com
I will not talk in class.
I will not talk in class.
I will not talk in class.
On the other hand, who knows what I'll do?
SCHULZ

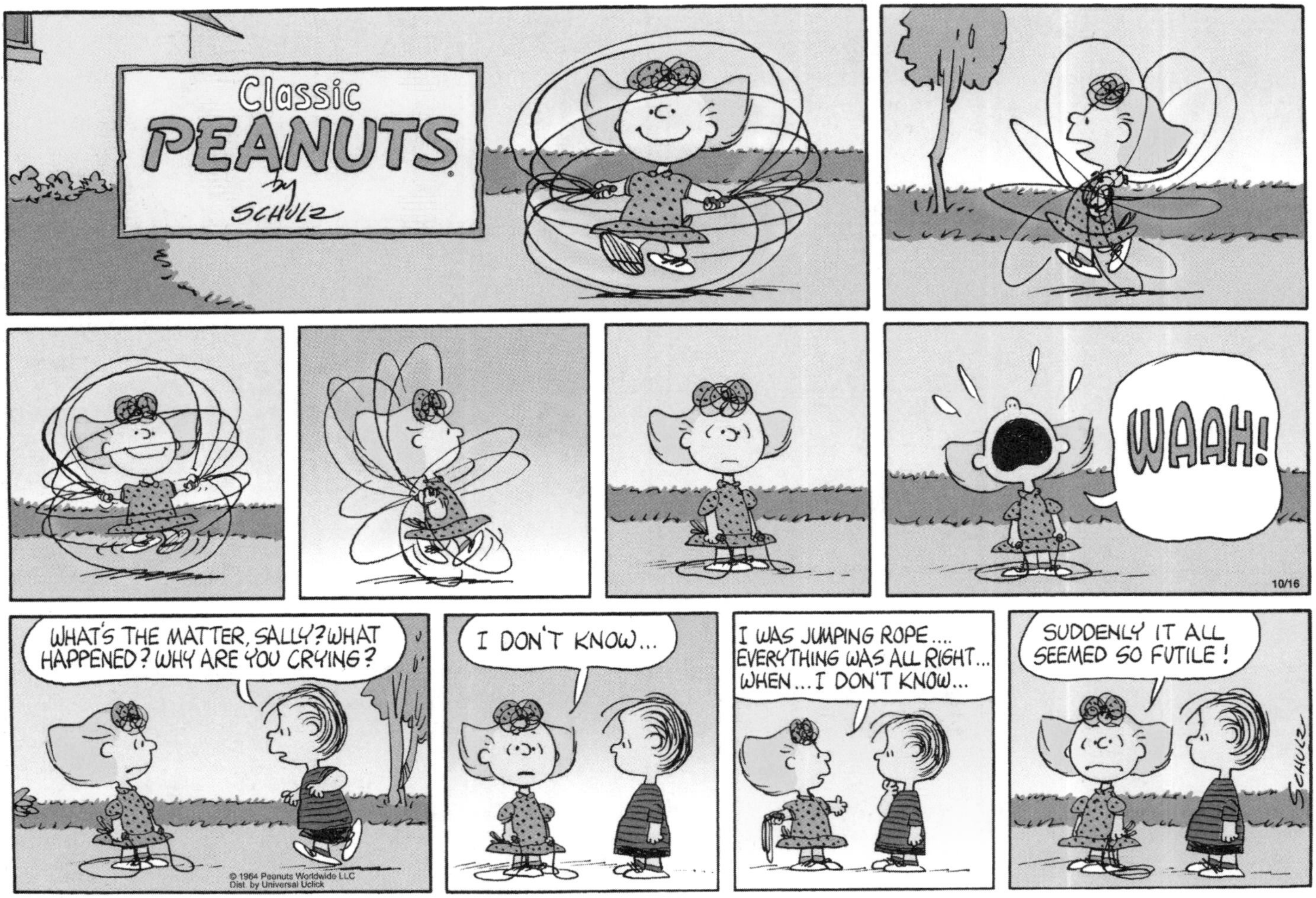
Classic
PEANUTS
by SCHULZ
WAAH!
10/16
WHAT'S THE MATTER, SALLY? WHAT HAPPENED? WHY ARE YOU CRYING?
© 1964 Peanuts Worldwide LLC
Dist. by Universal Uclick
I DON'T KNOW...
I WAS JUMPING ROPE.... EVERYTHING WAS ALL RIGHT... WHEN... I DON'T KNOW...
SUDDENLY IT ALL SEEMED SO FUTILE!
SCHULZ

10-8
EVERYONE HATES TO SEE WINTER COME...YOU KNOW THAT, DON'T YOU?
© 1965 Peanuts Worldwide LLC. Dist. by Universal Uclick
WELL, YOU GUYS DON'T HELP THINGS ANY...FALLING LEAVES ARE DEPRESSING!
www.snoopy.com
STAY UP THERE! STOP FALLING! STOP FALLING, I SAY! STAY UP THERE!
STUPID LEAVES!
SCHULZ

10-9
STAY UP THERE, YOU FOOL!
© 1965 Peanuts Worldwide LLC. Dist. by Universal Uclick
OH, GOOD GRIEF! YOU WOULDN'T LISTEN, WOULD YOU?
www.snoopy.com
NOW, IT'LL BE THE RAKE AND THE BURNING PILE...
YOU JUST CAN'T TELL THEM ANYTHING!
SCHULZ

HOW COME YOU NEVER GIVE ME ANY PRESENTS?
© 1965 Peanuts Worldwide LLC. Dist. by Universal Uclick
BECAUSE I THINK YOU'RE LOUD, MEAN, RUDE AND OVERBEARING!
www.snoopy.com
LOUD, MEAN, RUDE AND OVERBEARING PEOPLE LIKE PRESENTS, TOO, YOU KNOW!
SCHULZ
10/12

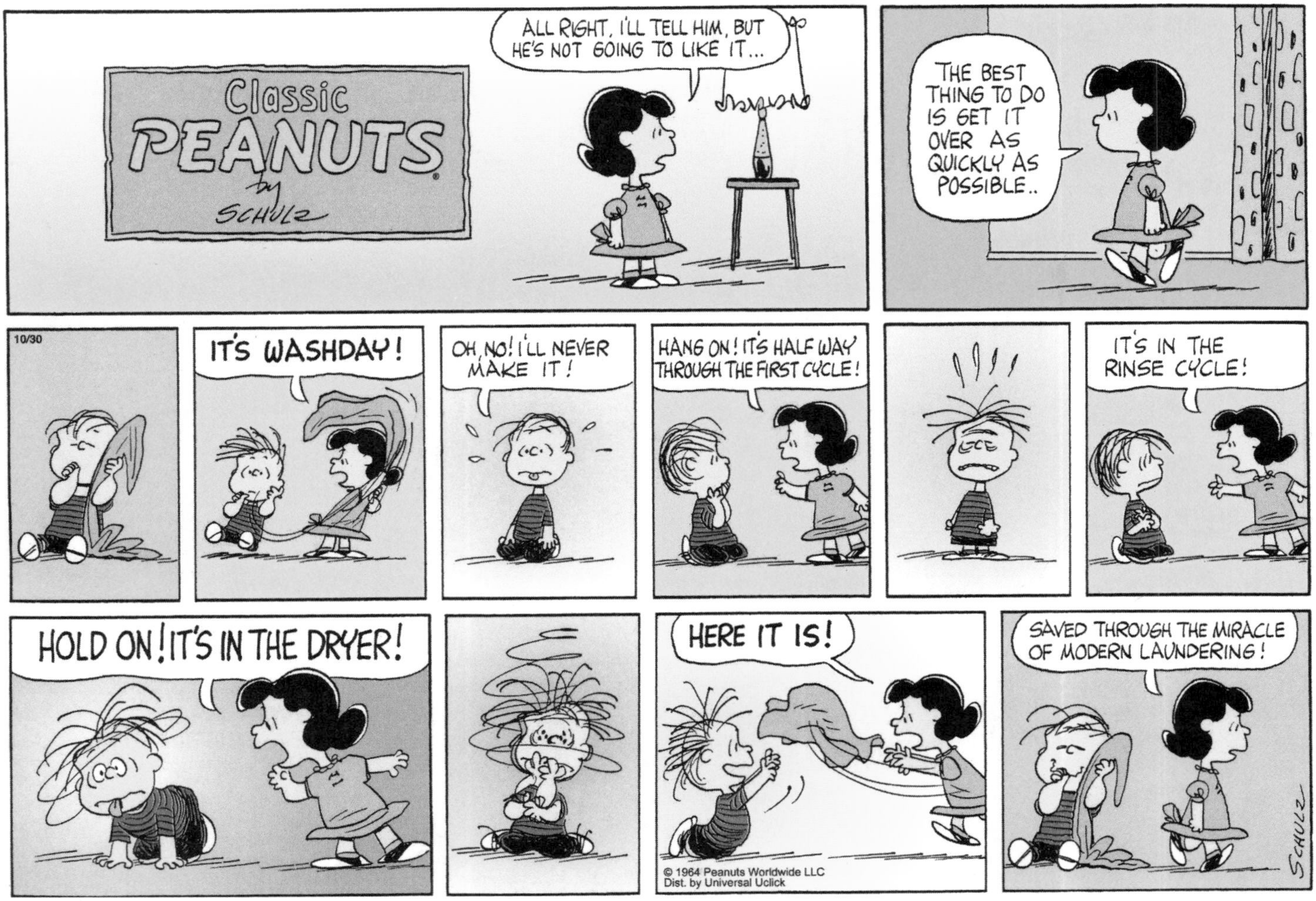
Classic PEANUTS by SCHULZ
ALL RIGHT, I'LL TELL HIM, BUT HE'S NOT GOING TO LIKE IT...
THE BEST THING TO DO IS GET IT OVER AS QUICKLY AS POSSIBLE..
10/30
IT'S WASHDAY!
OH, NO! I'LL NEVER MAKE IT!
HANG ON! IT'S HALF WAY THROUGH THE FIRST CYCLE!
IT'S IN THE RINSE CYCLE!
HOLD ON! IT'S IN THE DRYER!
HERE IT IS!
© 1964 Peanuts Worldwide LLC
Dist. by Universal Uclick
SAVED THROUGH THE MIRACLE OF MODERN LAUNDERING!
SCHULZ

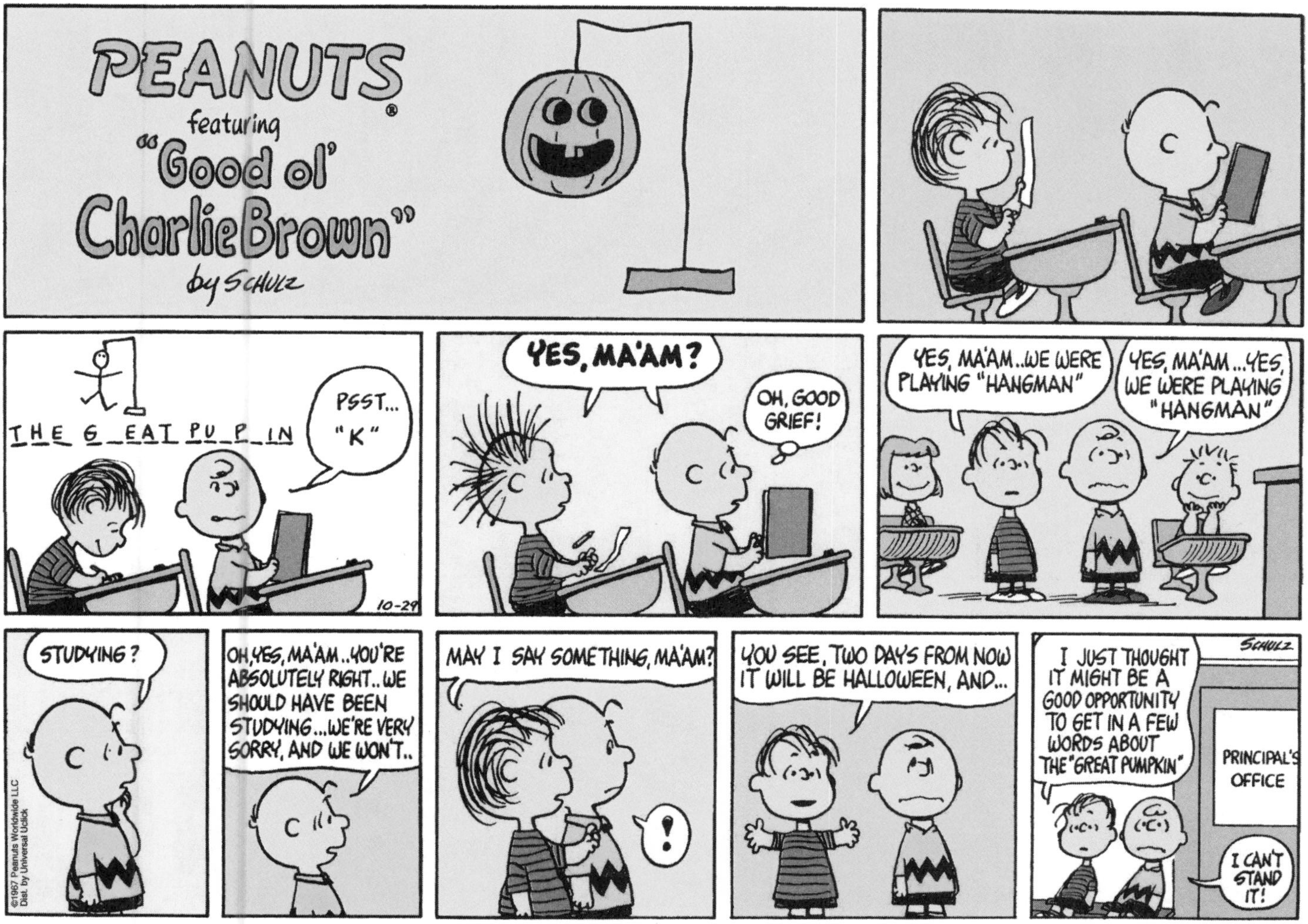
PEANUTS® featuring "Good ol' Charlie Brown" by SCHULZ
THE G_EAT PU_P_IN
PSST... "K"
10-29
YES, MA'AM?
OH, GOOD GRIEF!
YES, MA'AM..WE WERE PLAYING "HANGMAN"
YES, MA'AM...YES, WE WERE PLAYING "HANGMAN"
STUDYING?
©1967 Peanuts Worldwide LLC Dist. by Universal Uclick
OH, YES, MA'AM..YOU'RE ABSOLUTELY RIGHT..WE SHOULD HAVE BEEN STUDYING...WE'RE VERY SORRY, AND WE WON'T..
MAY I SAY SOMETHING, MA'AM?
!
YOU SEE, TWO DAYS FROM NOW IT WILL BE HALLOWEEN, AND...
SCHULZ
I JUST THOUGHT IT MIGHT BE A GOOD OPPORTUNITY TO GET IN A FEW WORDS ABOUT THE "GREAT PUMPKIN"
PRINCIPAL'S OFFICE
I CAN'T STAND IT!

LOOK, ROY... I GOT A LETTER FROM LINUS!
"DEAR PEPPERMINT PATTY...HOW HAVE YOU BEEN? IT OCCURRED TO ME THAT PERHAPS YOU HAVE NEVER HEARD OF THE 'GREAT PUMPKIN'"
© 1966 Peanuts Worldwide LLC, Dist. by Universal Uclick
THE GREAT PUMPKIN?! WHAT IN THE WORLD IS THAT? MAYBE I SHOULDN'T READ ANY MORE..I'M VERY SUPERSTITIOUS, YOU KNOW...
10-14
www.snoopy.com
THIS IS THE SORT OF THING THAT COULD CAUSE A PERSON TO GET A DEMON!
SCHULZ

HELLO?
HELLO, LUCILLE? THIS IS PEPPERMINT PATTY...SAY, I'M CALLING ABOUT A PECULIAR LETTER I GOT FROM YOUR BROTHER...IT HAS TO DO WITH A "GREAT PUMPKIN"
10-15
© 1966 Peanuts Worldwide LLC, Dist. by Universal Uclick
I SEE...WELL, LINUS IS GOING BY RIGHT NOW...DO YOU WANT TO TALK TO HIM?
www.snoopy.com
HERE HE IS!
STOMP
SCHULZ

HELLO?
HELLO, LUCILLE? YOUR KID BROTHER JUST LEFT HERE A FEW MINUTES AGO...MAYBE YOU CAN WATCH FOR HIM SO HE DOESN'T GET LOST... YEAH...HE AND THAT FUNNY LOOKING KID WITH THE BIG NOSE
10-24
© 1966 Peanuts Worldwide LLC, Dist. by Universal Uclick
YEAH, HE TOLD ME THAT WHOLE RIDICULOUS AND IMPOSSIBLE STORY ABOUT THE "GREAT PUMPKIN"... THAT'S THE WILDEST STORY I'VE EVER HEARD...
www.snoopy.com
BUT I BELIEVE IT!!
SCHULZ

?
HI, ROY! WELCOME TO THE PUMPKIN PATCH!
WHERE DID YOU GET ALL THE PUMPKINS?
I BOUGHT 'EM AT A FRUIT STAND!
© 1966 Peanuts Worldwide LLC, Dist. by Universal Uclick
BUT THAT'S HYPOCRISY! LINUS ONCE TOLD ME THAT THE "GREAT PUMPKIN" HATES HYPOCRISY...THIS IS WORSE THAN HYPOCRISY....
10-25
www.snoopy.com
THIS IS **COMMERCIAL**!
SCHULZ

SO I TOLD THEM ABOUT THE "GREAT PUMPKIN" AND THEY ALL LAUGHED!
AM I THE FIRST PERSON EVER TO SACRIFICE POLITICAL OFFICE BECAUSE OF BELIEF? OF COURSE, NOT! I SIMPLY SPOKE WHAT I FELT WAS THE TRUTH...
10-25
© 1964 Peanuts Worldwide LLC, Dist. by Universal Uclick
I'VE NEVER PRETENDED TO UNDERSTAND POLITICS, BUT I DO KNOW ONE THING...
www.snoopy.com
IF YOU'RE GOING TO HOPE TO GET ELECTED, DON'T MENTION THE "GREAT PUMPKIN"!
SCHULZ

DEAR GREAT PUMPKIN, SOMETHING HAS OCCURRED TO ME.
10-26
© 1965 Peanuts Worldwide LLC, Dist. by Universal Uc
YOU MUST GET DISCOURAGED BECAUSE MORE PEOPLE BELIEVE IN SANTA CLAUS THAN IN YOU.
www.snoopy.com
WELL, LET'S FACE IT... SANTA CLAUS HAS HAD MORE PUBLICITY.
BUT BEING NUMBER TWO, PERHAPS YOU TRY HARDER.
SCHULZ

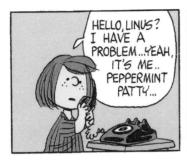

HELLO, LINUS? I HAVE A PROBLEM...YEAH, IT'S ME.. PEPPERMINT PATTY...
NOW, YOU TOLD ME THAT THE "GREAT PUMPKIN" WOULD APPEAR IF I HAD A VERY SINCERE PUMPKIN PATCH...NOW, YOU ALSO KNOW THAT I DIDN'T HAVE A PUMPKIN PATCH..
10-26
© 1966 Peanuts Worldwide LLC. Dist. by Universal Uclick
WELL, I WENT OUT AND BOUGHT TEN PUMPKINS, AND TRIED TO FAKE, IF YOU'LL PARDON THE EXPRESSION, A PUMPKIN PATCH...NOW, YOU TELL ME, AND TELL ME STRAIGHT...AM I A **HYPOCRITE** ?!!
www.snoopy.com
WHAT DO I TELL HER?
DON'T ASK ME.. YOU'RE THE THEOLOGIAN!
SCHULZ

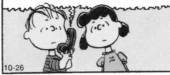

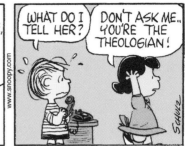

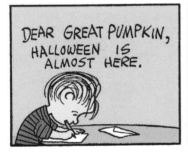

DEAR GREAT PUMPKIN, HALLOWEEN IS ALMOST HERE.
I'VE TOLD EVERYONE ABOUT YOUR COMING.
© 1964 Peanuts Worldwide LLC. Dist. by Universal Uclick
FORGIVE ME IF I SOUND BLUNT, BUT.......
www.snoopy.com
IF YOU DON'T SHOW UP THIS YEAR, **YOU'VE HAD IT!!**
SCHULZ
10-26

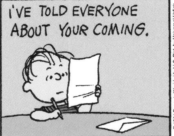

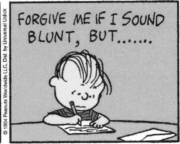

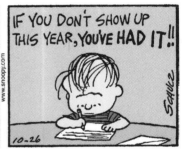

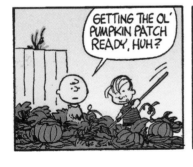

GETTING THE OL' PUMPKIN PATCH READY, HUH?
YES, SIR, BOY! EACH YEAR THE "GREAT PUMPKIN" RISES OUT OF THE PUMPKIN PATCH WHICH HE REGARDS AS THE MOST SINCERE
10-28
© 1964 Peanuts Worldwide LLC. Dist. by Universal Uclick
DO YOU THINK THIS PUMPKIN PATCH LOOKS SINCERE?
OH, YES, IT LOOKS VERY SINCERE
www.snoopy.com
WELL, IT DIDN'T LOOK **INSINCERE**!
SCHULZ

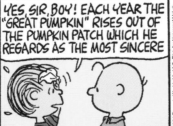

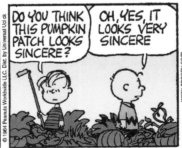

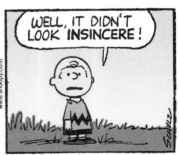

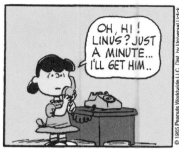

OH, HI! LINUS? JUST A MINUTE... I'LL GET HIM..
IT'S FOR YOU...IT'S CHARLIE BROWN..
I'M NOT SPEAKING TO HIM..HE INSULTED MY BELIEF!
I'M NOT SPEAKING TO ANYONE WHO DOESN'T BELIEVE IN THE "GREAT PUMPKIN"!
GOOD LUCK WITH THE WORLD!
© 1965 Peanuts Worldwide LLC. Dist. by Universal Uclick
www.snoopy.com
10-29
SCHULZ

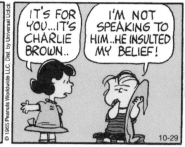

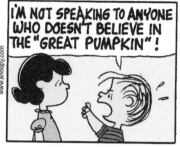

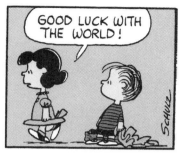

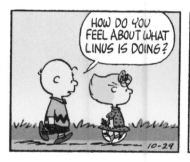

HOW DO YOU FEEL ABOUT WHAT LINUS IS DOING?
DOESN'T IT BOTHER YOU TO KNOW THAT ONE OF YOUR FRIENDS IS GOING TO SPEND HALLOWEEN NIGHT SITTING IN A PUMPKIN PATCH WAITING FOR THE "GREAT PUMPKIN"?
IT DOESN'T BOTHER ME BECAUSE IT DOESN'T AFFECT ME...
HORRORS! WHAT DO YOU WANT ME TO DO, GET **INVOLVED**?!
10-29
© 1964 Peanuts Worldwide LLC. Dist. by Universal Uclick
www.snoopy.com
SCHULZ

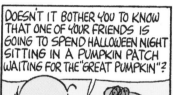

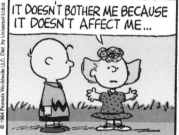

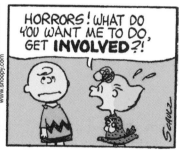

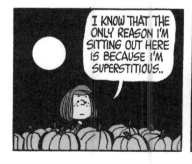

I KNOW THAT THE ONLY REASON I'M SITTING OUT HERE IS BECAUSE I'M SUPERSTITIOUS..
WHY ELSE WOULD I SIT IN A PUMPKIN PATCH ALL NIGHT WAITING FOR THE "GREAT PUMPKIN"?
OF COURSE, I'M THE TRUSTING TYPE, TOO... I'M TRUSTING AND FAITHFUL AND SUPERSTITIOUS...
LET'S FACE IT... I'M ALSO A LITTLE BIT STUPID!
10-31
© 1966 Peanuts Worldwide LLC. Dist. by Universal Uclick
www.snoopy.com
SCHULZ

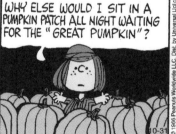

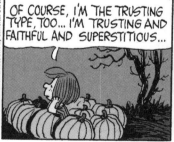

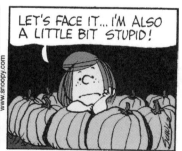

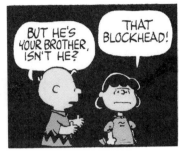

BUT HE'S YOUR BROTHER, ISN'T HE?
THAT BLOCKHEAD!
HE'S SITTING OUT THERE IN THAT PUMPKIN PATCH RIGHT NOW!
THAT BLOCKHEAD!
10-31
© 1964 Peanuts Worldwide LLC, Dist. by Universal Uclick
HE'LL END UP SITTING THERE ALL NIGHT WAITING FOR THE "GREAT PUMPKIN"! AREN'T YOU CONCERNED?
THAT BLOCKHEAD!
www.snoopy.com
HE'S GOING TO SIT THERE ALL NIGHT, AND NOBODY CARES...
THAT BLOCKHEAD!
SCHULZ

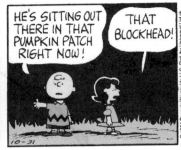

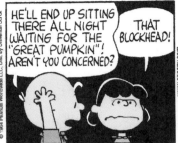

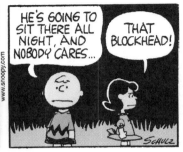

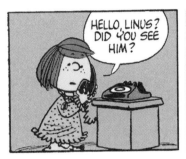

HELLO, LINUS? DID YOU SEE HIM?
DID YOU SEE THE "GREAT PUMPKIN"? I SAT IN THAT PUMPKIN PATCH UNTIL AFTER MIDNIGHT, BUT HE NEVER CAME
11-1
© 1966 Peanuts Worldwide LLC, Dist. by Universal Uclick
I'M PRETTY TIRED... HOW ABOUT YOU?
www.snoopy.com
MMM?
SCHULZ

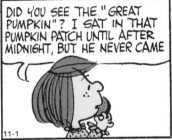

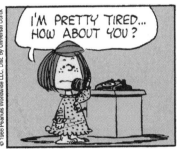

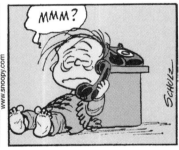

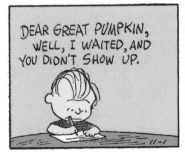

DEAR GREAT PUMPKIN, WELL, I WAITED, AND YOU DIDN'T SHOW UP.
11-1
IT'S A GOOD THING I'M YOUNG AND CAN STAND ALL THESE DISAPPOINTMENTS BECAUSE, FRANKLY, I'VE HAD IT!
© 1964 Peanuts Worldwide LLC, Dist. by Universal Uclick
THE ONES I FEEL SORRY FOR ARE THE OLDER PEOPLE WHO WAITED ALL NIGHT IN THEIR PUMPKIN PATCHES FOR YOU TO COME.
www.snoopy.com
IF I SOUND BITTER, IT'S BECAUSE I AM.
SINCERELY, LINUS VAN PELT
P.S. SEE YOU NEXT YEAR.
SCHULZ

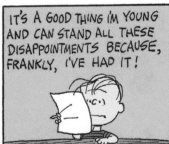

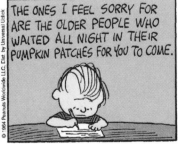

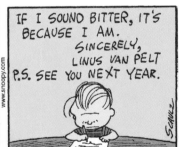

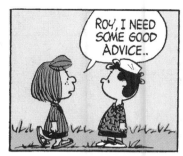

ROY, I NEED SOME GOOD ADVICE..
WHAT DO YOU DO WHEN SOMETHING YOU'VE COUNTED ON DOESN'T HAPPEN?
11-2
© 1966 Peanuts Worldwide LLC. Dist. by Universal Uclick
THIS THING I REALLY BELIEVED WAS GOING TO HAPPEN, DIDN'T HAPPEN...WHAT DO I DO?
www.snoopy.com
WELL, YOU COULD ADMIT YOU WERE WRONG...
BESIDES THAT, I MEAN
SCHULZ

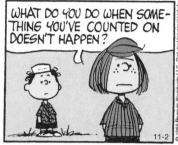

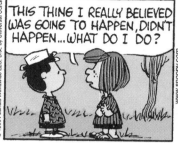

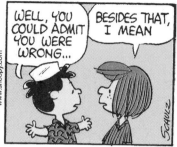

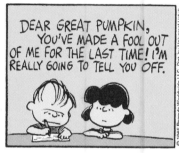

DEAR GREAT PUMPKIN, YOU'VE MADE A FOOL OUT OF ME FOR THE LAST TIME! I'M REALLY GOING TO TELL YOU OFF.
© 1965 Peanuts Worldwide LLC. Dist. by Universal Uclick
DON'T BURN ALL OF YOUR BRIDGES BEHIND YOU...
www.snoopy.com
SIGH!
11-3
SCHULZ

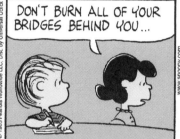

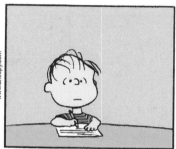

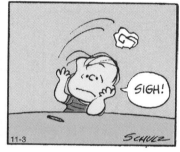

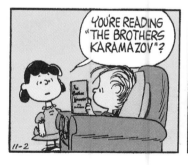

YOU'RE READING "THE BROTHERS KARAMAZOV"?
11-2
UH HUH... I FIND IT QUITE FASCINATING
© 1964 Peanuts Worldwide LLC. Dist. by Universal Uclick
DON'T ALL THOSE RUSSIAN NAMES BOTHER YOU?
www.snoopy.com
NO, WHEN I COME TO ONE I CAN'T PRONOUNCE, I JUST **BLEEP** RIGHT OVER IT!
SCHULZ

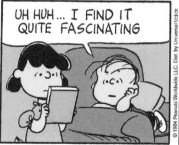

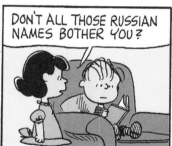

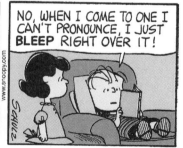

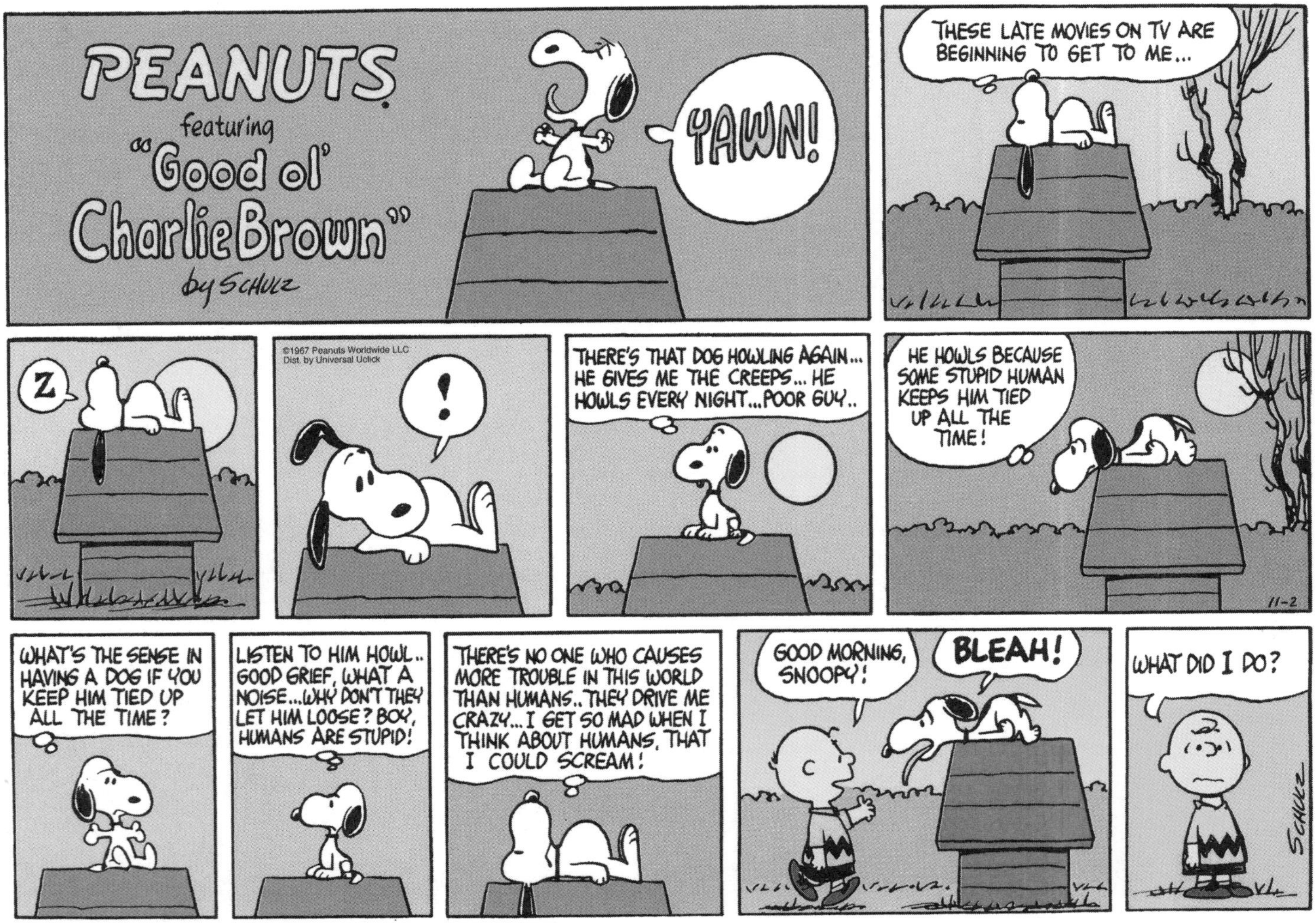
PEANUTS
featuring
"Good ol' Charlie Brown"
by SCHULZ
YAWN!
THESE LATE MOVIES ON TV ARE BEGINNING TO GET TO ME...
Z
©1967 Peanuts Worldwide LLC
Dist. by Universal Uclick
!
THERE'S THAT DOG HOWLING AGAIN... HE GIVES ME THE CREEPS... HE HOWLS EVERY NIGHT...POOR GUY..
HE HOWLS BECAUSE SOME STUPID HUMAN KEEPS HIM TIED UP ALL THE TIME!
11-2
WHAT'S THE SENSE IN HAVING A DOG IF YOU KEEP HIM TIED UP ALL THE TIME?
LISTEN TO HIM HOWL.. GOOD GRIEF, WHAT A NOISE...WHY DON'T THEY LET HIM LOOSE? BOY, HUMANS ARE STUPID!
THERE'S NO ONE WHO CAUSES MORE TROUBLE IN THIS WORLD THAN HUMANS..THEY DRIVE ME CRAZY...I GET SO MAD WHEN I THINK ABOUT HUMANS, THAT I COULD SCREAM!
GOOD MORNING, SNOOPY!
BLEAH!
WHAT DID I DO?
SCHULZ

ASK LUCY WHO TOOK THE LAST PIECE OF CAKE
© 1965 Peanuts Worldwide LLC, Dist. by Universal Uclick
TELL HIM WHAT HE DOESN'T KNOW WON'T HURT HIM...
www.snoopy.com
10-19
WHAT YOU DO NOT KNOW WILL NOT DO YOU ANY PHYSICAL DAMAGE!
SCHULZ

AN ENVELOPE FOR ME...
U.S. MAIL
© 1965 Peanuts Worldwide LLC, Dist. by Universal Uclick
WELL! THIS IS A NICE ONE...
10-20
www.snoopy.com
A BLANKET? HOW COME YOU'RE GETTING A BLANKET IN THE MAIL?
I JOINED THE "SECURITY-BLANKET-OF-THE-MONTH CLUB"
SCHULZ

YOU AND THAT STUPID BLANKET!
IF I WERE YOUR MOTHER, I'D SNATCH IT AWAY FROM YOU, AND THROW IT IN THE TRASH BURNER!
11-7
www.snoopy.com
© 1964 Peanuts Worldwide LLC, Dist. by Universal Uclick
"THE TACTICS OF EXTREMISM"
SCHULZ

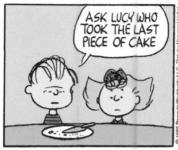

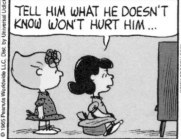

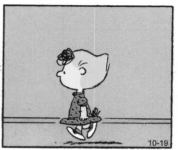

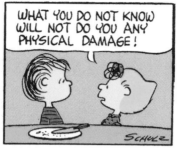

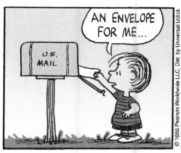

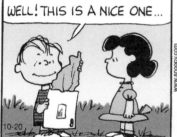

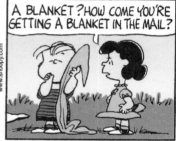

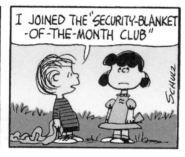

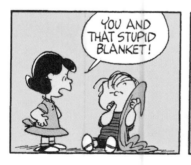

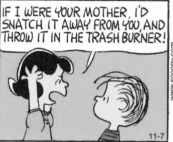

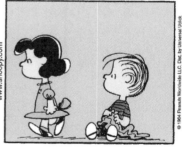

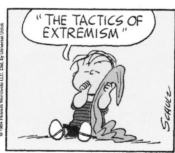

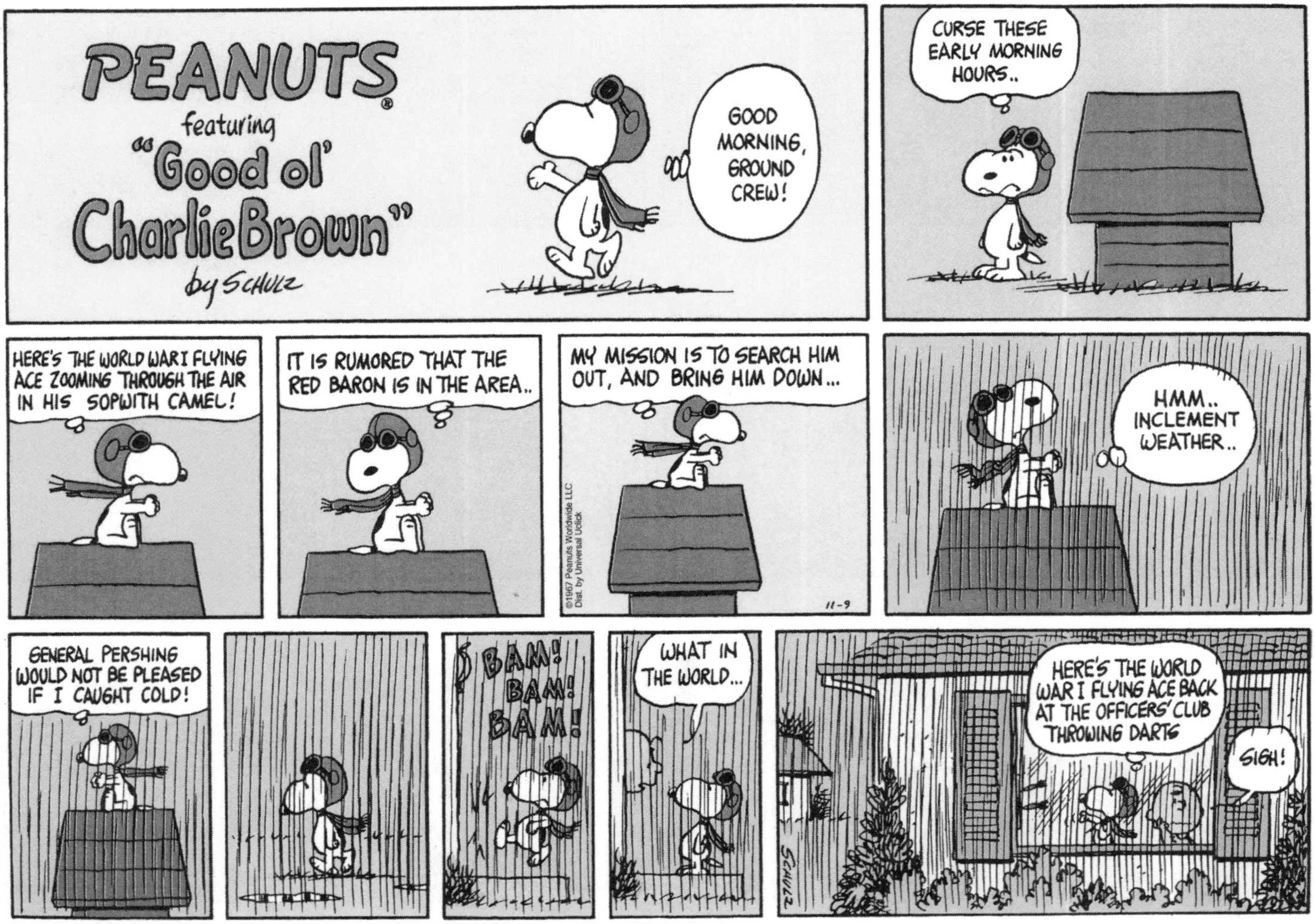
PEANUTS
featuring
"Good ol' Charlie Brown"
by SCHULZ
GOOD MORNING, GROUND CREW!
CURSE THESE EARLY MORNING HOURS..
HERE'S THE WORLD WAR I FLYING ACE ZOOMING THROUGH THE AIR IN HIS SOPWITH CAMEL!
IT IS RUMORED THAT THE RED BARON IS IN THE AREA..
MY MISSION IS TO SEARCH HIM OUT, AND BRING HIM DOWN...
©1967 Peanuts Worldwide LLC
Dist. by Universal Uclick
11-9
HMM.. INCLEMENT WEATHER..
GENERAL PERSHING WOULD NOT BE PLEASED IF I CAUGHT COLD!
BAM! BAM! BAM!
WHAT IN THE WORLD...
SCHULZ
HERE'S THE WORLD WAR I FLYING ACE BACK AT THE OFFICERS' CLUB THROWING DARTS
SIGH!

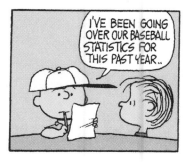

I'VE BEEN GOING OVER OUR BASEBALL STATISTICS FOR THIS PAST YEAR..
WHEN I THINK OF ALL THOSE GAMES WE LOST, I GET SICK..
11-3
© 1967 Peanuts Worldwide LLC, Dist. by Universal Uclick
WINNING ISN'T EVERYTHING, CHARLIE BROWN...
www.snoopy.com
THAT'S TRUE, BUT LOSING ISN'T **ANYTHING**!
SCHULZ

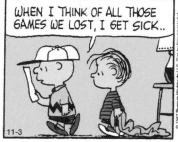

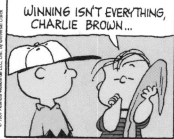

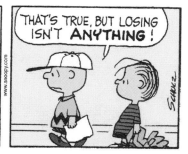

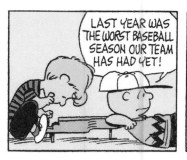

LAST YEAR WAS THE WORST BASEBALL SEASON OUR TEAM HAS HAD YET!
I'M REALLY WORRIED ABOUT OUR TEAM, SCHROEDER... I THINK WE'RE GETTING WORSE..
© 1967 Peanuts Worldwide LLC, Dist. by Universal Uclick
BEETHOVEN HAD HIS PROBLEMS, TOO!
11/4
www.snoopy.com
THAT'S WHAT I LIKE, A NICE RELEVANT STATEMENT..
SCHULZ

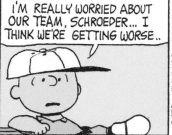

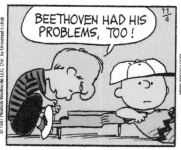

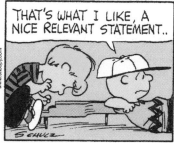

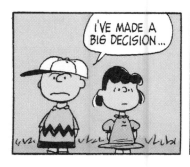

I'VE MADE A BIG DECISION...
THIS IS THE TIME OF YEAR WHEN ALL THE BIG BASEBALL TRADES ARE MADE...I'M GOING TO TRY TO IMPROVE OUR TEAM WITH A FEW SHREWD TRADES
© 1967 Peanuts Worldwide LLC, Dist. by Universal Uclick
THAT'S A GREAT IDEA, CHARLIE BROWN...
11-5
www.snoopy.com
WHY DON'T YOU TRADE YOURSELF?
SCHULZ

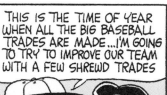

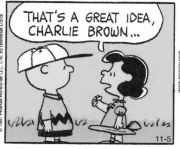

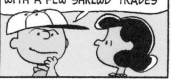

HELLO, PEPPERMINT PATTY? I WAS WONDERING IF YOU'D BE INTERESTED IN TRADING A FEW BASEBALL PLAYERS..
WELL, I DON'T KNOW, CHUCK...THE ONLY GOOD PLAYER YOU HAVE IS THAT LITTLE KID WITH THE BIG NOSE
YOU MEAN, SNOOPY? OH, NO, I COULD NEVER TRADE HIM... I WAS THINKING MORE OF LUCY...
HELLO? HELLO?
© 1967 Peanuts Worldwide LLC, Dst. by Universal Uclick
www.snoopy.com
11-6
SCHULZ

HOW ARE YOUR BASEBALL TRADES COMING, CHARLIE BROWN?
TERRIBLE..PEPPERMINT PATTY SAID THE ONLY PLAYER SHE'D BE INTERESTED IN WOULD BE SNOOPY...
I TOLD HER, "NO"... BUT MAYBE I WAS WRONG...
YOU MEAN YOU'D TRADE YOUR OWN DOG JUST TO WIN A FEW BALL GAMES?!
"WIN"...HAVE YOU EVER NOTICED WHAT A BEAUTIFUL WORD THAT IS? "WIN!" WHAT A WONDERFUL SOUND! "WIN!" "WIN!" "WIN!"
© 1967 Peanuts Worldwide LLC, Dst. by Universal Uclick
www.snoopy.com
11-7
SCHULZ

HELLO, PEPPERMINT PATTY? I'VE DECIDED TO TAKE YOU UP ON YOUR OFFER..
THAT'S GREAT, CHUCK...I'LL GIVE YOU FIVE PLAYERS FOR SNOOPY... I GUARANTEE IT'LL IMPROVE YOUR TEAM..WHY DON'T I BRING A CONTRACT OVER ON MONDAY, AND WE'LL SETTLE THE WHOLE DEAL, OKAY?
UH... YEAH... OKAY... OKAY...FINE..FINE.....
GOODBY...
WHAT HAVE I DONE? I'VE TRADED AWAY MY OWN DOG! I'VE BECOME A REAL MANAGER!!
11-8
© 1967 Peanuts Worldwide LLC, Dst. by Universal Uclick
www.snoopy.com
SCHULZ

OKAY, CHUCK..HERE'S THE CONTRACT... I'M TRADING YOU FIVE PLAYERS FOR SNOOPY...
I'M KIND OF NERVOUS... I'VE NEVER TAKEN PART IN ANY BIG BASEBALL TRADES BEFORE...MAYBE I SHOULD THINK ABOUT THIS A LITTLE WHILE, AND..
© 1967 Peanuts Worldwide LLC. Dist. by Universal Uclick
DON'T BE RIDICULOUS...YOU WANT TO BUILD A BETTER TEAM, DON'T YOU? COME ON, SIGN RIGHT HERE..
11-10
TRY NOT TO LET YOUR HAND SHAKE SO MUCH, CHUCK, YOU'RE SPILLING INK ALL OVER THE CONTRACT
www.snoopy.com
SCHULZ

SNOOPY, THIS IS A HARD THING FOR ME TO SAY..
I'VE TRADED YOU TO PEPPERMINT PATTY FOR FIVE NEW PLAYERS...ALL I ASK IS A LITTLE UNDERSTANDING AND SOME SIGN FROM YOU THAT YOU DON'T HATE ME...
11-11
© 1967 Peanuts Worldwide LLC. Dist. by Universal Uclick
BLEAH!!
THAT WASN'T IT!
www.snoopy.com
SCHULZ

YOU WHAT?!!
I TRADED SNOOPY TO PEPPERMINT PATTY FOR FIVE GOOD PLAYERS... HE'S THE ONLY PLAYER SHE'D TRADE FOR... I HAD TO DO IT...
© 1967 Peanuts Worldwide LLC. Dist. by Universal Uclick
BUT HE'S YOUR OWN DOG! DOES WINNING A BALL GAME MEAN THAT MUCH TO YOU?
11-12
I DON'T KNOW...I'VE NEVER WON A BALL GAME...
www.snoopy.com
SCHULZ

YOU TRADED YOUR OWN DOG!
I'M SO DISAPPOINTED IN YOU, CHARLIE BROWN, THAT I DON'T EVEN WANT TO TALK TO YOU!
11-13
© 1967 Peanuts Worldwide LLC, Dist. by Universal Uclick
SIGH
www.snoopy.com
AND STOP BREATHING ON MY BLANKET!
SCHULZ

HI, PAL..WELCOME TO MY TEAM...LET ME FILL YOU IN ON A FEW THINGS...
11-14
I'M A GREAT BELIEVER IN WINTER CONDITIONING! EVERY DAY BETWEEN NOW AND NEXT SPRING, IT'S GOING TO BE RUN, RUN, RUN, RUN...
© 1967 Peanuts Worldwide LLC, Dist. by Universal Uclick
SO LET'S GET GOING!
www.snoopy.com
I DON'T KNOW...HE MAY BE A GOOD PLAYER, AND I'M GLAD I HAVE HIM ON MY TEAM, BUT I STILL SAY HE'S THE FUNNIEST LOOKING KID I'VE EVER SEEN!
SCHULZ

I WAS WRONG.. I CAN SEE IT NOW...
I SIMPLY LOST ALL SENSE OF PROPORTION...THE THOUGHT OF POSSIBLY WINNING A FEW BALL GAMES BLINDED ME TO THE DUTY I HAVE TO LOVE AND PROTECT MY DOG
11-15
© 1967 Peanuts Worldwide LLC, Dist. by Universal Uclick
LOOK, SNOOPY, I'M TEARING UP THE CONTRACT...I'M GOING TO TELL PEPPERMINT PATTY THE DEAL IS OFF!
www.snoopy.com
WHAT DID YOU SAY?
OH, GOOD GRIEF!!
SCHULZ

!
WHAT'S THIS? YOU'VE TORN UP OUR CONTRACT, CHUCK..
YOU MUST HAVE GOT MY MESSAGE
MESSAGE?
© 1967 Peanuts Worldwide LLC. Dist. by Universal Uclick
11-17
THOSE FIVE PLAYERS I WAS SUPPOSED TO TRADE TO YOU SAID THEY'D GIVE UP BASEBALL BEFORE THEY'D PLAY ON YOUR TEAM!
www.snoopy.com
SORRY, CHUCK..THE DEAL'S OFF... I HOPE YOUR FEELINGS AREN'T HURT..
I'M CRUSHED!
SCHULZ

?
LOOK WHAT I FOUND..HERE'S A BRAND NEW SHIRT THAT YOU'VE NEVER WORN...
www.snoopy.com
YOU GOT THIS FOR YOUR BIRTHDAY OVER A YEAR AGO...WHY HAVEN'T YOU WORN IT?
11-15
© 1964 Peanuts Worldwide LLC. Dist. by Universal Uclick
IT WAS TOO MUCH TROUBLE TAKING ALL THE PINS OUT!
SCHULZ

11-17
© 1965 Peanuts Worldwide LLC, Dist. by Universal Uclick
www.snoopy.com
"HEEL"!
SIGH
SCHULZ

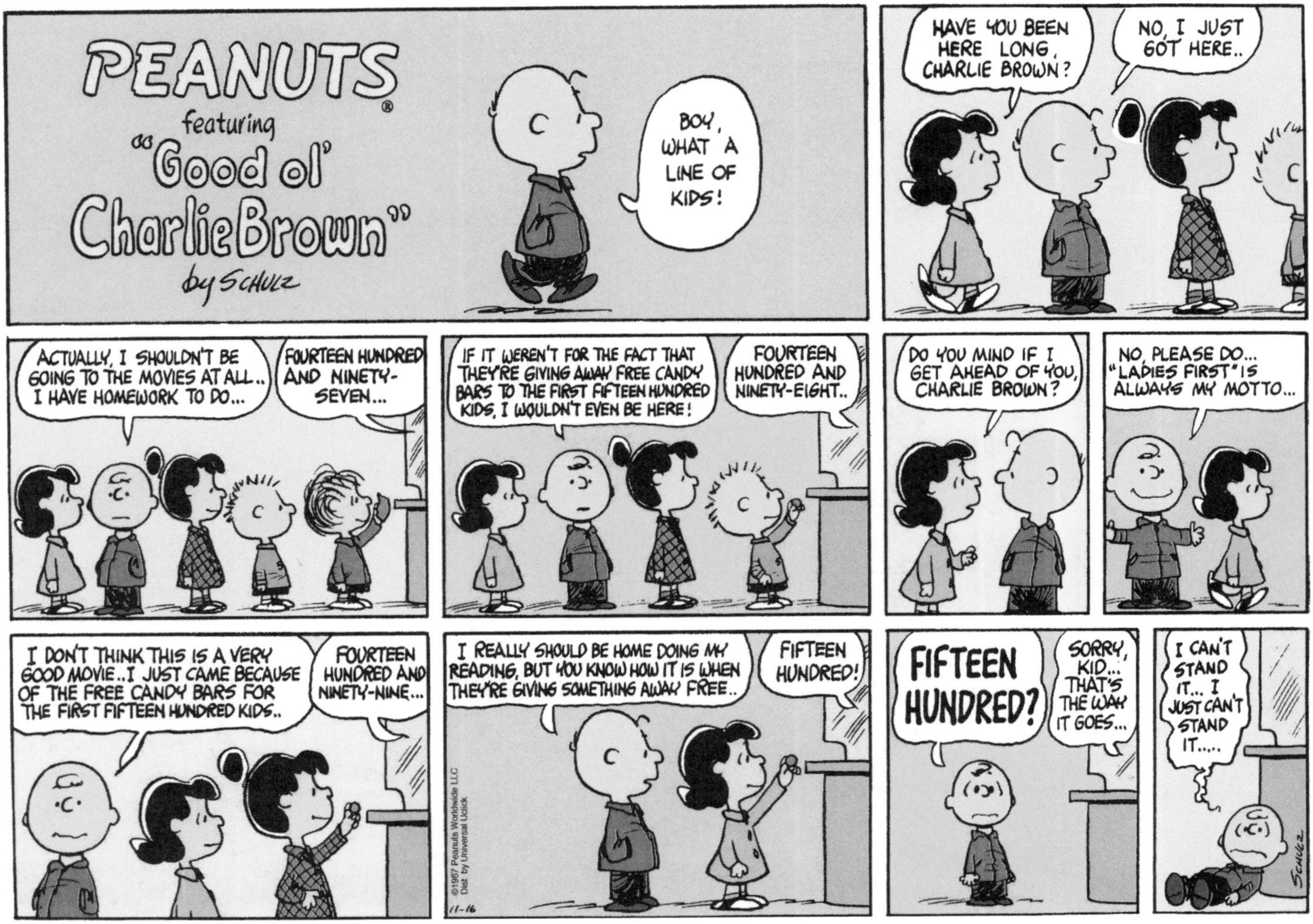
PEANUTS
featuring "Good ol' Charlie Brown"
by SCHULZ
BOY, WHAT A LINE OF KIDS!
HAVE YOU BEEN HERE LONG, CHARLIE BROWN?
NO, I JUST GOT HERE..
ACTUALLY, I SHOULDN'T BE GOING TO THE MOVIES AT ALL.. I HAVE HOMEWORK TO DO...
FOURTEEN HUNDRED AND NINETY-SEVEN...
IF IT WEREN'T FOR THE FACT THAT THEY'RE GIVING AWAY FREE CANDY BARS TO THE FIRST FIFTEEN HUNDRED KIDS, I WOULDN'T EVEN BE HERE!
FOURTEEN HUNDRED AND NINETY-EIGHT..
DO YOU MIND IF I GET AHEAD OF YOU, CHARLIE BROWN?
NO, PLEASE DO... "LADIES FIRST" IS ALWAYS MY MOTTO...
I DON'T THINK THIS IS A VERY GOOD MOVIE..I JUST CAME BECAUSE OF THE FREE CANDY BARS FOR THE FIRST FIFTEEN HUNDRED KIDS..
FOURTEEN HUNDRED AND NINETY-NINE...
I REALLY SHOULD BE HOME DOING MY READING, BUT YOU KNOW HOW IT IS WHEN THEY'RE GIVING SOMETHING AWAY FREE..
FIFTEEN HUNDRED!
©1967 Peanuts Worldwide LLC Dist. by Universal Uclick
11-16
FIFTEEN HUNDRED?
SORRY, KID... THAT'S THE WAY IT GOES...
I CAN'T STAND IT... I JUST CAN'T STAND IT.....
SCHULZ

LINUS! MOM SAYS TO COME IN, AND GET WASHED UP FOR SUPPER!
www.snoopy.com
11-17
GOOD GRIEF! WHAT HAVE YOU GUYS BEEN PLAYING?
© 1964 Peanuts Worldwide LLC. Dist. by Universal Uclick
TOUCH FOOTBALL!
SCHULZ

SPRING RAINS ARE INSPIRING
SUMMER RAINS ARE INVIGORATING...
© 1967 Peanuts Worldwide LLC. Dist. by Universal Uclick
FALL RAINS ARE QUIET AND RESTFUL...
11-18
www.snoopy.com
NOVEMBER RAINS ARE NOTHING!
SCHULZ

YOU KNOW WHAT ANNOYS ME ABOUT YOU?
THE WAY YOU LIVE WITHOUT RESPONSIBILITY
© 1967 Peanuts Worldwide LLC. Dist. by Universal Uclick
THAT REALLY ANNOYS ME!
11-19
www.snoopy.com
WE ALL HAVE OUR HANG-UPS!
SCHULZ

I WONDER IF I WOULDN'T BE MORE POPULAR IF I HAD A NEW NAME...
11-20
THE WRONG NAME CAN BE A REAL HINDRANCE TO A PERSON'S FUNCTIONING IN SOCIETY..I THINK A NAME WHICH IS CONSISTENT WITH A PERSON'S PERSONALITY IS IMPORTANT
© 1967 Peanuts Worldwide LLC, Dist. by Universal Uclick
I WONDER WHAT WOULD BE A GOOD NAME FOR ME...
HOW ABOUT "SUPERMOUTH"?
www.snoopy.com
I'VE GOT TO STOP THIS BUSINESS OF TALKING WITHOUT THINKING...
SCHULZ

ALL RIGHT, NOW LET'S SEE YOU WRITE THE NUMBER SENTENCE FOR, "ONE IS LESS THAN FIVE"
11-20
© 1965 Peanuts Worldwide LLC, Dist. by Universal Uclick
1 < 5
www.snoopy.com
THAT'S RIGHT!
IT IS?!
I'VE SOLVED THE NEW MATH!!
SCHULZ

DEAR PENCIL PAL, I AM DISTURBED.
11-21
ACCORDING TO WHAT I READ, YOUR COUNTRY HATES MY COUNTRY AND MY COUNTRY HATES YOUR COUNTRY.
© 1967 Peanuts Worldwide LLC, Dist. by Universal Uclick
I DON'T HATE YOU, AND I DON'T THINK YOU HATE ME. I THINK ABOUT THIS A LOT.
www.snoopy.com
IT MAKES SLEEPING AT NIGHT VERY DIFFICULT.
SCHULZ

LITTLE BROTHERS SHOULD STAND WHEN BIG SISTERS ENTER THE ROOM...
YOU'RE RIGHT...I BEG YOUR PARDON...
© 1967 Peanuts Worldwide LLC. Dist. by Universal Uclick
11-22
LITTLE BROTHERS ARE THE NEW YORK METS OF LIFE!
www.snoopy.com
SCHULZ

THAT'S NOT ART!
11-24
THAT'S A TERRIBLE DRAWING! YOU HAVE ABSOLUTELY NO TALENT!
© 1967 Peanuts Worldwide LLC. Dist. by Universal Uclick
NO ONE EVER LISTENS TO US CRITICS...
www.snoopy.com
SCHULZ

YOU DON'T LIKE ME, DO YOU?
NO, I NEVER HAVE LIKED YOU, AND I DOUBT VERY MUCH IF I EVER WILL LIKE YOU!
© 1967 Peanuts Worldwide LLC. Dist. by Universal Uclick
11-26
www.snoopy.com
I CAN TELL YOU DON'T LIKE ME...
SCHULZ

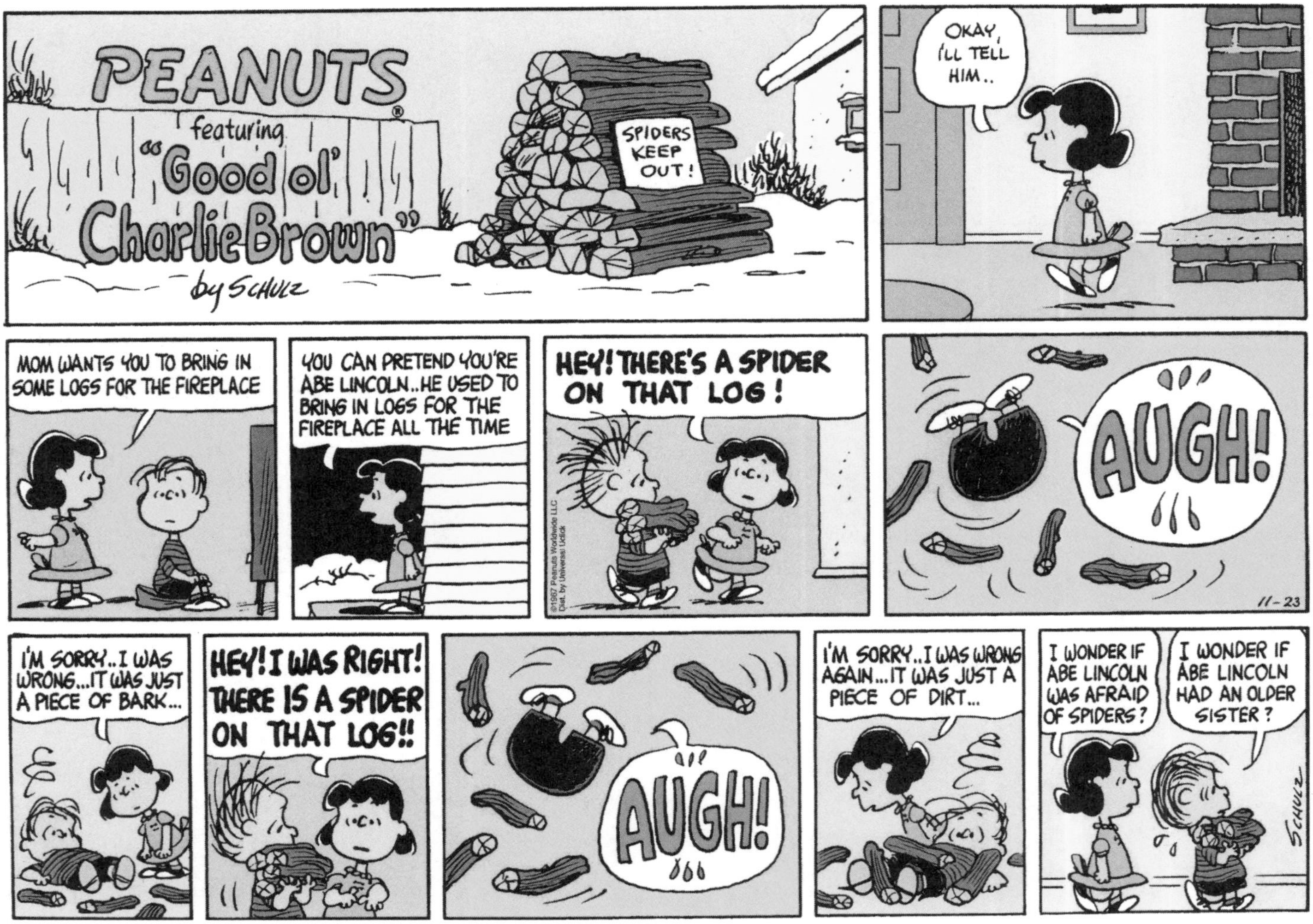
PEANUTS
featuring
"Good ol' Charlie Brown"
by SCHULZ
SPIDERS KEEP OUT!
OKAY, I'LL TELL HIM..
MOM WANTS YOU TO BRING IN SOME LOGS FOR THE FIREPLACE
YOU CAN PRETEND YOU'RE ABE LINCOLN..HE USED TO BRING IN LOGS FOR THE FIREPLACE ALL THE TIME
HEY! THERE'S A SPIDER ON THAT LOG!
©1967 Peanuts Worldwide LLC
Dist. by Universal Uclick
AUGH!
11-23
I'M SORRY..I WAS WRONG...IT WAS JUST A PIECE OF BARK...
HEY! I WAS RIGHT! THERE IS A SPIDER ON THAT LOG!!
AUGH!
I'M SORRY..I WAS WRONG AGAIN...IT WAS JUST A PIECE OF DIRT...
I WONDER IF ABE LINCOLN WAS AFRAID OF SPIDERS?
I WONDER IF ABE LINCOLN HAD AN OLDER SISTER?
SCHULZ

HERE'S THE WORLD WAR I FLYING ACE ZOOMING THROUGH THE AIR IN HIS SOPWITH CAMEL
11-25
I FEEL SORRY FOR THOSE POOR BLIGHTERS IN THE TRENCHES DOWN BELOW...
© 1967 Peanuts Worldwide LLC. Dist. by Universal Uclick
I THINK I'LL WAVE TO THEM...
www.snoopy.com
BLIGHTERS ALWAYS FEEL BETTER WHEN YOU WAVE TO THEM!
SCHULZ

HURRY UP... WE'LL BE LATE FOR SCHOOL!
DID YOU BRUSH YOUR TEETH?
I'M GOING TO
© 1966 Peanuts Worldwide LLC. Dist. by Universal Uclick
AND COMB YOUR HAIR... IT LOOKS LIKE A RAT'S NEST!
11-25
www.snoopy.com
RATS HAVE TO HAVE A PLACE TO LIVE, TOO, YOU KNOW!
SCHULZ

AN EYE PATCH? WHY IN THE WORLD SHOULD I PUT ON AN EYE PATCH?
© 1965 Peanuts Worldwide LLC. Dist. by Universal Uclick
BECAUSE I'M GOING TO TEST YOU FOR "LAZY EYE"... THIS IS ONLY A HOME TEST, BUT IT'S VERY IMPORTANT..
11-26
www.snoopy.com
HERE, PUT ON THE EYE PATCH..
YO HO HO AND A BOTTLE OF RUM!
SCHULZ

11-26
IT WON'T GO...IT JUST LIES THERE!
SCHULZ

11-29
I'M TOO FEMININE FOR THIS GAME!
SCHULZ

11-30
HOW COME YOU DON'T GO WHERE I POINT YOU?
SCHULZ

DON'T LOOK AT ME LIKE THAT, OR I'LL LET ALL YOUR AIR OUT!

I SUPPOSE YOU'RE WONDERING WHY I'M WEARING THIS EYE PATCH, EH LINUS?

YOU PROBABLY HAVE AMBLYOPIA EX ANOPSIA..THE VISION IN YOUR RIGHT EYE IS DIM SO THE DOCTOR HAS PATCHED THE LEFT ONE, THUS FORCING THE RIGHT EYE TO WORK...

ACTUALLY, TREATMENT OF AMBLYOPIA IS ONE OF THE MOST REWARDING IN MEDICINE...WITHOUT MEDICATION OR SURGERY OR HOSPITALIZATION A CHILD CAN BE GIVEN EYESIGHT IN AN EYE WHICH OTHERWISE MIGHT HAVE NO SIGHT...

YOU DRIVE ME CRAZY!!

YOU SHOULD HAVE HEARD ME TODAY AT "SHOW AND TELL" TIME

I TOLD THE WHOLE CLASS ALL ABOUT "AMBLYOPIA" AND WHY I WEAR THIS EYE PATCH..I EXPLAINED HOW MY "LAZY EYE" IS BEING STRENGTHENED BY BEING FORCED TO WORK WHILE MY OTHER EYE IS COVERED...

THEN I URGED THEM ALL TO GO SEE THEIR OPHTHALMOLOGISTS FOR EYE TESTS IMMEDIATELY!

DID YOU GET A GOOD GRADE?

I GOT A "B" FROM MY TEACHER AND AN "A" FROM MY OPHTHALMOLOGIST!

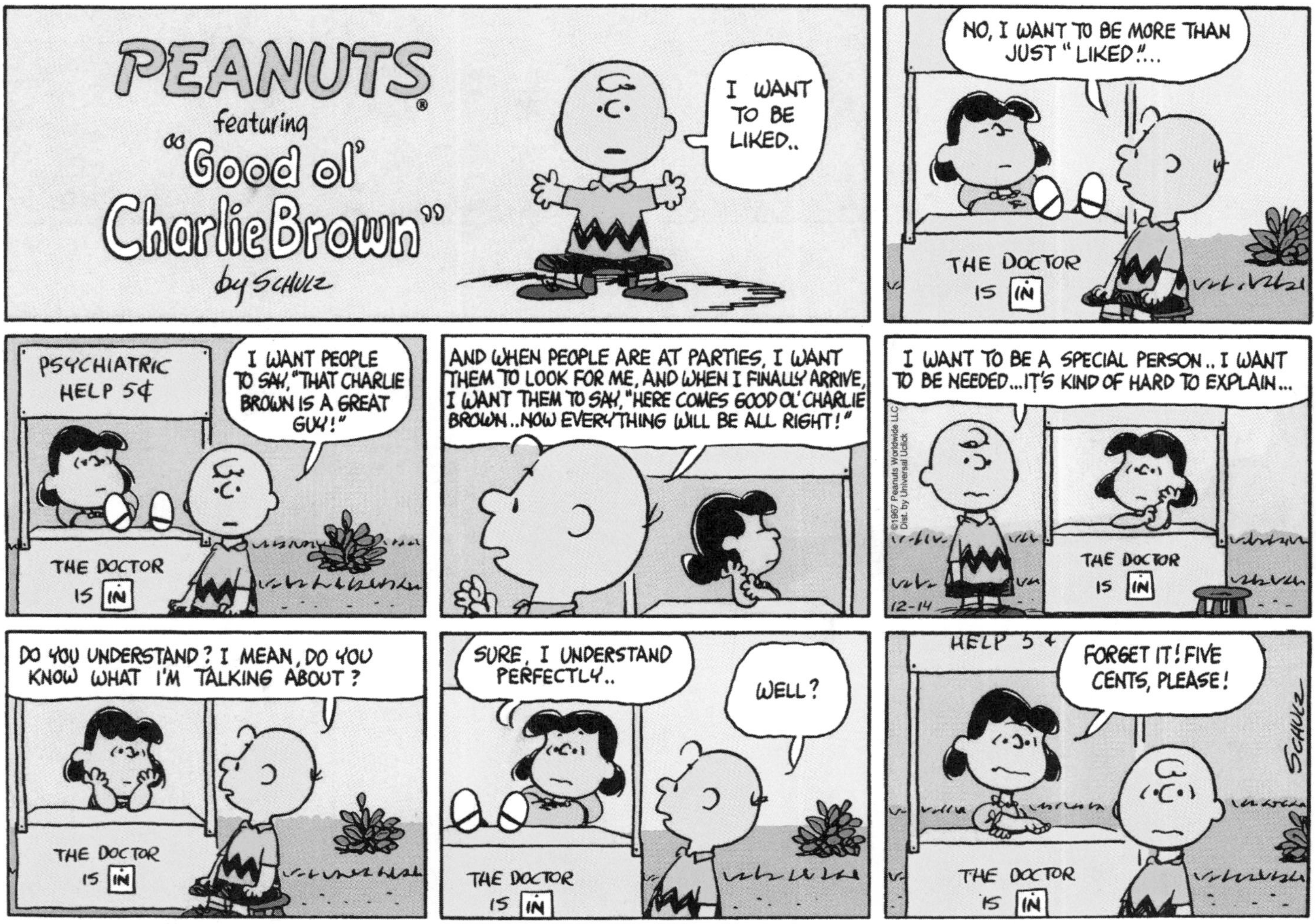
PEANUTS®
featuring
"Good ol' Charlie Brown"
by SCHULZ
I WANT TO BE LIKED..
NO, I WANT TO BE MORE THAN JUST "LIKED"!...
THE DOCTOR IS IN
PSYCHIATRIC HELP 5¢
I WANT PEOPLE TO SAY, "THAT CHARLIE BROWN IS A GREAT GUY!"
THE DOCTOR IS IN
AND WHEN PEOPLE ARE AT PARTIES, I WANT THEM TO LOOK FOR ME, AND WHEN I FINALLY ARRIVE, I WANT THEM TO SAY, "HERE COMES GOOD OL' CHARLIE BROWN..NOW EVERYTHING WILL BE ALL RIGHT!"
I WANT TO BE A SPECIAL PERSON..I WANT TO BE NEEDED...IT'S KIND OF HARD TO EXPLAIN...
©1967 Peanuts Worldwide LLC Dist. by Universal Uclick
12-14
THE DOCTOR IS IN
DO YOU UNDERSTAND? I MEAN, DO YOU KNOW WHAT I'M TALKING ABOUT?
THE DOCTOR IS IN
SURE, I UNDERSTAND PERFECTLY..
WELL?
THE DOCTOR IS IN
HELP 5¢
FORGET IT! FIVE CENTS, PLEASE!
SCHULZ
THE DOCTOR IS IN

HEY! GET UP! AREN'T YOU GOING TO SCHOOL?
I DON'T THINK SO...
I'VE GOT A PAIN..
TELL MOM I THINK MY STOMACH IS BROKEN!
www.snoopy.com
12-6
© 1964 Peanuts Worldwide LLC, Dist. by Universal Uclick
SCHULZ

WHAT'S THIS BOARD FOR?
THAT'S NOT A BOARD..THAT'S A TRAP DOOR
IF YOU LIFT THAT TRAP DOOR, YOU'LL FIND A LONG STAIRWAY GOING DOWN FOURTEEN FLIGHTS AND LEADING TO HUGE STOREROOMS FILLED WITH TOYS AND ALL SORTS OF CANDY...
© 1966 Peanuts Worldwide LLC, Dist. by Universal Uclick
12-7
YOU'RE PUTTING ME ON!
www.snoopy.com
SCHULZ

MOM SAYS TO GET STARTED ON YOUR HOMEWORK
© 1965 Peanuts Worldwide LLC, Dist. by Universal Uclick
TELL HER I'M CONDUCTING AN EXPERIMENT TO SEE WHAT WOULD HAPPEN TO SOMEONE WHO NEVER DID HIS HOMEWORK, BUT JUST SAT AND WATCHED TV EVERY EVENING...
www.snoopy.com
MOM SAYS TO GET STARTED ON THAT HOMEWORK RIGHT NOW!
I SHOULD THINK THE RESULTS OF SUCH AN EXPERIMENT COULD PROVE TO BE QUITE VALUABLE...
SCHULZ
12-7

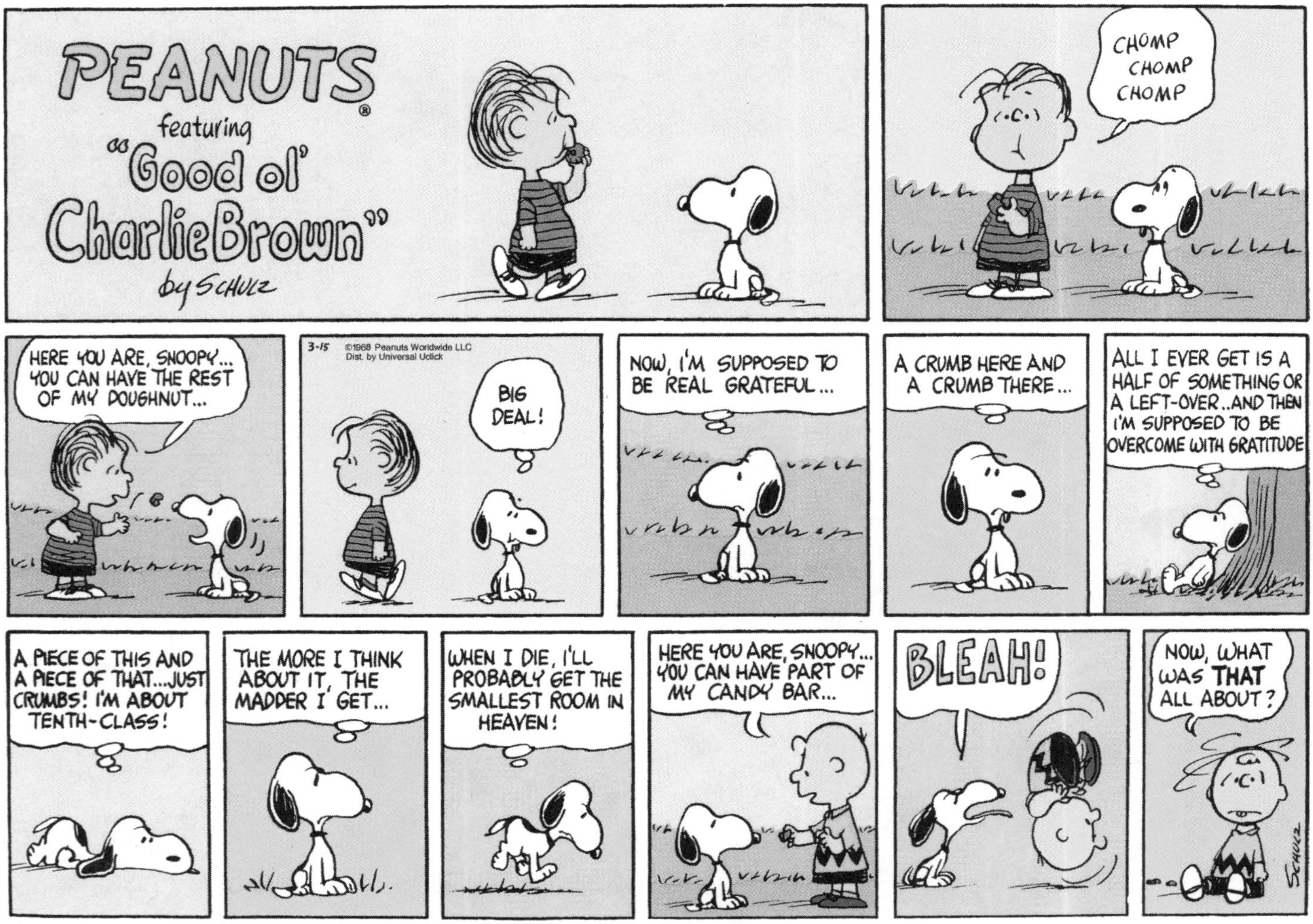
PEANUTS®
featuring
"Good ol' CharlieBrown"
by SCHULZ
CHOMP CHOMP CHOMP
HERE YOU ARE, SNOOPY... YOU CAN HAVE THE REST OF MY DOUGHNUT...
3-15 ©1968 Peanuts Worldwide LLC Dist. by Universal Uclick
BIG DEAL!
NOW, I'M SUPPOSED TO BE REAL GRATEFUL...
A CRUMB HERE AND A CRUMB THERE...
ALL I EVER GET IS A HALF OF SOMETHING OR A LEFT-OVER..AND THEN I'M SUPPOSED TO BE OVERCOME WITH GRATITUDE
A PIECE OF THIS AND A PIECE OF THAT...JUST CRUMBS! I'M ABOUT TENTH-CLASS!
THE MORE I THINK ABOUT IT, THE MADDER I GET...
WHEN I DIE, I'LL PROBABLY GET THE SMALLEST ROOM IN HEAVEN!
HERE YOU ARE, SNOOPY... YOU CAN HAVE PART OF MY CANDY BAR...
BLEAH!
NOW, WHAT WAS THAT ALL ABOUT?
SCHULZ

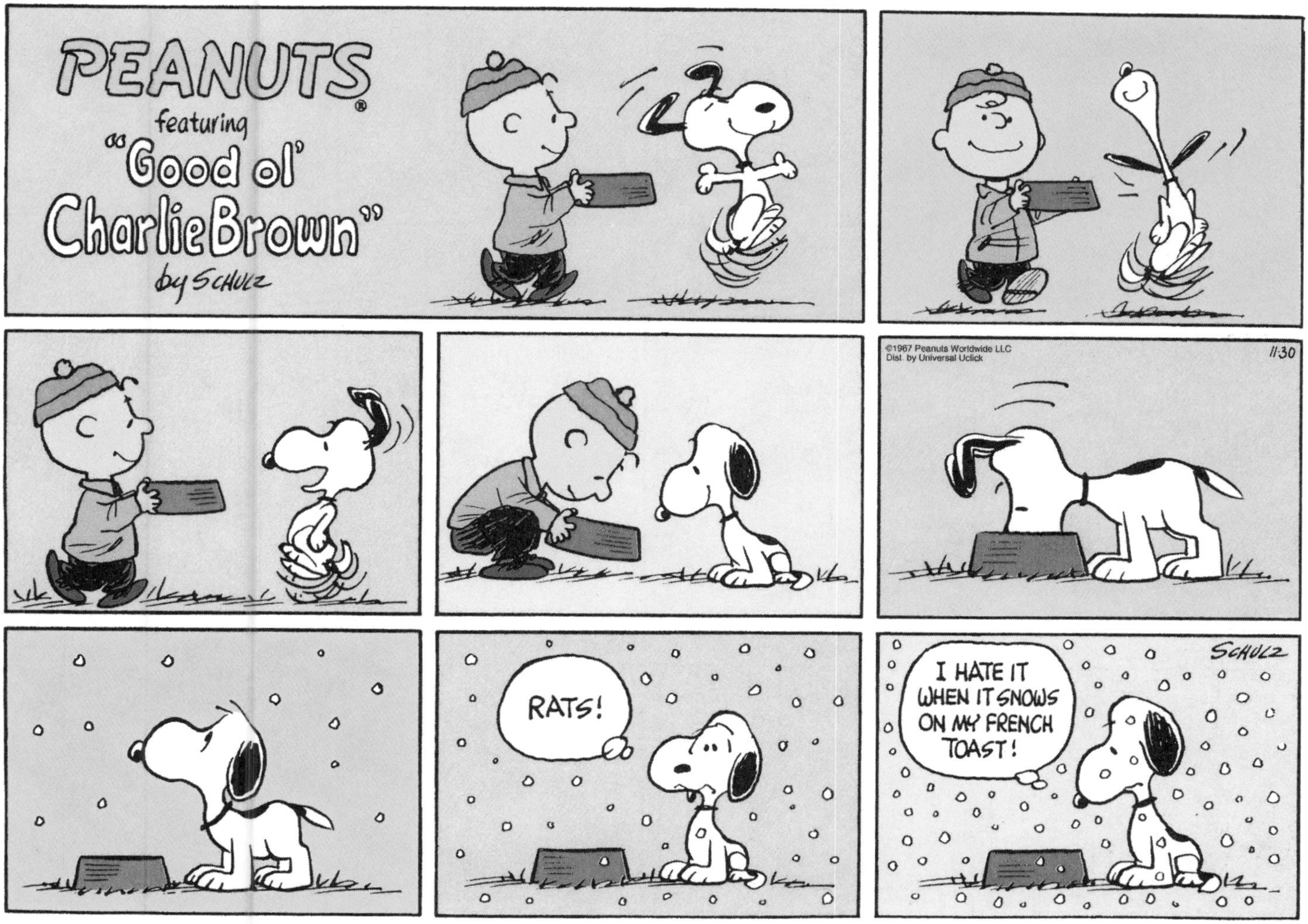
PEANUTS
featuring
"Good ol' CharlieBrown"
by SCHULZ
©1967 Peanuts Worldwide LLC
Dist. by Universal Uclick
11-30
RATS!
SCHULZ
I HATE IT WHEN IT SNOWS ON MY FRENCH TOAST!

SNOW?!
BUT I'M NOT READY FOR WINTER!
MY BLOOD'S TOO THIN! I STILL HAVE MY SUMMER FUR!
© 1967 Peanuts Worldwide LLC. Dist. by Universal Uclick
STOP SNOWING! STOP IT, I SAY! STOP THIS STUPID SNOWING!
11-28
www.snoopy.com
RATS!
SCHULZ

11-29
© 1967 Peanuts Worldwide LLC. Dist. by Universal Uclick
www.snoopy.com
HOW IN THE WORLD DO YOU FIND A SNOW-COVERED SUPPER DISH?!
SCHULZ

DEAR SANTA CLAUS, HOW ARE ALL YOUR REINDEER? ARE THEY WELL FED?
12-14
© 1965 Peanuts Worldwide LLC. Dist. by Universal Uclick
IS YOUR SLEIGH IN GOOD SHAPE? ARE THE RUNNERS OILED?
www.snoopy.com
THEN GO, MAN... GO!!!
I DON'T THINK I'D BETTER SEND THAT...
SCHULZ

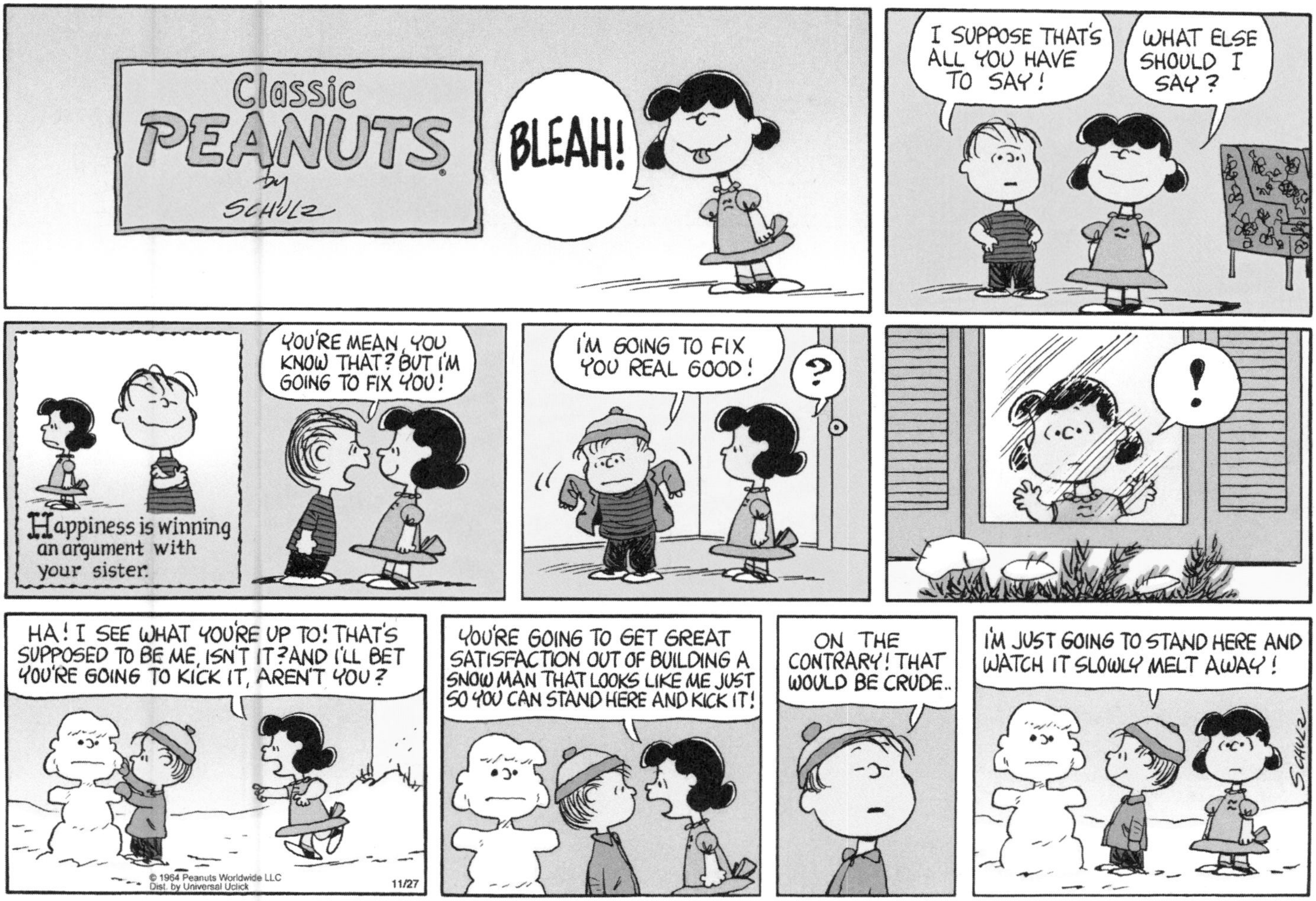
Classic PEANUTS by SCHULZ
BLEAH!
I SUPPOSE THAT'S ALL YOU HAVE TO SAY!
WHAT ELSE SHOULD I SAY?
Happiness is winning an argument with your sister.
YOU'RE MEAN, YOU KNOW THAT? BUT I'M GOING TO FIX YOU!
I'M GOING TO FIX YOU REAL GOOD!
?
!
HA! I SEE WHAT YOU'RE UP TO! THAT'S SUPPOSED TO BE ME, ISN'T IT? AND I'LL BET YOU'RE GOING TO KICK IT, AREN'T YOU?
© 1964 Peanuts Worldwide LLC Dist. by Universal Uclick
11/27
YOU'RE GOING TO GET GREAT SATISFACTION OUT OF BUILDING A SNOW MAN THAT LOOKS LIKE ME JUST SO YOU CAN STAND HERE AND KICK IT!
ON THE CONTRARY! THAT WOULD BE CRUDE..
I'M JUST GOING TO STAND HERE AND WATCH IT SLOWLY MELT AWAY!
SCHULZ

I MISS SKATING WITH SONJA HENIE...
12-1
© 1967 Peanuts Worldwide LLC. Dist. by Universal Uclick
www.snoopy.com
SCHULZ

HERE'S THE WORLD FAMOUS FIGURE SKATER PRACTICING HIS "OUTSIDE EIGHTS"
HE REALIZES THAT HE MUST PRACTICE DILIGENTLY IF HE IS TO WIN A GOLD MEDAL AT THE OLYMPICS...
ACTUALLY, VERY FEW BEAGLES ARE EVER INVITED TO THE OLYMPICS!
12-2
© 1967 Peanuts Worldwide LLC. Dist. by Universal Uclick
www.snoopy.com
SCHULZ

REAL FIGURE SKATERS SMILE A LOT...
MAYBE JUST A PLEASANT GRIN WOULD BE BETTER..
12-3
© 1967 Peanuts Worldwide LLC. Dist. by Universal Uclick
www.snoopy.com
SCHULZ

I HEAR YOU'RE PRACTICING FOR THE OLYMPICS...
DID YOU KNOW THEY'RE BEING HELD IN GRENOBLE, FRANCE?
12-4
© 1967 Peanuts Worldwide LLC. Dist. by Universal Uclick
DO YOU KNOW WHERE GRENOBLE IS?
I DON'T EVEN KNOW WHERE FRANCE IS!
www.snoopy.com
SCHULZ

BEING A GOOD FIGURE SKATER IS HARD WORK
12-5
RIGHT NOW I'M PRACTICING MY "OUTSIDE FORWARD ROLL"
© 1967 Peanuts Worldwide LLC. Dist. by Universal Uclick
LATELY I'VE HAD TO DO MY PRACTICING AT NIGHT...
OTHERWISE I'M SURROUNDED BY FLOCKS OF ADMIRING GIRLS...
www.snoopy.com
SCHULZ

SNOOPY, I'VE DECIDED TO TAKE UP A COLLECTION TO SEND YOU TO THE OLYMPICS..
AND JUST TO SHOW YOU HOW SINCERE I AM, I'M GOING TO START BY PUTTING IN A NICKEL.. WHAT DO YOU THINK OF THAT?
12-6
© 1967 Peanuts Worldwide LLC. Dist. by Universal Uclick
WHAH!
WE FIGURE SKATERS ARE VERY EMOTIONAL!
www.snoopy.com
SCHULZ

HERE'S THE WORLD FAMOUS FIGURE SKATER PRACTICING FOR THE OLYMPICS IN GRENOBLE..

12-8

TODAY I'M WORKING ON MY "DOUBLE AXEL"

THEY'RE GOING TO LOVE ME IN GRENOBLE!

DID YOU KNOW THAT YOUR STUPID DOG THINKS HE'S GOING TO GRENOBLE TO SKATE IN THE OLYMPICS?

GRENOBLE IS IN FRANCE! HOW CAN HE GO TO GRENOBLE?

12-9

HOW CAN A STUPID BEAGLE EVER GO TO GRENOBLE?!

WE BEAGLES DO A LOT OF PECULIAR THINGS!

STUPID DOG!

GRENOBLE?

I'M TAKING UP A COLLECTION TO SEND SNOOPY TO THE OLYMPICS..

HOW MUCH DO YOU HAVE SO FAR?

EIGHTEEN CENTS

EIGHTEEN CENTS?! HOW IN THE WORLD IS HE GOING TO GET TO FRANCE ON EIGHTEEN CENTS?

12-10

DOES HE HAVE TO GO FIRST-CLASS?

134

I'M TAKING UP A COLLECTION TO SEND SNOOPY TO FRANCE TO SKATE IN THE OLYMPICS..
I DON'T SUPPOSE YOU'D CARE TO CONTRIBUTE?
© 1967 Peanuts Worldwide LLC. Dist. by Universal Uclick
SURE, I WOULD, BUT WHY STOP THERE? HERE'S A QUARTER... SEND HIM TO THE **MOON**!!
12-11
www.snoopy.com
SILLY GIRL...SHE SHOULD KNOW THEY DON'T HAVE FIGURE SKATING ON THE MOON
STUPID BEAGLE!!
SCHULZ

"GOODBY"?
YOU'RE NOT SERIOUS?!
YOU'RE REALLY GOING TO FRANCE FOR THE OLYMPICS? I DON'T BELIEVE IT! THIS IS RIDICULOUS!!
© 1967 Peanuts Worldwide LLC. Dist. by Universal Uclick
BESIDES, THE OLYMPICS DON'T BEGIN UNTIL FEBRUARY! YOU'RE GOING TO MISS CHRISTMAS AND EVERYTHING! WHY DO YOU HAVE TO LEAVE **NOW**?
12-12
www.snoopy.com
IT'S A LONG WALK!
SCHULZ

THIS IS ALL YOUR FAULT! YOU WERE THE ONE WHO TOOK UP THAT **COLLECTION**!
NOW MY DOG HAS LEFT!! HE'S OFF SOMEWHERE WANDERING ACROSS THE COUNTRY! I'LL NEVER SEE HIM AGAIN! HE'S GONE!
12-13
© 1967 Peanuts Worldwide LLC. Dist. by Universal Uclick
BUT HE **WANTED** TO GO, CHARLIE BROWN! HE WANTED TO!
THAT'S RIDICULOUS! HE DOESN'T HAVE ANY IDEA WHAT HE'S DOING!
www.snoopy.com
HERE'S THE WORLD-FAMOUS FIGURE SKATER ON HIS WAY TO FRANCE TO COMPETE IN THE OLYMPICS...
SCHULZ

HELLO? I'D LIKE TO RUN AN AD IN YOUR PAPER, PLEASE
MY DOG IS GONE...WELL, I DON'T KNOW IF HE'S LOST OR NOT, BUT HE'S SURE GONE.... UH HUH...
12-15
© 1967 Peanuts Worldwide LLC. Dist. by Universal Uclick
WELL, HE'S MOSTLY WHITE WITH LONG BLACK EARS, AND HE'S GOT HIS SUPPER DISH ON HIS HEAD, AND HE'S ON HIS WAY TO........
www.snoopy.com
... BRACE YOURSELF, PLEASE... I JUST **KNOW** YOU'RE NOT GOING TO BELIEVE THIS...
SCHULZ

HOW CAN I ADDRESS CHRISTMAS CARDS WHEN I'M DEPRESSED?
12-16
HOW CAN I ENJOY CHRISTMAS WHEN MY DOG IS OUT WANDERING ACROSS THE COUNTRY SOMEWHERE?
SNIF!
© 1967 Peanuts Worldwide LLC. Dist. by Universal Uclick
HE MAY EVEN BE INJURED OR LOST OR STARVING OR MAYBE HE'S LOCKED UP SOME PLACE! OH, MY POOR DOG! MY POOR POOR DOG!
www.snoopy.com
♫ IT'S A LONG WAY TO TIPPERARY... ♫
SCHULZ

HE'S GONE! I CAN'T BELIEVE IT! HE'S GONE!
MY DOG HAS GONE TO FRANCE TO SKATE IN THE OLYMPICS...HOW DOES HE THINK HE'S GOING TO GET TO FRANCE? IT'S RIDICULOUS!
© 1967 Peanuts Worldwide LLC. Dist. by Universal Uclick
INCIDENTALLY, DID YOU HAVE A GOOD TIME ON BEETHOVEN'S BIRTHDAY?
GOOD GRIEF...
12-17
www.snoopy.com
I FORGOT!
SCHULZ

HERE'S THE WORLD-FAMOUS FIGURE SKATER ON HIS WAY TO FRANCE TO SKATE IN THE OLYMPICS..
NO ONE TOLD ME ANYTHING ABOUT AN OCEAN...
© 1967 Peanuts Worldwide LLC, Dist. by Universal Uclick
12-18
www.snoopy.com
SCHULZ

MY DOG IS BACK!! HE'S BACK!
OH, IT'S GOING TO BE A MERRY CHRISTMAS AFTER ALL! MY DOG IS BACK!
WHEN DID HE COME BACK? WHAT HAPPENED?
I THOUGHT HE WAS ON HIS WAY TO GRENOBLE, FRANCE, TO SKATE IN THE OLYMPICS... WHAT MADE HIM DECIDE TO COME BACK?
WELL, THERE WAS THIS OCEAN, SEE....
© 1967 Peanuts Worldwide LLC, Dist. by Universal Uclick
12-19
www.snoopy.com
SCHULZ

12-8
I GOT A QUARTER FROM THE TOOTH-FAIRY LAST NIGHT..
WHAT DO YOU SUPPOSE SHE DOES WITH ALL THOSE TEETH?
I THINK SHE SELLS THEM TO SOME FIRM IN THE EAST THAT MANUFACTURES BILLIARD BALLS
IF THAT'S TRUE, WE HAVE A GOOD COURT CASE BECAUSE WE SHOULD BE GETTING ROYALTIES!
© 1965 Peanuts Worldwide LLC, Dist. by Universal Uclick
www.snoopy.com
SCHULZ

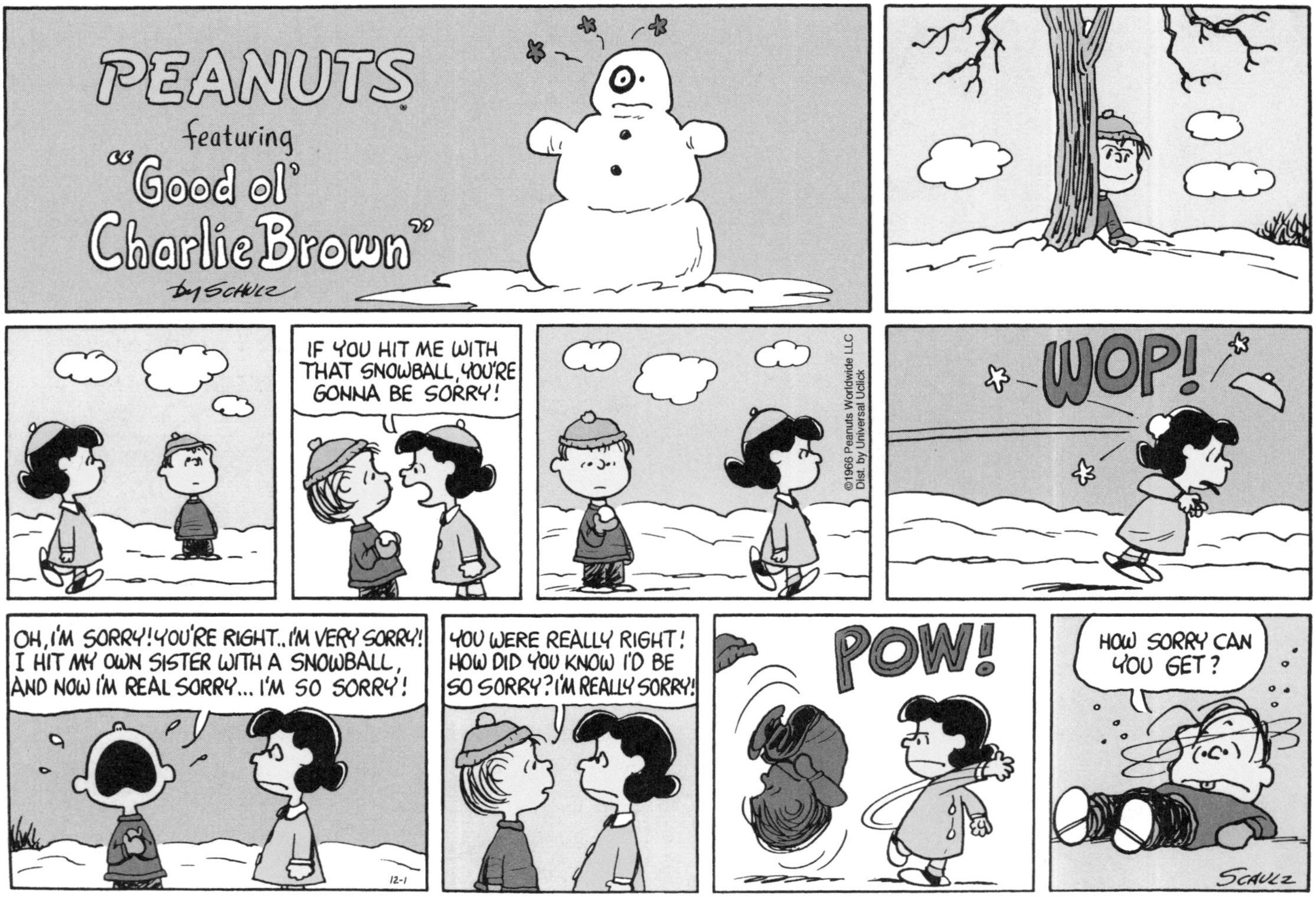
PEANUTS
featuring "Good ol' Charlie Brown"
by SCHULZ
IF YOU HIT ME WITH THAT SNOWBALL, YOU'RE GONNA BE SORRY!
©1966 Peanuts Worldwide LLC
Dist. by Universal Uclick
WOP!
OH, I'M SORRY! YOU'RE RIGHT.. I'M VERY SORRY! I HIT MY OWN SISTER WITH A SNOWBALL, AND NOW I'M REAL SORRY... I'M SO SORRY!
12-1
YOU WERE REALLY RIGHT! HOW DID YOU KNOW I'D BE SO SORRY? I'M REALLY SORRY!
POW!
HOW SORRY CAN YOU GET?
SCHULZ

12-9
© 1966 Peanuts Worldwide LLC, Dist. by Universal Uclick
www.snoopy.com
HI, SHORTY!
SCHULZ

12-10
© 1966 Peanuts Worldwide LLC, Dist. by Universal Uclick
www.snoopy.com
CHARGE!
SCHULZ

12-11
© 1966 Peanuts Worldwide LLC, Dist. by Universal Uclick
www.snoopy.com
SCHULZ
TODAY THE NEIGHBORHOOD, TOMORROW THE WORLD!

© 1966 Peanuts Worldwide LLC. Dist. by Universal Uclick
12-12
www.snoopy.com
SCHULZ

I AM YOUR LEADER!
12-13
IF YOU WILL FOLLOW ME, YOU WILL BE INVINCIBLE! THERE IS NOTHING THAT CAN STOP US!
© 1966 Peanuts Worldwide LLC. Dist. by Universal Uclick
NOTHING! NOTHING!
www.snoopy.com
SCHULZ

12-20
I'M WRITING A LAST-MINUTE LETTER TO SANTA CLAUS...
I SEE..
© 1967 Peanuts Worldwide LLC. Dist. by Universal Uclick
www.snoopy.com
MISTAKE!
SCHULZ

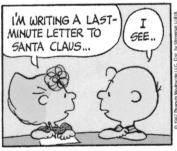

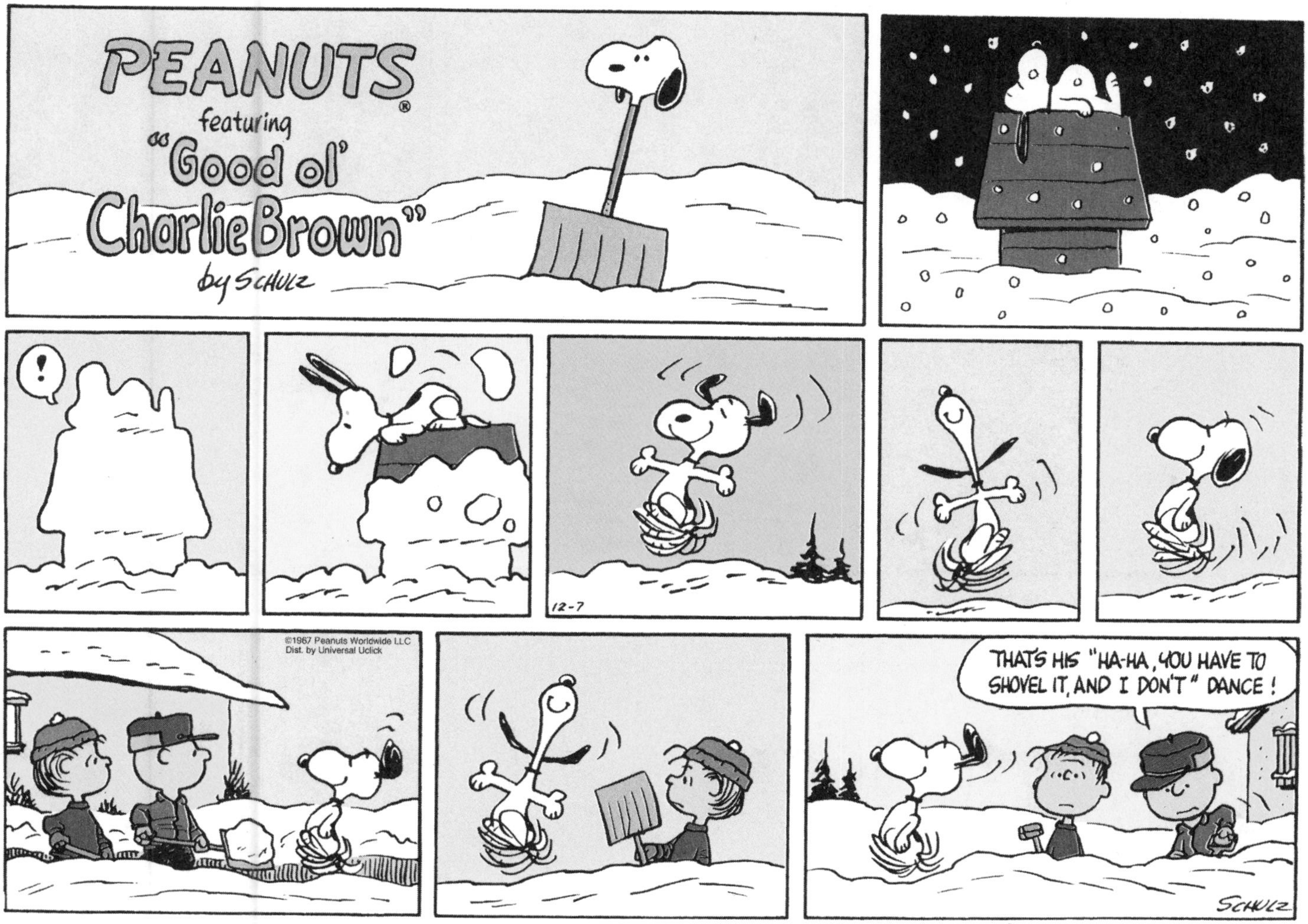
PEANUTS®
featuring
"Good ol' Charlie Brown"
by SCHULZ
!
12-7
©1967 Peanuts Worldwide LLC
Dist. by Universal Uclick
THAT'S HIS "HA-HA, YOU HAVE TO SHOVEL IT, AND I DON'T" DANCE!
SCHULZ

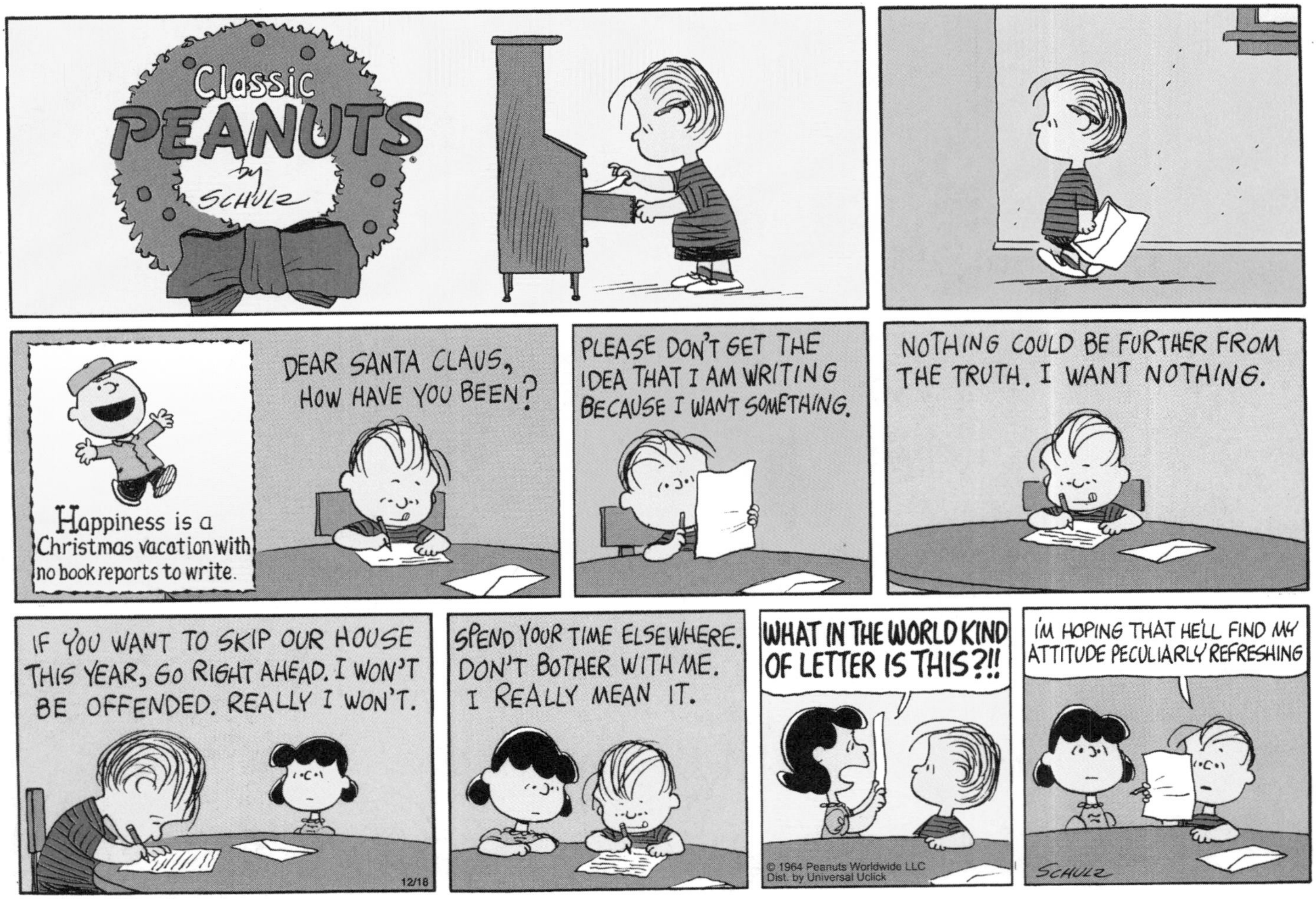
Classic
PEANUTS
by SCHULZ
Happiness is a Christmas vacation with no book reports to write.
DEAR SANTA CLAUS, HOW HAVE YOU BEEN?
PLEASE DON'T GET THE IDEA THAT I AM WRITING BECAUSE I WANT SOMETHING.
NOTHING COULD BE FURTHER FROM THE TRUTH. I WANT NOTHING.
IF YOU WANT TO SKIP OUR HOUSE THIS YEAR, GO RIGHT AHEAD. I WON'T BE OFFENDED. REALLY I WON'T.
12/18
SPEND YOUR TIME ELSEWHERE. DON'T BOTHER WITH ME. I REALLY MEAN IT.
WHAT IN THE WORLD KIND OF LETTER IS THIS?!!
© 1964 Peanuts Worldwide LLC
Dist. by Universal Uclick
I'M HOPING THAT HE'LL FIND MY ATTITUDE PECULIARLY REFRESHING
SCHULZ

DEAR SANTA CLAUS,
JUST A LITTLE NOTE BEFORE YOU TAKE OFF.
12-20
© 1965 Peanuts Worldwide LLC, Dist. by Universal Uclick
I ALWAYS WORRY ABOUT YOU. I HOPE YOU ARE IN GOOD HEALTH. PLEASE DRIVE CAREFULLY.
www.snoopy.com
HAVE A GOOD TRIP.
AFFECTIONATELY YOURS,
LUCY VAN PELT
(YOUR FRIEND)
P.S. MERRY CHRISTMAS
LUCY (YOUR VERY GOOD FRIEND)
XXXXXXXXX ← KISSES
BLEAH!
SCHULZ

Dear Santa Claus,
12-21
Just a last note before you take off.
© 1966 Peanuts Worldwide LLC, Dist. by Universal Uclick
I hope you have a nice trip.
www.snoopy.com
Don't forget to fasten your seat belt.
SCHULZ

12-21
© 1965 Peanuts Worldwide LLC, Dist. by Universal Uclick
www.snoopy.com
SCHULZ

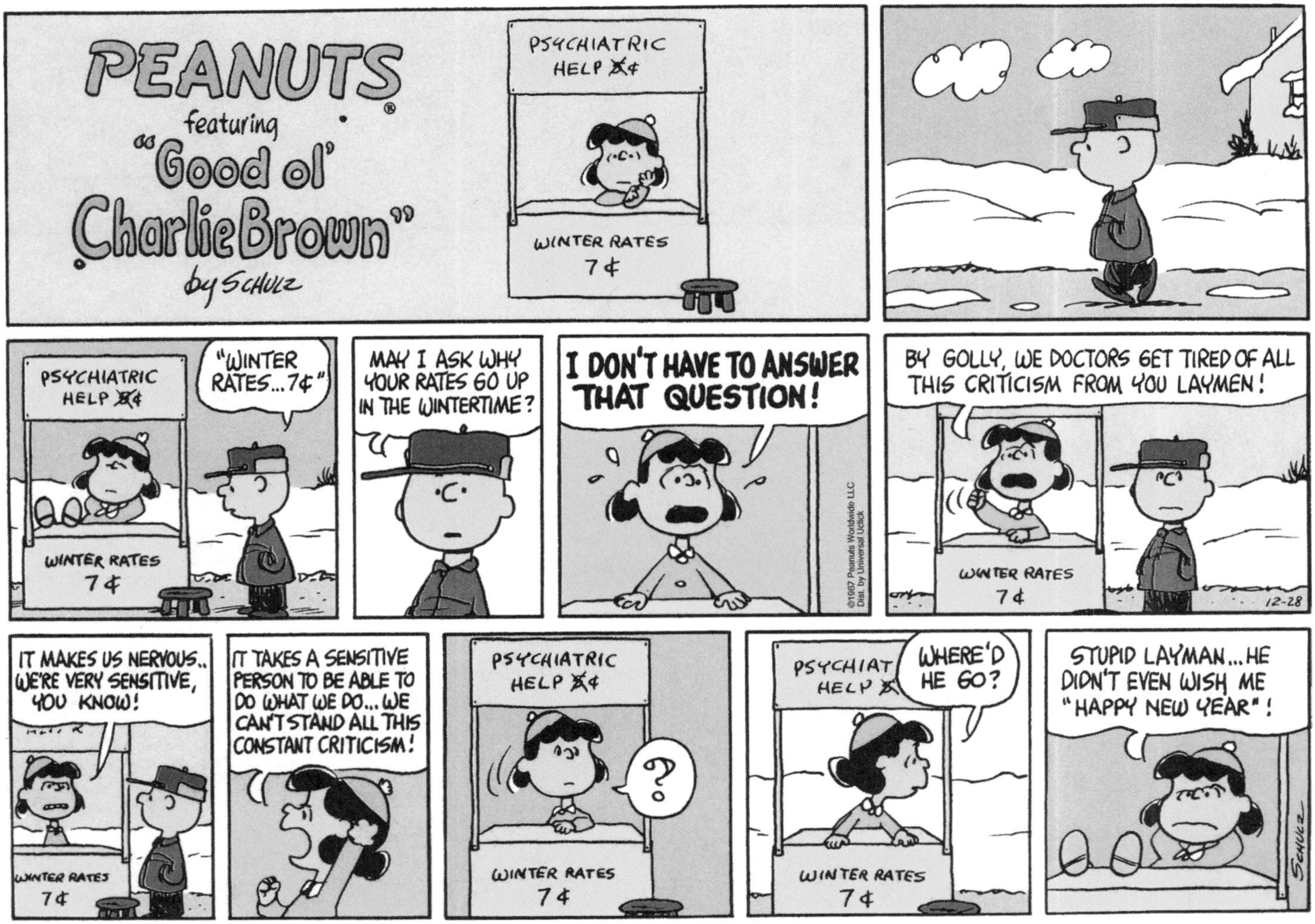
PEANUTS
featuring
"Good ol' Charlie Brown"
by SCHULZ
PSYCHIATRIC HELP 5¢
WINTER RATES 7¢
PSYCHIATRIC HELP 5¢
WINTER RATES 7¢
"WINTER RATES...7¢"
MAY I ASK WHY YOUR RATES GO UP IN THE WINTERTIME?
I DON'T HAVE TO ANSWER THAT QUESTION!
©1967 Peanuts Worldwide LLC
Dist. by Universal Uclick
BY GOLLY, WE DOCTORS GET TIRED OF ALL THIS CRITICISM FROM YOU LAYMEN!
WINTER RATES 7¢
12-28
IT MAKES US NERVOUS.. WE'RE VERY SENSITIVE, YOU KNOW!
WINTER RATES 7¢
IT TAKES A SENSITIVE PERSON TO BE ABLE TO DO WHAT WE DO... WE CAN'T STAND ALL THIS CONSTANT CRITICISM!
PSYCHIATRIC HELP 5¢
?
WINTER RATES 7¢
PSYCHIAT HELP
WHERE'D HE GO?
WINTER RATES 7¢
STUPID LAYMAN... HE DIDN'T EVEN WISH ME "HAPPY NEW YEAR"!
SCHULZ

12-20
WHEN JULIET ASKS, "O ROMEO, ROMEO, WHEREFORE ART THOU ROMEO?" SHE IS NOT WONDERING WHERE HE IS...
RATHER, SHE IS COMMENTING ON THE FACT OF HIS BEING NAMED ROMEO!
NOW THAT I KNOW THAT, WHAT DO I DO?
© 1966 Peanuts Worldwide LLC. Dist. by Universal Uclick
www.snoopy.com
SCHULZ

"THE ORIGIN OF THE BEAGLE IS NOT KNOWN"
"THE NAME, HOWEVER, IS TAKEN FROM THE FRENCH WORD 'BEGLE' "
IS THAT RIGHT?
12-27
OUI!
© 1967 Peanuts Worldwide LLC. Dist. by Universal Uclick
www.snoopy.com
SCHULZ

ACTUALLY, THEY ALL LOOK ALIKE TO ME!
12-22
© 1967 Peanuts Worldwide LLC. Dist. by Universal Uclick
www.snoopy.com
SCHULZ

BUT FIFTY IS MORE THAN TWENTY-FIVE!
YOU SIMPLY DON'T UNDERSTAND DIVISION..NO WONDER YOU'VE BEEN GETTING SUCH POOR GRADES...
12-23
© 1967 Peanuts Worldwide LLC, Dist. by Universal Uclick
YOU CAN'T MAKE FIFTY GO INTO TWENTY-FIVE!
www.snoopy.com
YOU CAN IF YOU PUSH IT!
SCHULZ

FIFTEEN SNOWBALLS?
12-25
YOU MUST BE KIDDING! THAT'S RIDICULOUS!
© 1967 Peanuts Worldwide LLC, Dist. by Universal Uclick
BEHIND A TREE, YOU SAY? OH, COME ON NOW!
www.snoopy.com
HOW COULD I POSSIBLY HIDE FIFTEEN SNOWBALLS BEHIND A TREE?
SCHULZ

GRAMMA SAYS WHEN SHE WAS LITTLE, SHE USED TO HANG UP HER STOCKING ON CHRISTMAS EVE..
THEN, WHEN CHRISTMAS MORNING CAME, SHE'D RUN DOWNSTAIRS, AND FIND IT FILLED WITH APPLES AND ORANGES...
© 1966 Peanuts Worldwide LLC, Dist. by Universal Uclick
www.snoopy.com
I CAN SEE IT NOW... THREE GRAPES!
12-23
SCHULZ

WHY IS THERE NO MISTLETOE AROUND HERE?

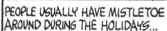

PEOPLE USUALLY HAVE MISTLETOE AROUND DURING THE HOLIDAYS...

WHEN I SAW YOU COMING, I TOOK IT DOWN.. THEN I THREW IT IN THE TRASH BURNER, AND I BURNED IT, AND I STOOD THERE WATCHING IT BURN TO MAKE SURE IT WAS DESTROYED, AND IT WAS! I DESTROYED IT COMPLETELY!!

12-24

THAT'S VERY PECULIAR.... USUALLY MUSICIANS ARE QUITE FOND OF MISTLETOE...

IF YOU REALLY LIKED ME, YOU'D GIVE ME PRESENTS..

IF YOU REALLY LIKED **ME**, YOU WOULDN'T EXPECT PRESENTS!

EITHER WAY, I END UP NOT GETTING ANY PRESENTS!

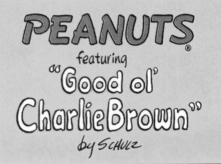

PEANUTS
featuring
"Good ol' Charlie Brown"
by Schulz

HERE'S THE WORLD WAR I FLYING ACE IN HIS SOPWITH CAMEL ZOOMING OVER ENEMY LINES..

PRESIDENT WILSON SAID WE'D BE HOME BY CHRISTMAS... HA!

HERE'S THE WORLD WAR I FLYING ACE SITTING IN A LITTLE FRENCH CAFE DRINKING ROOT BEER ..HE IS DISGUSTED..

ACTUALLY, WORLD WAR I FLYING ACES VERY SELDOM DRANK ROOT BEER ..

©1987 Peanuts Worldwide LLC
Dist. by Universal Uclick

WE'LL NEVER GET HOME BY CHRISTMAS! THIS STUPID WAR WILL GO ON FOREVER!

I THINK I'LL TAKE A BOTTLE OF ROOT BEER OVER TO THE ENLISTED MEN ... POOR CHAPS, THEY PROBABLY NEED A LITTLE CHEERING UP...

HMM...IT'S BEGINNING TO SNOW...

WHAT'S THAT? THE ENLISTED MEN ARE SINGING CHRISTMAS CAROLS!

12-21

THOSE POOR BLIGHTERS ARE CHEERING THEMSELVES UP! THEY DON'T NEED ME!

SUDDENLY THE LONELINESS OF HIS DAYS BECOMES TOO MUCH FOR THE FLYING ACE TO BEAR.. HE CRIES OUT IN TERRIBLE ANGUISH ...

AAUGH!!

WHAT IN THE WORLD WAS THAT?

LET'S NOT SING ANY MORE CHRISTMAS CAROLS..

IF YOU'RE A LONG WAY FROM HOME, THEY CAN BE VERY DEPRESSING..

SOMETIMES I HAVE NO IDEA WHAT HE'S TALKING ABOUT ???

YOU KNOW, YOU AMAZE ME...YOU REALLY DO...
HERE YOU ARE, VIRTUALLY FAILING IN MATH, AND YOU DON'T SEEM TO CARE!
© 1967 Peanuts Worldwide LLC. Dist. by Universal Uclick
WHAT DO YOU MEAN, I DON'T CARE? OF COURSE, I CARE!
WELL, IT DOESN'T SEEM TO BOTHER YOU...
12-24
www.snoopy.com
I TRY NOT TO TAKE IT PERSONALLY!
SCHULZ

4-18
NOW, SAY WE CUT AN APPLE IN HALF...
WE HAVE TWO HALVES, DON'T WE? NOW...
© 1966 Peanuts Worldwide LLC. Dist. by Universal Uclick
THAT'S FRACTIONS!! YOU'RE TRYING TO TEACH ME FRACTIONS!
www.snoopy.com
YOU KNOW I'LL NEVER UNDERSTAND FRACTIONS! WHAT ARE YOU TRYING TO DO TO ME? I'LL GO CRAZY! I'LL...
SCHULZ

FOR THREE MONTHS I COUNTED THE DAYS UNTIL CHRISTMAS..
12-26
THEN LAST WEEK I STARTED TO COUNT THE HOURS...
www.snoopy.com
THEN ON CHRISTMAS EVE I STARTED TO COUNT THE MINUTES; THEN THE SECONDS...I COUNTED EVERY SECOND UNTIL CHRISTMAS...
© 1964 Peanuts Worldwide LLC. Dist. by Universal Uclick
AND NOW IT'S ALL OVER!
SCHULZ

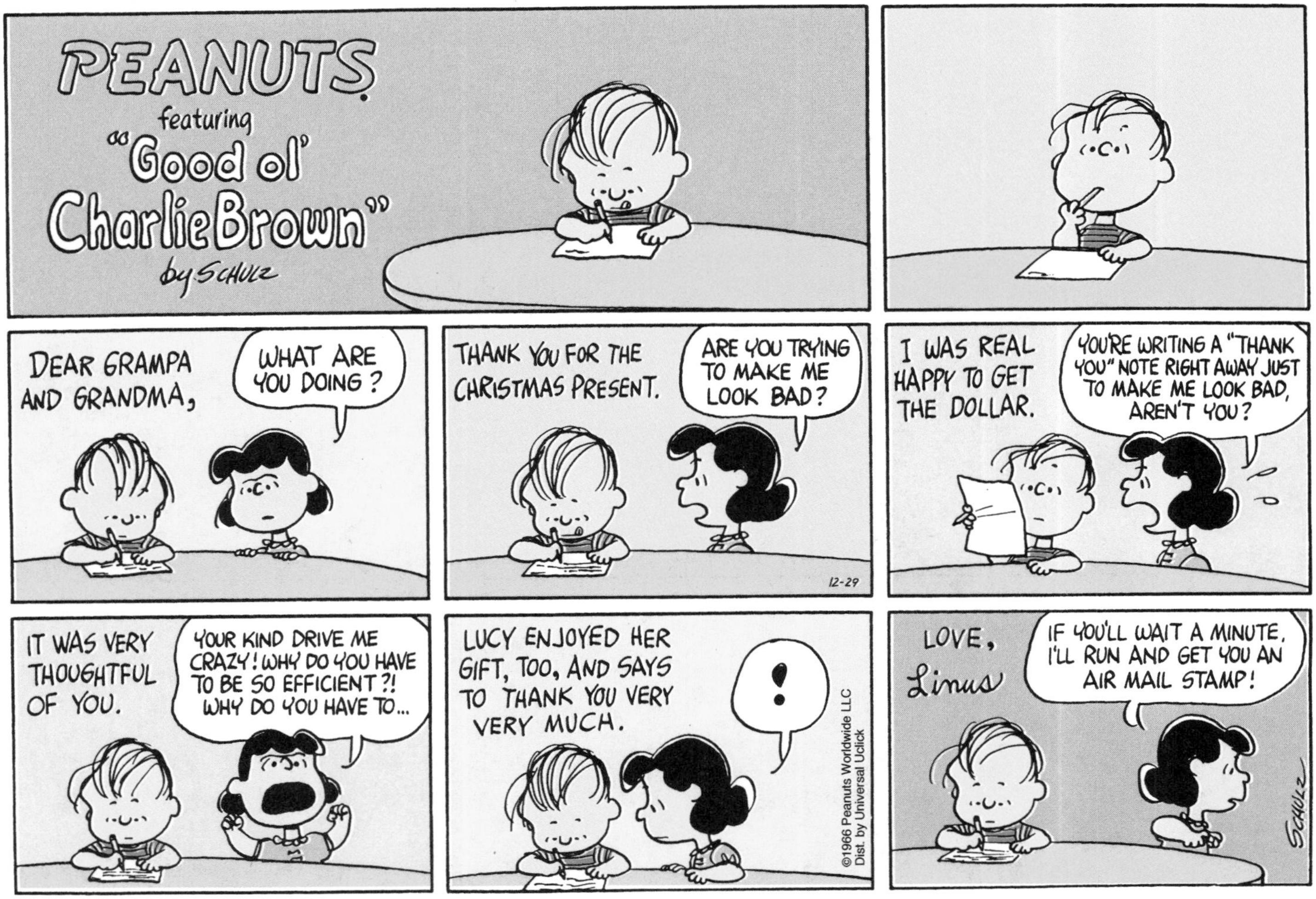
PEANUTS
featuring "Good ol' Charlie Brown"
by SCHULZ
DEAR GRAMPA AND GRANDMA,
WHAT ARE YOU DOING?
THANK YOU FOR THE CHRISTMAS PRESENT.
ARE YOU TRYING TO MAKE ME LOOK BAD?
12-29
I WAS REAL HAPPY TO GET THE DOLLAR.
YOU'RE WRITING A "THANK YOU" NOTE RIGHT AWAY JUST TO MAKE ME LOOK BAD, AREN'T YOU?
IT WAS VERY THOUGHTFUL OF YOU.
YOUR KIND DRIVE ME CRAZY! WHY DO YOU HAVE TO BE SO EFFICIENT?! WHY DO YOU HAVE TO...
LUCY ENJOYED HER GIFT, TOO, AND SAYS TO THANK YOU VERY VERY MUCH.
!
©1966 Peanuts Worldwide LLC
Dist. by Universal Uclick
LOVE,
Linus
IF YOU'LL WAIT A MINUTE, I'LL RUN AND GET YOU AN AIR MAIL STAMP!
SCHULZ